JG MONTGOMERY

HAUNTED BRITAIN

Supernatural Realms of the United Kingdom

Schiffer Publishing Ltd

4880 Lower Valley Road • Atglen, PA 19310

Other Schiffer Books by the Author:
Haunted Australia: Ghosts of the Great Southern Land. ISBN: 978-0-7643-5228-7

Other Schiffer Books on Related Subjects:
Haunted London: English Ghosts, Legends, and Lore. E. Ashley Rooney. ISBN: 978-0-7643-3149-7

Lancashire Folk: Ghostly Legends and Folklore from Ancient to Modern. Melanie Warren. ISBN: 978-0-7643-4983-6

Ireland's Ghosts, Legends, and Lore. E. Ashley Rooney. Photography by Ciaran McHugh. ISBN: 978-0-7643-4508-1

Published by Schiffer Publishing, Ltd.
4880 Lower Valley Road
Atglen, PA 19310
Phone: (610) 593-1777; Fax: (610) 593-2002
E-mail: Info@schifferbooks.com
Web: www.schifferbooks.com

For our complete selection of fine books on this and related subjects, please visit our website at www.schifferbooks.com. You may also write for a free catalog.

Schiffer Publishing's titles are available at special discounts for bulk purchases for sales promotions or premiums. Special editions, including personalized covers, corporate imprints, and excerpts, can be created in large quantities for special needs. For more information, contact the publisher.

We are always looking for people to write books on new and related subjects. If you have an idea for a book, please contact us at proposals@schifferbooks.com.

Thank you to my mother, Jill,

for instilling in me a wonder and curiosity

about the world that surrounds us.

Contents

INTRODUCTION
†
Personal Encounters and Thoughts

*If a man harbors any sort of fear, it percolates through all his thinking,
damages his personality, makes him landlord to a ghost.*

—Lloyd Douglas

In my previous book *A Case for Ghosts* I managed to visit many reputedly haunted sites in Wales, England, and all across Australia. In addition I looked at historical hauntings and tried to place these in a modern context by way of comparison in what has happened, or has been happening at these sites today, or at least, in the recent past. I also spent some time interviewing and talking to numerous people from all walks of life about their experiences with the supernatural or paranormal, and could only come to the conclusion that these people were not lying about what they witnessed or experienced.

But if this is the case and all these people had genuine supernatural experiences, then surely ghosts must be real? And not only real but almost common, after all, it seems that everyone has a ghost story of their own, whether it be something about living in an old spooky house when they were a child, to tales of loved ones who somehow make their presence known after death.

In my case, I have had a number of what I can call supernatural experiences. Some I can rationalise to a point whereby I can almost convince myself that nothing untoward actually happened and that the circumstances I was experiencing at the time were due to atmospheric or weather conditions or a sense of hyper-arousal and sensitivity due to the site itself. And yet, even with this rationalisation I cannot fully discount the fact that *something* strange, whether explainable or not, happened.

To illustrate this I shall recount a sighting of what I can only describe as a ghost in the town of Montgomery, Wales, in the northern summer of 2007.

Montgomery, apart from being where my distant forebears once lived, is a picturesque town just on the Welsh side of the border with England. It is a small rural town and was once an important strategic point for the Normans with a motte and bailey castle standing high above it. Later this castle was replaced with a larger and more substantial stone castle, which was to play an important part in the defence of England during the 1200s. However, after 1295 and the final Welsh War of the thirteenth century, the castle became more of a military backwater, and was used as a prison rather than its original role as a front line fortress.

In 1402, Welsh forces led by Owain Glyndŵr attacked the walled town, and it was sacked and burned. Although the castle survived, it was reduced to a ruin, which is how it remained until being rebuilt some 200 years later. However, by the Civil War the castle was made largely redundant due to advances in military tactics and equipment. Apart from this the new nobility favoured stately homes and fortified manors over castles. However, with the outbreak of war, castles like Montgomery again became important and it was rebuilt and refortified although, sadly for the future of the castle, its inhabitants sided with the monarchy, and in the resulting defeat the castle was once again destroyed to deny any remaining loyalists a rallying point.

And so, with such a history of war and associated death for over 800 years, it could be suggested that, if anywhere, this castle could be haunted. Yet my visit to the castle one late afternoon when a cold drizzle fell upon the ancient stones and the sun struggled to appear low on the horizon, provided me with no proof whatsoever that ghosts exist.

True, it was cold, windy, and eerie, but what more could one expect on such a dreary Welsh afternoon where the grey skies seemed to penetrate your very soul, and the wet stones that once provided the castle with walls gave the site an overall menacing and malevolent feel?

And yet, for all of this, it was not the castle where I was to experience my supernatural encounter. Instead my encounter was to come in the comparative warmth and comfort of the Dragon Inn, which sits quietly nestled against the hill on which the castle stands, a quaint but substantial Tudor-era building with white-washed walls, heavy oak beams, and a shingle roof.

A former coaching inn, this building now caters to tourists, and although no longer the hub of the community as it was in its heyday, it still attracts numerous visitors. Indeed, that night as I sat in the restaurant dining on a particularly excellent meal whilst drinking Welsh ale, I was surprised at the number of diners given that it was midweek.

In the restaurant is a huge open fireplace created from an old bread oven that still burns much as it did over 300 years ago. Near the front entrance a pane of glass said to have been signed by the hangman who presided over the last public hanging in the town sits as a grisly reminder of the past. Indeed, it is believed that the hangman made the inn his regular drinking spot.

In my previous book I talked about the *stone tape* theory of ghosts and hauntings, which basically states that ghosts in a historical context are somehow a recording of the past that is replayed in the present by some unknown means but believed to be the very stones of the building where the ghost itself exists. But if this is true, then why is it that there are so little reports and literature of ghosts in the ruins of Montgomery Castle itself? Given that there are countless stories of haunted inns and castles where murders, grisly torture, and death have occurred on a regular basis in the past, surely the castle *must* be haunted in some way?

Of course, the question here is somewhat similar to asking whether or not, when a tree has fallen in a forest, has it actually fallen? That is, how can one be sure if one has not witnessed it? This holds true for the ruins of the castle given its decrepit state and relative obscurity. Simply put, visitors, few as they are, spend a relatively short time at the site and so the chances of them experiencing something of a supernatural origin are considerably lessened when compared to a hotel, or popular tourist attraction.

And so it would seem to be for the Dragon Inn, which, not incidentally, was constructed from much of the ruins of the old castle itself. Given this, is it possible then for the ghosts of the old castle to be somehow connected to the material of the building, meaning that they would now be expected to haunt the inn rather than the castle?

And so, with this is mind we can now turn to one of my few apparent supernatural experiences. After my meal I retired to an old but comfortable guest bedroom. While lying in bed under the inviting warmth of a huge fluffy doona, or duvet, the rain tapped incessantly against the old glass-paned windows, and the building itself emitted strange creaking and groaning noises. At times, as the wind and rain increased in intensity, it seemed as if a wolf could be heard howling in the distance. And yet, in the relatively quiet periods when the rain ceased and the wind dropped, the quietness was eerie and spine tingling and my senses seemed at the very limit of their abilities.

At this point one could very much believe in ghosts and spirits and all things unspeakable that roam graveyards and other places of ill repute at night looking for wayward souls to steal. This is where suggestion takes over, and the imagination, if allowed, can run wild. It is a very childlike feeling that everyone at some time has experienced, lying under the covers, eyes straining to see in the darkness that surrounds you, ears tingling at the slightest sound, your body frozen and your breathing almost non-existent. You see, in this environment, ghosts are very, very real and frightening.

And yet as adults, we can dismiss this irrational fear of the dark and the unknown, even in this environment, as one still must sleep, which I did.

Sometime in the very early morning, around 4:00 a.m., I awoke. It was still dark but the wind and rain had stopped and the room was quiet. As I lay there in the dark I imagined that I saw movement, a shadow perhaps, near the bathroom door. My heartbeat quickened and my body tensed, and for a moment I held my breath, straining to hear and see into the dark. There, not five or so metres away was the distinct form of a person, a man of about six feet in height wearing a hooded robe like a Cistercian monk from the middle ages.

I lay there in the darkness not moving and barely breathing for what seemed an eternity, but was probably less than a minute. My heart was pounding as I squinted into the darkness; could I really be seeing a ghost? And not just a fleeting shadow or flash in the corner of the eye but a full, life-sized figure in distinct dress, indeed, I have no doubt it was a hooded robe.

And then, in time, my eyes slowly adjusted to the dark and I became fully awake. As I did the figure seemed to disappear until I was left somewhat apprehensive but confused as to what it was I thought I had seen. Could I really have witnessed a hooded figure near the door to the bathroom? And where was it now? Was it a dream? Or a nightmare?

Whatever the case, it was now gone and I got out of bed and wandered into the bathroom to get a drink of water. As I lay back in bed I thought about this dark shape. Did I really see something or did the surroundings provide a suggestion to my brain while I was sleeping and in the process of waking up I had somehow blurred reality with dream, thus conjuring up the shape of a nondescript ghostly monk? Or was it simply a vivid dream?

Although this is only one of my apparent supernatural encounters, I find this one the easiest to explain—not because I disbelieve in ghosts, or even doubt that ghosts exist, but more so because I can rationalise what happened and, with some effort, almost convince myself that nothing untoward had actually happened. This is because of a combination of factors. During the day I had explored the old town before climbing the steep gravel road to the dreary ruins of the castle that lay like silent sentinels in the grey landscape above the town. At the castle site I wandered quietly through the ruins fully aware of the bleakness and the eeriness that seemed to be present in the place. And then later in the inn I had read of the hangman and his penchant for drinking in the very inn I was to stay at. Not only this, his victims were often hung outside the very front door of the inn itself.

And so, with these things in my mind I went to bed. Outside the weather was wild, which simply added to the picture, layering more and more suggestions in my brain like one of the old masters delicately and deliberately building up the background of a painting. By the time I was ready for sleep my mind was primed for a supernatural experience of some kind. If anything, in hindsight it would have surprised me if something *hadn't* happened given the circumstances.

And so, ghost or not? While I can rationally argue that I didn't see a ghost or experience anything out-of-this-world, I also cannot blithely dismiss it as simply suggestion and dream. Is it possible that I really did see a ghost that night in the Dragon Inn? Of course, as we shall see in later chapters, nothing is as simple as it seems when you are dealing with matters of a supernatural or paranormal origin.

And yet, as much as I can rationally argue against this apparent ghost sighting, I cannot do so for others.

In my early teens I lived for a period of time in Virginia in the United States. The house was a fairly standard upper-middle-class house in a reasonably affluent area and sat on the top of a small hill in suburbia surrounded by lush trees to the sides and a deep, heavily vegetated creek gully to the back. And it appeared to be haunted, or at least, that's what I believed, as did my younger brother and sister, all of whom relayed this information to me a couple of decades after we moved out of the place. Before this we had never spoken about it, which sort of affirms my feelings about ghosts in that how can so many people with no links whatsoever or prior knowledge of a site, report seeing the same thing over so many years?

This encounter, in this so normal of circumstances, was possibly my first real and unexplainable encounter with the supernatural, or at least, something unexplainable. And whereas my encounter in the Dragon Inn can be explained by a number of circumstances, this one it seems cannot.

Put simply, one night, while sitting alone on a lounge in the downstairs part of the house while watching the football on television, I distinctly heard a deep, gruff voice say something in my left ear. And by distinctly I mean that it was so close, and so obviously human-like that a sharp chill ran up my spine. What it said I have no idea, but it appeared to be literally *in my ear*. As previously mentioned both my sister and brother later confirmed that other strange events had happened to them in the house which somewhat legitimises what I heard.

But if this encounter is unexplainable, then others, like the Dragon Inn, are quite explainable, even if, again, somewhat like the Dragon Inn, they are not completely convincing.

In the late 1970s and early 1980s I attended a boarding school in Victoria, Australia. The school was built in the 1920s, and was reputed to be haunted by the ghost of a young school boy who died from fever. Late at night as we lay silently in our beds, the moonlight flooding the dormitory with an eerie grey light; we would hear what sounded like footsteps slowly striding up and down the wooden floors. Doors would mysteriously open as if an unseen hand had turned the handle and pushed it open, and organ music could sometimes be heard late at night coming from the locked and deserted chapel.

Of course, this could also be the product of an overactive imagination in combination with an old, eerie building that, if I think back now, was simply a stereotype for what we would expect a haunted building to be. And yet, the footsteps were real as was the eerie organ music. Is it possible that the place was haunted, not by just the ghost of a young boy but someone else, someone older, sterner and more likely to walk in deliberate, slow footsteps along a wooden floor? Is it possible the spirit of some long dead master still strode down those lonely corridors checking to see if boys were in bed and not getting up to hijinks or mischief? In hindsight, it is certainly possible.

At around the same time I experienced the frightening disembodied voice in suburban America, I also experienced the just as unnerving cornfields of Civil War Gettysburg, which I visited in the late 1970s. This was a place where the wind seemed to whisper urgent secrets and the corn stalks hid something unknown. But once again, these voices and feelings were surely a figment of my imagination spurred on by the history and isolation of the place . . .

Or maybe not? Gettysburg has long been known as being haunted, and not just by the odd ghost of a Civil War soldier but at times by whole battalions. Is it possible that the rustling of the corn in the soft breeze was something more? Could the ghosts of the American Civil War still be fighting a battle that ended over a century ago? Could they still be crawling through the fields, hoping, and praying not to be shot and to return once again to loved ones?

Not surprisingly, given its tragic history, Gettysburg itself is considered to be one of the most haunted sites in the world. Fought between 1 July and 3 July 1863 in and around the town of Gettysburg in Pennsylvania, it had the largest amount of casualties in any battle in the American Civil War. Indeed, the battle was so significant that it has been described as the turning point of the war as Union Major General George Gordon Meade's Army of the Potomac defeated repeated attacks by Confederate General Robert E. Lee's Army of Northern Virginia, ending Lee's invasion of the North.

Almost unbelievably, the two armies suffered between 46,000 and 51,000 casualties over the three days of intense fighting. Overall Union casualties were 23,055 with 3,155 killed, 14,531 wounded, and 5,369 captured or missing while Confederate casualties are unknown to this day but could have been as many as 28,000 with nearly 5,000 killed, and over 12,000 wounded.

And so, in this place of incredible and unbelievable human slaughter where the folly of war was brutally exposed for all to see, is it possible that I experienced just a small part of this battle, somehow transported through time and manifesting itself in the whispers and sounds of the cornfields that now lie serenely over the killing grounds?

Of course, once again, this could simply be put down to expectation and imagination, although at the time I was not fully aware of the extent of this tragic battle, indeed, all I knew at the time was that some sort of Civil War battle had taken place on the site some 115 years earlier.

Having said this, reports of ghosts at the battleground are not only numerous but also incredibly detailed, including strong smells of vanilla and peppermint, which were used by the townspeople after the battle to try and cover the stench of dead and dying bodies. Apart from this, the Farnsworth House, now a working bed-and-breakfast with original rafters, walls, flooring, and bullet holes in the walls from the battle, is reputed to be one of the most haunted houses in the area with disembodied footsteps, intense presences, and mysterious harp music that emanates from the top floor. In addition the ghostly image of a woman in period clothes is also regularly seen, although she rapidly disappears if approached.

But this is not the only haunted house in the area. The Jennie Wade House is named after twenty-year-old Marie Virginia "Ginnie" Wade, the only known civilian killed in the battle. She was tragically hit by a stray bullet and killed instantly while inside her house making bread.

Strange happenings have been regularly reported around the house, and the ghost of a young woman, believed to be Ginnie is often seen, accompanied by the smell of freshly baked bread and rose-scented perfume. In addition, children's voices have been heard in the house, and the ghost of an unknown man is said to haunt the upper floor.

These, however, only make up a small part of the overall supernatural landscape of Gettysburg. At Little Round Top a headless horseman is often seen, while at Culp Farm, a house located directly on the battlefield, footsteps can be heard on the second floor pacing back and forth. As well, at Devil's Den, reports of the ghosts of soldiers, and also of ancient Native American warriors are commonplace with unexplained drum rolls, voices, and gunshot sounds common in the area. Almost unbelievably people have reported meeting a soldier who they describe as being like a re-enactor and who they have spoken to at length and who has then simply and mysteriously disappeared.

But if my experience in the quiet cornfields of Gettysburg can be simply explained as suggestion, imagination, and anticipation leading to a sense of hyper-arousal whereby every sound is magnified and every movement misconstrued as something it is not, then what of my next supernatural encounter: a strange, and unnerving experience I had whilst exploring the Hellfire Caves in Buckinghamshire in England. So strange was this encounter that it took me months to realise what had happened, and that possibly, just possibly, I had seen and spoken to a ghost. Indeed, my experience there still has me scratching my head as to what I may, or may not have seen and experienced, or may have misinterpreted.

Commissioned by Sir Francis Dashwood and finished in 1752, the Hellfire Caves in Buckinghamshire took local workmen six years to complete, extending a natural cave system to the half-mile-long tunnel complex that exists today. Visitors pay a small entry fee and then can enter the caves and follow the long winding passage deep below the ground past various small chambers finally leading to an Inner Temple, 100 metres directly below St. Lawrence's church, which sits on a ridge above the magnificent Gothic entrance to the caves.

Although used by Dashwood and his colleagues as the meeting place for the infamous and mysterious Hellfire Club, it is also thought that the caves were once the site of a pagan altar in more ancient times.

Dashwood was introduced to freemasonry while travelling in Europe, and upon returning to England decided to start his own society called the Monks of Medmenham, later to be called the Hellfire Club. Those involved included John Wilkes, Lord Sandwich, many senior aristocrats and statesmen, and Benjamin Franklin, who was a close friend of Dashwood.

The main activity of the Hellfire Club appears to have included drinking copious amounts of alcohol, debauchery, and holding occult rituals, and it is these black magic rituals that are thought to be one of the reasons for the supernatural activity in the Hellfire Caves.

In particular, poet Paul Whitehead gave Dashwood fifty pounds to put his heart in an urn after he died with the express instructions that the heart be kept in the caves. However, even though the urn is still in the caves today, the heart was stolen by an Australian soldier and was never recovered. Whitehead's ghost is said to wander the caves and the grounds looking for his stolen heart.

Aside from the ghost of the heartless Whitehead, the most famous of the ghosts is that of a local girl who was tragically murdered in the caves. Sukie was a chambermaid at a local pub, and held ambitions to marry into the gentry. As such she spurned the advances of local boys, eventually accepting a proposal from a wealthy local man. One night she received a note asking her to meet him in the caves so that they could elope, but upon her arriving in her wedding dress, she discovered that some local boys had tricked her. Consumed with anger the girl started throwing rocks at the boys until one of them threw back a rock which knocked her unconscious. The boys panicked and carried her back to the inn where she died later that night. Her ghost is now said to haunt the eerie tunnels of the cave, dressed in white, and still searching for her betrothed.

Apart from this the caves are reported to experience extreme drops in temperature in some places and strange lights and orbs have also been reported. Ominously, visitors sometimes emerge from the caves shaken, apparently due to strange misty shapes that approach them in the semi-darkness.

And so it was that I came to experience something quite odd in that, even today, it still puzzles me. While walking down a length of the cave that led to a junction that split to the left and right, I came across a short, thin, apparently middle-aged woman in old clothes. She was standing against the wall at the end of the corridor and did not appear to notice me approach in the semi-darkness. When I reached her I said hello but she didn't move, just stood there with her head slightly bowed in a strange, almost unexplainable way.

As she didn't acknowledge me or move, I simply slid past her into the next part of the cave when it occurred to me that she seemed somewhat brown or misty, or *not properly* there, if you can understand what I mean. I turned around, and to my surprise she had disappeared. And not only from the spot where she was standing only seconds ago but there was also no sign of her in the corridor from which I'd come, the only place she could have gone. Put simply, she had disappeared into thin air.

So, what am I to make of this strange occurrence? Is it possible I literally said hello to a ghost? And if so, who was this ghost as it certainly wasn't a young and forlorn girl in a wedding dress nor was it a poet searching for his stolen heart? Maybe it was simply a shy tourist, albeit, one who seemed to possess the ability of disappearing into thin air. Over time, as I thought more about this encounter, it occurred to me that the woman was somewhat see-through, like a hologram projected in front of the stone wall. As such, today I cannot be sure whether what I saw was a real person, or some sort of apparition. Maybe over time I have convinced myself that something was amiss due to the underlying eeriness of the place. But then again, maybe not.

Ghost or not, it seems that the Hellfire Caves, along with numerous other places across England are haunted, which leads me to one final supernatural-like encounter I experienced, this time at the London Dungeon.

Although the London Dungeon sounds terrifying, it is really just a theme park in an old warehouse. However, it is a theme park with a difference as it carefully and accurately chronicles the dark and grisly history of London, including displays about the great plague, Jack the Ripper, the fire of London, and a boat ride through a mock Traitor's Gate, interestingly not really that far from the real Traitor's Gate on the River Thames.

Entering the London Dungeon one is surprised by the darkness, noise, and displays, which are quite convincing and realistic, even to the point that my partner, Kirsten, said she felt slightly ill with the depictions of plague, blood, gore, and grisly, violent death. But as interesting as this was, it was a small incident during a butcher surgeon recreation performance that really caught my attention.

Kirsten and I stood there in the darkness and watched while an actor demonstrated how surgeons would have operated in the early to mid-1800s. To be accurate it was somewhat like watching a part from the movie *Sweeny Todd* especially as doctors in those days were considered barber/surgeons and only had a rudimentary knowledge of human physiology. However, this is not what we are interested in as, to my surprise, halfway through the performance I distinctly felt three sharp, urgent prods in my right side ribcage. Thinking that someone was next to me and was feeling nauseous by the blood-drenched performance, I stepped back to let them pass.

Imagine my surprise when there was no one there. A shiver went up my spine and after collecting my thoughts and replaying the incident in mind, I was no closer to explaining it than at first. Yes, I had definitely felt three sharp, urgent prods in my ribs. Yes, I had thought that it was someone next to me trying to get my attention. And yet, there was no one there, in fact, no one within a few metres.

I whispered to Kirsten that something had prodded me in the ribs, but she was more enthralled by the performance than my apparent brush with the supernatural. After we had finished going through the place and were safely back on the bustling streets of London I again brought it up. Both of us were at a loss as to explain what had happened and promptly dismissed it and went to the pub for a pint or two.

However, a couple of months later while back at home in Canberra, Australia, I happened to be watching a television documentary about the London Dungeon. You can imagine my surprise when the host mentioned that the mortuary room was a place where people often report being poked in the ribs by an unseen hand.

But if the London Dungeon, as we have seen, a modern-day recreation of medieval and Victorian London, is haunted, then why? Some quick research revealed to me that it had been built under some of the existing arches of the London and Greenwich Railway line which was opened in 1836. Its old brick corridors and curved stone walls made it a suitably atmospheric location for the historically-themed display.

Some 800 years previous to this the Hospital of St. Thomas the Martyr stood on the site and was run by a mixed order of nuns and monks providing shelter and treatment for the poor, sick, and homeless. By the seventeenth century the area to the south of London Bridge had become a place of crime and prostitution renowned for bear, dog, and cockfighting. In addition it was hit terribly by the Great Plague that swept through England in the 1660s. It is believed that thousands of people could have died on the very spot where the Dungeon now exists.

During the Second World War the area became one of the most bombed places in Britain and the railway arches were used as air raid shelters. However, in 1941, the arches were hit and it is believed that up to 300 people could have been killed with many of the bodies never recovered.

With this sort of a history, the reader will agree with me that it is not surprising that the Dungeon is reputed to be haunted.

But my slightly un-nerving experience is not the only of its kind in these dark tunnels and corridors. Shadowy figures have been seen behind the displays, and a male figure dressed completely in black has frightened the life out of visitors. Some have even speculated that this figure is no less than the ghost of Jack the Ripper, although one must ask what his spirit is doing in a recreation of Victorian England, especially as it is not known who he was or where he died. Is it possible that this most vile of humans died somewhere in the area, and now his ghost haunts the displays, perhaps searching for one last unsuspecting victim?

In other areas, members of staff have reported seeing a ghostly group of children playing Ring-a-Ring-o'-Roses while the mortuary room, where I had my strange encounter, has also been the scene of shadowy and slightly menacing figures that appear to hover over the mock operating table.

As well, it has been reported by staff that electrical equipment mysteriously stops and starts of its own accord, unexplained lights appear in several places, and people are often touched on the neck, tapped on the shoulder or poked in the ribs by unseen entities. To add, it has also been reported that doors often open and close apparently of their own accord, mannequins change position when the dungeon is closed, and people experience feelings of panic, which is really not surprising given the dreary atmosphere of the place.

As such, we must ask, is the London Dungeon haunted? In my case, I can see no reason to doubt that I had been poked in the ribs by something completely unknown to me. However, this is not to say that the spirit of a dead person suddenly decided to poke its fingers into my side, but more so to say that I have no explanation as to what happened, except maybe to suggest that it could have been of a supernatural origin, that being a ghost.

And so, where does this leave us in terms of supernatural or paranormal experiences? Of all the experiences I have had, I have been able to rationalise some as possibly being something much more mundane than an actual ghost. However, can this be the case for everyone that has had such an experience?

In *A Case for Ghosts* I interviewed a woman who was seemingly subjected to a paranormal attack in a nursing home by what she believed was a ghostly entity. I also spoke at lengths to another woman who was convinced that her bedroom and a doll were possessed by some sort of spirit. Both these women were adamant that what they had experienced was not normal, and that it was somehow connected with the supernatural world.

Of course, in *A Case for Ghosts* I tried to find explanations for their experiences and yet, as thorough as my explanations may have been, they still don't quite seem to answer the questions put forward.

That is, how can it be that so many people can experience so many events or happenings that appear to be totally the domain of the paranormal or supernatural? How is it that so many normal and sane people can report seeing things that apparently can't exist? And more so, how can so many people with no prior knowledge of things or links to each other report the same phenomena over and over again?

Many have commented that I am much more sceptical than they expected. This statement is true. When I started to write about ghosts, I was convinced that pretty much all reported ghostly activity was the result of genuine paranormal activity. However, over time and after delving deeper into the subject, I came to realise that most phenomena can be explained by simple means and that they are no more supernatural than the workings of a computer.

However, even if one is to discount ninety percent of sightings or reports of ghosts or ghostly phenomena, then we are left with the sobering fact that there are still literally thousands and thousands of reports that *cannot* be explained. This begs the question, what is it that we are really dealing with?

Whereas in my first book I took a philosophical approach to examining the phenomena from all angles, in this book I intend more to cover a wide variety of ghosts, apparitions, spirits, and hauntings without attempting to explain in detail what could be the cause of the happenings. Rather, I intend to present the stories, legends, and tales to the reader and allow them to make up their own minds. And if the reader wishes to do so, they may visit the places that I have written about and see for themselves what all the fuss is about.

As such, I hope that this book, much like my previous books, will shed just a little more light on the subject. I also hope it will allow for more research into the topic and just as importantly, an open mind into the subject.

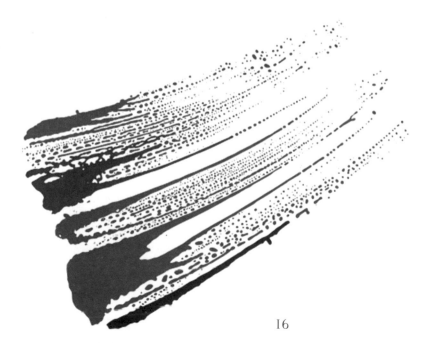

CHAPTER 1

†

Castles and Ghosts and a Tower in London

Horses did neigh, and dying men did groan,
And ghosts did shriek and squeal about the streets.

—William Shakespeare

The sun is shining merrily through high wispy clouds and the day is warm. The scent of an English spring wafts pleasantly past your nostrils, and small sparrowlike birds chatter incessantly in the bushes and hedgerows. I park the hired car and my partner Kirsten and I get out and walk along a crunchy gravel path that winds its way through stunning gardens of beautifully manicured lawns, regimented hedges, and imposing trees. We then follow the path as it runs parallel to a small brook that cheerfully babbles its way through this wonderful landscape. Next to the brook are peacocks in full plumage, and in the brook a large pike waits in ambush for its next meal.

And then, majestically standing out from the forested gardens is the imposing and stunningly beautiful Leeds Castle. Located just south east of Maidstone in Kent and sitting on two small islands in a large but shallow lake, it has survived for nearly a thousand years and is one of the most significant and historically-important buildings in English history.

Originally named after Led, the chief minister of King Ethelbert IV of Kent, it was the site of a manor house built in 857 by Saxon kings. The original castle, an earthwork enclosure with a timber palisade and two timber towers, was mentioned in the Domesday Book. Later, King Edward the Confessor granted the manor to the powerful house of Godwin, and over the next several hundred years the castle became the centre of sieges and fighting, many which resulted in a change of ownership.

By 1119, the Norman Crevecoeur family possessed the castle and Robert Crevecoeur started rebuilding it in stone. In 1278, it was given to King Edward I of England and this began a long line of royal ownership. King Edward I quickly added a fortified mill and barbican and made extensive alterations to the castle, including the moat. He also enlarged the castle by building an outer stone wall around the edge of the larger island including cylindrical open-backed towers. The gatehouse was also improved.

The castle fell in battle to King Edward II in 1321 and from then after was never again besieged as it developed a reputation as being a ladies' castle. Over time the castle has claimed to be the home of six medieval queens of England.

During the reign of Henry VIII large amounts of money were spent on improvements, much like other castles of the era, and it was from here that the King started his historic meeting at the Fields of the Cloth of Gold with Francis I of France in 1520.

Over the next 100 or so years the castle was owned by Sir Anthony St. Leger, the Lord Deputy of Ireland, and the Culpeper family, who were supporters of Parliament during the Civil War, which probably allowed Leeds Castle to remain intact when many castles at the time were razed. Later the castle was occupied by the 6th Lord Fairfax who gothicised the main house, and even entertained King George III in 1778.

Over time the castle has been constantly inhabited and rebuilt, although most of what exists today is the result of the nineteenth-century additions and reconstruction. In 1926, Lady Baillie bought the castle and filled it with high-quality medieval furnishings, ceramics, tapestries, and art works. In addition she created the Leeds Castle Foundation to maintain the castle, garden, and park, and today it remains a national treasure.

Strangely enough, even with such a rich history, Leeds Castle does not appear to have a great deal of literature or even tradition of ghosts and hauntings as its only ghost seems to be a large black dog, although like other black dogs or devil dogs, it is reputed to be an omen of death.

Having said that, there is a legend about a woman who was once saved by the appearance of the hound as she sat in a bay window. Apparently, when she saw the ghostly dog, she jumped back from the window just as it collapsed into the moat.

Although Leeds Castle has some history of battle and warfare, it is not renowned for its brutal past, and so, after a lovely day exploring the castle and grounds, we walk back to our waiting car in the late afternoon warmth past the shallow babbling brook. As we do, I wonder why such a place is not haunted? Why is it that one castle can be seemingly overrun by ghosts, for instance the Tower of London, and others not so? Is it possible that grisly brutal death has something to do with it? But even if this is so, surely Leeds, with its ancient history would qualify? Or maybe ghosts and hauntings disappear over time, which could explain why Leeds appears unhaunted?

Whatever the case, as ancient as Leeds Castle is, its apparent lack of ghostly legend demonstrates that it is not simply the age of a place that contributes to ghostly apparitions and visitations.

The suggestion that all castles are haunted is familiar to us through film and literature. However, this is most obviously not the case as amply demonstrated by Leeds Castle. When one considers the history of some castles, especially in Britain, then it is not that surprising that ghostly stories exist given that violent death, murder, rape, incarceration, and torture were all common occurrences.

But if Leeds Castle appears relatively unhaunted, then what are we to make of Hever Castle, which is located only a relatively short drive away?

Hever Castle is a truly wondrous and beautifully evocative place. Whereas Leeds Castle is a stunning and imposing fortress of stone seemingly floating on a shallow lake, and invokes visions of the Arthurian Avalon, Hever is more gentile, more cultured, and one would think, less likely to have seen bloody struggles for power and associated death. As such, one would suspect it to be much less haunted.

And yet Hever Castle has its own ghosts, and not just the ghost of some nondescript woman in grey or a lonely sentry that patrols the ancient battlements. No, Hever Castle has no less than Anne Boleyn as its resident and most well-known ghost.

Born sometime between 1501 and 1507, although some reports suggest an earlier date of 1499, Anne was the daughter of Thomas Boleyn, who later became the earl of Wiltshire, and his wife, Lady Elizabeth Howard, the daughter of Thomas Howard, the second duke of Norfolk. Thomas Boleyn was a talented and respected diplomat who spoke many languages and was a favourite of Henry VII of England. As such, life for the Boleyn family was one of privilege and lack of want.

Although it is thought that Anne was born at Blickling Hall in Norfolk, remarkably little is known about her early years except that she spent part of her childhood at the court of the Archduchess Margaret. From there, she later moved to the household of Mary, Henry VIII's sister, who was married to Louis XII of France.

At this stage Anne's sister, Mary, was in the French queen's attendance although when Louis died, Mary returned to England leaving Anne in France to attend Claude, the new French queen. It is believed that Anne then remained in France for the next six or seven years. During her stay in France she learned to speak fluent French and developed a taste for French clothes, poetry, and music. In addition, due to her position in the French royal household, it is quite possible that she was at the Field of the Cloth of Gold, the famous meeting between Henry VIII and the French king, Francis I.

And yet for all the history associated with Anne and her early days, it is her liaison and later marriage, and execution, at the hands of Henry VIII that interests us. Exactly when and where Henry VIII first noticed Anne is unknown although it is suggested that soon after they had met Henry attempted to make Anne his mistress, as he had with her sister Mary years before.

However, much to Henry's chagrin, Anne denied him sexual favours. Instead, it appears that Anne became fixated on being queen, and so it was a case of "queen or nothing" for Anne, which presented an obvious problem for Henry who was at the time married to Catherine of Aragon, the youngest surviving child of Ferdinand and Isabella, the joint rulers of Spain.

Although the court quite reasonably suspected that Henry would just take Anne as his mistress, they were unaware of his true feelings for her, which was later revealed in seventeen love letters he wrote to her while she was away from court. By 1527, the unimaginable happened and Henry began to seek an annulment of his marriage to Catherine, which would leave him free to marry Anne.

Henry and Anne were secretly married in January 1533, even though the King's marriage to Catherine was not yet dissolved. This obviously created a huge scandal, although in the mind of Henry this was not an issue, having thoroughly convinced himself on the invalidity of his previous marriage. On 23 May 1533, the Archbishop officially proclaimed that the marriage of Henry and Catherine was invalid.

Life as queen was pleasant enough for Anne. She was crowned at Westminster Abbey in June, and by August preparations were being made for the birth of a child. However, the child, expected to be a boy and heir to Henry's throne, was a girl, Princess Elizabeth. Interestingly, the princess' white christening robes have regularly been on display at Sudeley Castle in Gloucestershire, another place with a rich history of ghosts and hauntings.

With Henry desperate to have a son, Anne was pregnant again in January 1534, although tragically the child was either miscarried or stillborn. In 1535, she became pregnant again but once again failed to carry for the full term, miscarrying by the end of January. Even more tragically, especially for Henry, was that the child was reported to be a boy.

Unable to produce a healthy son for the king, and realising that the inability to do so was a threat to her own life, Anne's world began to unravel. Indeed, around this time Henry appeared to have lost some interest in her and was actively pursuing one of her ladies-in-waiting, Jane Seymour. In addition, during her time as queen, Anne had made many enemies, and they now plotted against her to bring charges of treason.

In April 1536, one of Anne's friends, a musician by the name of Mark Smeaton, was arrested and tortured into confessing to relationships with the queen. Soon after, her brother, George Boleyn, Lord Rochford, was also arrested and taken to the Tower of London, as was Sir Henry Norris, a courtier in Henry's privy chamber who was also accused of adultery with the queen.

By May, Anne herself had been arrested and held in the Tower of London with pending charges of adultery, incest, and plotting to murder the King. The fairy tale life had now become a grotesque nightmare with little or no expectation of a happy ending.

More arrests followed with Sir Francis Weston and William Brereton charged with adultery with the queen. On 12 May 1536, they were put on trial with Smeaton and Norris at Westminster Hall and, unable to defend themselves against the charges, were found guilty and were sentenced to be hanged, drawn, and quartered, the usual punishment for treason.

On Monday 15 May, Anne and her brother were put on trial at the Tower. Anne denied all charges against her. Her brother was then tried with his own wife testifying against him. Both were found guilty even though the evidence against them was limited and obviously biased, and they were sentenced to either be burnt at the stake, the punishment for incest, or beheaded, at the discretion of the King.

George Boleyn was executed on Tower Hill on 17 May. The other four condemned to be hanged, drawn, and quartered had their sentences commuted to the less horrific beheading by axe as all were in service of the court.

On 19 May 1536, Anne was taken to the Tower Green where she was afforded the dignity of a private execution. She made a short speech before kneeling on the scaffold and removing her headdress after which her ladies tied a blindfold over her eyes. Rather than an axe, her head was removed with one stroke of a sword.

Apparently, Anne's body then lay unattended for quite some time until her body and head were put into an arrow chest and buried in an unmarked grave in the Chapel of St. Peter ad Vincula, which adjoined the Tower Green. And as such, it is not surprising that this place is famously known for sightings of the ghostly queen. Indeed, while awaiting her death Anne penned the following:

Oh Death
Rock me asleep
Bring on my quiet rest
Let pass my very guiltless ghost
Out of my careful breast
Ring out the doleful knell
Let it sound
My death tell
For I must die.

However, whereas Anne wished that her guiltless ghost be allowed to rest, it appears that it has done anything but. Her ghost seems to be one of the most, if not the most, reported ghosts of all time and, according to Hever Castle, holds the record for the most sighted spirit. And yet, one must ask, if Anne's ghost is regularly reported to have been seen at the Tower of London why is it she seems to appear all over the place, including Blickling Hall in Norfolk, Rochford Hall in Essex, and floating across the gardens and wooden bridges of Hever Castle in Kent?

And so it is with some trepidation that I step into the oddly atmospheric bedroom on the first floor of the castle. Rumoured to be Anne's bedroom that she may have shared with her sister, Mary, one gets an intense feeling of history as if it has seeped into the very walls of the building, and leaning against the fireplace one cannot help but realise that Anne herself must have done the same at some stage. Indeed, looking out the window is to see the landscape that Anne must have loved so much as a child, albeit, restored and remodelled over the years.

It is quiet and peaceful in the bedroom, and for an instant I am able to be alone in this truly splendid and magical place. I gaze out of the window at the lush lawns and mature trees that sit peacefully in the warmth and sunlight of an early English summer. Turning around I feel as if someone or something is in the room with me, as if watching quietly from a corner, unseen and unheard.

But of course, there is no one there, and somewhere in the distance a crow calls, lonely, and plaintively, and my serenity is broken by the arrival of a family with day packs and cameras and noisy children. The moment is gone, there are no ghosts in this room, and yet, for a fleeting moment, one could believe they exist.

Apart from Hever Castle, Anne has been reported to appear once a year at Blickling Hall in Norfolk on the anniversary of her execution, on this occasion not on her own but travelling in a coach pulled by a headless horse driven by a headless horseman with her severed head in her lap. Once the coach reaches the hall it is said it disappears leaving the sad and pathetic figure of Anne alone on the steps until she too disappears only to be seen again in the halls and corridors of the great house. Local folklore also suggests that these ghostly visions are said to be followed by eerie blue lights through the back roads of Norfolk. What they are is unknown.

Similarly, at Rochford Hall in Essex, once belonging to Thomas Boleyn and the marital home of Anne's sister, Mary, it is said that a headless woman dressed in silk and thought to be a witch haunts the grounds for the twelve days after Christmas. This spirit is also said to be Anne.

And yet for all these reports Anne is mostly seen at the Tower of London, the place of her grisly and untimely death. Indeed, it was reported that in 1817 a sentry reportedly died of a heart attack after encountering her ghost on a stairway. Later, in 1864, a soldier was court-martialled for being found seemingly asleep on duty near the Lieutenant's lodgings. Apparently, the soldier encountered the figure of a lady dressed in white and challenged her. When she did not respond and moved towards him he thrust his bayonet into her, which caused a shock to run through his body causing him to faint. At his trial he was reputed to have said, "It was the figure of a woman wearing a queer-looking bonnet, but there wasn't no head inside the bonnet."

An officer claimed to have seen the whole event and added that the ghostly woman walked straight through the unconscious sentry as if he were not there and as if she didn't even acknowledge his presence.

Over the years many witnesses have come forward and stated that they have seen a strange woman dressed in white in various areas of the Tower. Almost all of them agree that this must be Anne. Indeed, in 1933, she walked into a guard post scaring the guard so much that he dropped his weapon and fled.

But Anne is not always seen without her head as, in 1882, a captain of the guard saw a light burning in the locked Chapel Royal and, wondering how this could be given the place was locked and silent, went to investigate. When he opened the door he witnessed a figure who he thought was Anne leading a slow, stately procession of knights and ladies in plush medieval clothing. Strangely in this case, although Anne had a head, the man reported that she appeared to not

have a face or that it was averted in some way. The complete procession then disappeared leaving a slightly shaken and confused witness.

Of interest here is the report that, although the figure had a head, it appeared to not have a face, or if it did, its features were somewhat indistinguishable, which matches with numerous other ghost reports from all over the world where apparitions are reported as being almost as if flesh and blood but without facial features. Of course, if a ghost is lacking facial features then one must ask, how is it that a person can identify who the ghost is? Is it the case that, knowing that the ghost of Anne Boleyn is said to haunt these corridors, a witness seeing something simply assumes that it is her ghost? And if so, then who is to say that this ghost is not Anne but someone else? After all, it is not as if Anne was the only person ever horribly killed, tortured, imprisoned, or executed in the Tower.

Just before Anne's execution on charges of adultery, her marriage to Henry was dissolved and declared invalid. As such, one must wonder how it is she could commit adultery when she was never actually married?

But if Anne's ghost is seen all over the place from the Tower of London to Blickling Hall and Hever Castle, is there any other evidence that ghosts can haunt more than one place? Is it possible that ghosts are not simply the spirit of a dead person and are something much more complex, for instance, a memory or event in history that has somehow become attached to a place, somewhat like a holographic recording? Two ghostly stories of hugely famous historical figures would suggest so.

Sir Francis Drake, the English vice admiral, politician, and sailor of the Elizabethan era, died at sea of dysentery in 1596 while anchored off the coast of Portobello in Panama, and yet bizarrely his ghost is reported to haunt the wild moorlands of Dartmoor in central Devon where, on dark stormy nights, he heads a pack of hounds or devil dogs seeking out the souls of the unbaptised and unworthy.

Just as puzzling is the case of Sir Walter Raleigh, the English soldier, poet, courtier, and explorer who was well known for either introducing or at least popularising tobacco into England. His ghost is regularly seen in the Tower of London grounds and yet he was executed many miles away at Old Palace Yard at the Palace of Westminster. Is it possible that Raleigh's spirit still lingers in his cell at the Tower?

After his death, Raleigh's head was embalmed and gruesomely presented to his wife. And whereas his body was to be buried in the local church in Beddington Surrey, the home of Lady Raleigh, it was finally buried in St. Margaret's at Westminster. After his wife died some twenty-nine years later, his head was returned to his tomb and interred at St. Margaret's Church. As such, one must ask, why is it that Anne Boleyn seems to appear in numerous places and yet Raleigh, imprisoned in the Tower of London, executed in another place, then buried headless in a different location, is only seen at the place of his imprisonment?

Or is he? Some believe that Raleigh's ghost, although still seen in the Tower of London, is also present in Beddington. Indeed, in *A History of Beddington,* written in 1923 by the Reverend Thomas Bentham, there is mention that Raleigh's ghost "haunts the walk behind the old yew tree in the churchyard."

Bentham also stated that a student of his who had an interest in the paranormal once staged a vigil over several nights in hope of catching a glimpse of the ghost. However, although he never saw anything, he came away from the whole experience believing it to be true. Local modern folklore also suggests that Raleigh's ghost walks around the churchyard three times on Christmas Eve. Of course, again one must ask, how is it known that this apparition is actually Raleigh? Could it be some other lonely spirit that died around the same time? Maybe even a seafarer like Raleigh himself?

It is alleged that the Church at Beddington sits on the corner of a ley line and is connected to another church not far away in Addiscombe. Although outside the scope of this book, ley lines are said to be a concept of straight lines of some sort of energy within the landscape that connect ancient and sometimes sacred sites, such as Stonehenge, Avebury, and other Neolithic sites. Whether this has anything to do with ghostly seafarers is a matter for another discussion but remains a point of interest all the same.

But not all of these out-of-place ghosts appear in medieval English castles or dwellings as, in Canberra at the Australian War Memorial in the Hall of Memory, the ghost of a soldier is often reported to staff, even though no one is buried there, and the place only opened relatively recently in 1941. Is it possible, as in the case of Anne Boleyn and Walter Raleigh, that this ghost has somehow returned without his remains to this most poignant of places? Why does his spirit haunt these hallowed halls and not the green overgrown battlefields of First World War France? Or is it something else? Is the significance of the place something that can generate intense emotions, enough to somehow produce what one could call a ghost? And if this is the case, then is this really a ghost or do we need to re-adjust our beliefs as to what ghosts really are?

It would seem, given what we have read, that ghosts are more than just the souls of the tormented dead. Indeed, it would seem that they are something much more substantial and even less understandable, and this is something that we shall look at further as we delve into this strange and misunderstood world. But whereas Anne Boleyn and Raleigh's ghost are well known at the Tower of London, what of other, less well-known entities?

In a previous book on the same subject, I spoke at length of the numerous and quite unbelievable stories of ghosts and supernatural happenings that have been reported over the years at the Tower of London and within the grounds themselves. At this stage I had not actually visited the Tower due to a lack of time and scheduling and instead had wandered around its perimeter marvelling at the ancient and significant building.

And so it was that, two years after my previous visit to London, I was determined that I would visit the Tower this time around. And I would have to say that, apart from the masses of tourists, I was not disappointed.

Reputedly the most haunted building in England, if not the entire world, the Tower of London is a spectacular set of buildings and grounds on the banks of the iconic Thames River in the London Borough of Tower Hamlets. Originally commissioned by William the Conqueror in 1078 and completed some nineteen years later, it has, without doubt, one of the bloodiest histories known to any building in the world.

Kirsten and I visit the Tower one cool and overcast day in May. A slight drizzle is falling and the pavements and roads that run along the artificial banks of the Thames are shiny and slippery with water. The river itself is grey and angry and a strong tide creates waves that lap loudly against the stone banks and moored boats. In such weather one is inclined to believe in ghosts.

We wander by Traitor's Gate and stop to take some photos. The gate itself is old and worn with rusted hinges and fittings and sits ominously in the greyish green waters of the river. Surrounding this, the stone walls are old and eroded and at lower levels covered in moss and river slime. The tide is quite low so we can see the full extent of the infamous structure that only acquired its name over the past 400 or so years due to the number of prisoners accused of treason who passed through it on their way to incarceration, torture, and probable death in the Tower.

Designed by a medieval architect on the orders of King Edward I between 1275 and 1279 as part of St. Thomas's Tower, it was originally built to provide a new water-gate by which the King and royalty could arrive at the Tower by river. St. Thomas's Tower was originally spare accommodations for visiting dignitaries and other royalty. However, after the Tower was discarded as a Royal residence, it became a place of torture, imprisonment, and death, and the gate took on a more menacing reason for being.

The journey of these terrified prisoners was once made by barge along the River Thames, sometimes taking them past London Bridge where the heads of recently executed traitors were displayed on spikes on the roof of the stone gatehouse. It was here that no less than the head of Sir Thomas More was displayed for all to see.

Sir Thomas More, also known as Saint Thomas after his unjust execution at the hands of King Henry VIII, had his head cut off in 1535 after he refused to take the oath required by the First Succession Act because the act disparaged the power of the pope and Henry's marriage to Catherine of Aragon. Before his execution More requested that his foster daughter be given his headless corpse to bury and he was buried in an unmarked grave in the chapel of St. Peter ad Vincula in the Tower of London. His head, as was the custom for traitors, was fixed upon a pike over London Bridge for a month and would have been simply thrown into the river after this time if his daughter Margaret Roper had not bribed a night watchman and rescued it.

More's skull is now believed to lie in the Roper Vault of St. Dunstan's Church in Canterbury, though it has also been claimed that it might be within the tomb he erected for himself in Chelsea Old Church. Surprisingly, and unlike Anne Boleyn and Walter Raleigh, his ghost does not appear to haunt the place of his death and has been reported at Baynards Park in Surrey, although the original historically important Tudor manor was destroyed by fire in 1979. Sadly, at the time of writing, the site is now under the threat of development as only the tower and gatehouse remain, and one wonders if in the future new tenants in their newly purchased modern dwellings will report seeing a wise-looking old man in Tudor clothes?

The rain is still a persistent drizzle, heavy enough to drench you if you remain in it for long enough, but not heavy enough to wet you if you are out in it for a short while. As such, Kirst and I decide to visit the Tower and get out of the gloom.

Once inside we are surprised and delighted to see the legendary ravens of the Tower of London and indeed the equally legendary Beefeaters, which reminds me of a *Goodies* episode where the poor Beefeaters no longer have any beef to eat and so they eat the ravens instead. Legend has it that if the resident ravens ever leave the grounds of the Tower, then the kingdom and Tower will fall. The resident birds now have their wings clipped so they cannot escape, not that I could imagine why they would want to escape given the care that is heaped upon them by their keepers.

Having said that, some ravens have escaped and others have been dismissed. One by the name of George was removed from the Tower for eating television aerials, and another, suitably named Grog, was last seen enjoying himself immensely outside a pub in the East End.

Interestingly, and with no hint of the supernatural, it has been suggested that the legend of the ravens, believed to have been instigated by Charles II, may be more of a legend than previously thought. Historian Geoff Parnell scoured the records for 1,000 years and could trace the ravens back no further than the late nineteenth century. Parnell, the official Tower of London historian and a member of the Royal Armouries staff, is convinced that the legend is a typical piece of Victorian romance.

Even worse, Parnell found that in at least one point in the Tower's history, the ravens did not exist at all with a blunt statement in the records stating, "there are none left." Unsurprisingly, the monarchy and the tower have somehow survived this calamity. But as cute as the large black birds are, it is the Tower that we have come to see.

From first views the Tower sits ominously over the River Thames, its four distinctive turrets designed to strike fear and submission into the residents of medieval London. Often called the White Tower, for obvious reasons, its primary function was as a royal palace but over time it became a prison for high status or royal prisoners with many executions being held on the green outside the tower, including William of Hastings in 1483, Anne Boleyn in 1536, and Lady Jane Grey in 1554. The last person to be executed in the Tower was a German spy by the name of Josef Jakobs who was shot in 1941.

Apart from Anne Boleyn, who seems to appear quite regularly, and Sir Walter Raleigh, the Tower has a plethora of ghostly inhabitants ranging from Thomas a'Becket, Catherine Howard, whose ghost has been seen running down the hallway screaming for help, and Guy Fawkes. Other strange sightings include funeral carriages and an unknown, "lovely veiled lady that upon closer look proves to have a black void where her face should be."

The Tower was also the scene of the disappearance and probable murder of the young princes Edward V and Richard Duke of York in 1483. Edward was twelve years of age at the time and Richard only ten. Legend has it that sometime after their deaths guards witnessed the ghostly figures of two small boys on some stairs in the Tower. It wasn't until 1674 that some workmen found a hidden chest containing two small skeletons which were presumed to be those of the missing boys. They were subsequently given a royal burial.

In addition to the ghostly boys, Lady Jane Grey, who ruled England for just nine days before being executed in 1554 for refusing to recant her religion, is also believed to haunt the ancient building. Her ghost was last seen by two guardsmen in 1957 on the anniversary of her death. The ghost of her husband, Lord Guildford Dudley, who was also executed, has been seen in another tower weeping for his lost love.

At one stage in its history the Tower was the home to the Royal menagerie, which included lions, birds, monkeys, an elephant, and bears, and in one bizarre story from 1815 a sentry saw a ghostly bear emerge from a doorway. Lunging at it with a bayonet the sentry found the weapon going straight through thin air.

And yet as strange as this encounter may have been, the most grisly of all ghostly visions in the Tower would have to be that of the seventy-year-old countess of Salisbury, last of the Plantagenets, who was executed in 1541 for political reasons. When she was taken for execution she refused to put her head on the block and tried to run away, forcing the executioner to run after her and hack her to death. Her ghost has been seen reliving this gruesome scene, and some have reported seeing the shadow of an executioner's axe chopping down at the scene of her execution.

But as interesting as these stories are, the Tower itself is a wonder, ghosts or no ghosts, as it contains a wealth of treasures from weaponry to armour to the Crown Jewels. A visit to London would not be complete without a tour of the grounds and Tower itself, where one can admire the iconic Beefeaters or walk along these ancient battlements knowing that, at some stage in history a king, queen, or royal dignitary once walked on the very same stone.

But it is not just high-profile places like the Tower of London that appear to be plagued by ghostly apparitions and, as Kirst and I walk out through the huge wooden doors and back onto the London streets, we notice that the Thames tide has slowly but surely risen. Now the ancient Traitor's Gate, where so many people were previously brought by boat to meet their fate at the hand of a gleaming executioner's axe, is now half hidden by the greenish-tinged water. In the drizzle of a grey London day it is a grim and thought-provoking sight.

Later that day, as we sit in a quiet and very old pub near Covent Garden, we are reminded as to why this great city is regarded as being so haunted and steeped in stories of the supernatural. The city has been in existence for nearly 2,000 years in one form or another and is possibly the best known city in the world, if not best known in history. Over this time it has seen massive social change, war, death, destruction, plague, and human misery. And although it is seen today as a glamorous hub of finance, fashion, and culture, it hides a tragic and brutal past, one that does not take much investigation to discover.

But if London's history is old and bloody, then what of other places not so old and not so bloody? Indeed, what if it were a genteel Georgian country house in the lush green countryside of rural Wiltshire or a place without death and bloodshed, nor it would appear anything of a tragic nature that could lead one to suspect that it may be haunted?

CHAPTER 2

†

A Georgian Country House, Haunted Manors, and a Castle in Dunster

The more enlightened our houses are, the more their walls ooze ghosts.

—Italo Calvino

The village of Avebury sits quietly in the rural landscape of Wiltshire. In the mornings the cool air is thick with misty fog and any sounds coming from the surrounding countryside are muffled and somewhat hollow. Sheep graze quietly in the lush green paddocks and the village exudes nothing but stereotypical bucolic English charm.

Set on the site of an ancient crossroads, the village contains Avebury Manor, which was believed to have been built around 1551 by Sir William Dunch, auditor of the Royal Mint for both Henry VIII and Edward IV. Over its history, the Manor, although not as prestigious as most country houses, has been a significant part of the village. It is surrounded by high boundary walls with formal gateways and retains an air of opulence with its old-world charm consisting of impressive gables, deep mullion windows, tall imposing chimneys, and beautiful landscaped gardens. And not surprisingly for such an ancient building, it is reputed to be haunted.

Among these spirits is Sir John Stawell of Cothelstone, a staunch Royalist who purchased the manor from Dunch in 1640. Stawell played a significant role in the English Civil War raising five regiments to fight on the side of Charles I. This allegiance to the Crown was to prove his undoing as he was captured by the Parliamentarians in 1646 and refused to swear that he would not bear arms against Parliament. As a result, his possessions and estates were to be sequestered, including Avebury Manor.

He was later committed to Newgate Prison on a charge of high treason and then held in the Tower of London where he remained until 1660. While imprisoned in the Tower, the manor was sold to George Long. On the restoration of Charles II to the throne, Stawell was released and returned to Avebury. However, he was a broken man and died soon after in 1662.

His ghost is said to haunt his bedroom, gazing longingly out of a window at the grounds and gardens. He has also been seen standing quietly and motionless next to the fireplace in the room and has been described as being solid in appearance and dressed in Cavalier finery, as befitted a high-standing person from those times. Witnesses have reported that he may be weeping, and his appearances sometimes seem to be preceded by the fragrant smell of roses as rose water during that time was often used to disguise body odour. Some visitors have reported being overcome by feelings of intense sadness in this room, a not uncommon occurrence in the case of many ghosts and supernatural reports. In addition, his ghost has also been seen in the gardens, a place he apparently loved while alive.

Another bedroom in the manor, in the eastern extension and built sometime between 1580 and 1600, also has an eerie and possibly malevolent spirit. A recent report suggests that a woman visitor was overcome by something in the room and, whilst in a trancelike state, started to shake and speak in a low, guttural voice in a language that no one could understand. When removed from the room, she apparently recovered. Whether or not this was a supernatural occurrence or a simple fit is debatable, but the fact that the woman was overcome by something in a room where others have reported feeling threatened and uneasy, and that she recovered upon being removed from the room makes for a curious happening. Other guides have refused to enter this room on the pretence that something evil is present.

Of course, a stately manor in rural England would not be complete without a ghostly woman who suffered from some tragic past, and so is the case for Avebury Manor where the house and gardens are reputedly haunted by a beautiful young woman dressed in white. Not surprisingly called "The White Lady," she is arguably the most active of the manor's ghosts, and although her identity is uncertain, it is believed that she may have been a ward of Sir John Stawell.

Stawell, before his untimely imprisonment at the hands of the Parliamentarians, was believed to have run an exceptionally strict house, especially in regards to protecting a young lady's integrity and virtues. Sadly, it is said that the woman fell in love with a man who worked on the estate and would meet secretly with him. Stawell was appalled and tried to put a stop to the clandestine meetings, but the young woman was not dissuaded.

When the Civil War erupted the young couple were torn apart as the man joined the regiment of the Royalists and went away to fight. In time the woman received news that he had been killed in battle, and in a fit of despair she committed suicide by leaping from a second-floor window, suffering internal injuries and a broken neck. She is now said to wander the grounds searching for her dead lover by tapping men, often with beards, on the shoulder in an attempt to identify them. When the person turns around there is no one there.

Although she is most often seen at the south gate close to the pet cemetery, she is also regularly seen by guides and visitors descending the main stairway inside the manor. Dressed in a flowing floor-length white gown she is described by those who have seen her as being stunningly beautiful.

But apart from these ghosts, Avebury Manor apparently has another interesting spirit, that of a cat. Staff on occasions have reported hearing the cries of a cat, and when investigated have found the room where the sound was coming from, empty. Interestingly, in medieval times cats were sometimes walled up as there was a belief that a dead cat in a wall would help prevent rodent infestations. Even more interesting is that in the Stables Museum on the grounds of the manor is an exhibit of a mummified cat, discovered in one of the manors walls during restoration work.

Although the manor itself was not constructed until the mid-sixteenth century, previous to this it is believed the site may have held a building for monastic purposes. And as such, it is not that surprising that the place has a resident phantom hooded monk, although the identity of the monk is completely unknown. This apparition is said to haunt the kitchen, the parlour, the east garden, and the churchyard of St. James, which stands adjacent to the manor.

In a fascinating and documented encounter in 1557, William Dunch reputedly encountered the ghostly monk one evening while waiting for a meal. The ghost is still reported to this day crossing the passage that connects the kitchen to the west garden door, even though the door was bricked up some considerable time ago.

St. James Church, apart from being visited by ghostly monks, is also the scene of numerous other supernatural figures, including a mysterious female figure and a little boy dressed in Victorian clothes who has been described as being solid in appearance and dressed in a short brown jacket with matching knickerbockers. Apart from that he has also been described as having rosy-cheeks and wearing white stockings and a brown cap.

A woman who encountered the little boy described how she thought he was part of a local play or recreation but when she approached, he took no notice of her as if she didn't exist. Then, to her shock and surprise he looked up at her, smiled, and simply vanished, leaving her completely bewildered.

But from one haunted manor in Wiltshire to another in Gloucestershire is where one cannot be but taken by the beauty and majesty of the surrounding landscape where rolling green fields are intersected by lush forests and fat cows stand happily in the warm sunshine. The spring time is stunningly beautiful with green grass in the fields, leaves on the trees, and small flowers swaying gently in the warm breeze on the roadsides. A small brook running through an unknown village brings childhood memories of Kenneth Grahame's *The Wind in the Willows*. And soon enough, in the lush green forests, one comes across a rare gem in the world of the supernatural.

Woodchester Mansion is an incomplete neo-Gothic mansion that was built upon an earlier seventeenth-century Georgian country house on the edge of the Cotswolds just twenty kilometres south of Gloucester. The exact date of commencement of the current buildings is unknown but is believed to be around 1857 or 1858; suffice to say that by 1866, the main building had been roofed. To get there one must walk a couple of kilometres along a thin winding country lane that is bordered by a tall deciduous forest complete with ferns and undergrowth on each side. At times the sun is completely blocked by the lush foliage overhead and at other times filters dappled light that trickles gently down to the ground and while stunningly beautiful and tranquil it might be, it is easy to imagine how spooky it could be to walk along this lane at night. The mansion itself looms out of the forest like a haunted house from an old horror movie from the 1950s with a richness of architectural form and an interesting blend of domestic structure and monastic design. Without doubt it is one of the most impressive buildings of this style in the area. Or, at least, it would be, if it had actually been finished.

The building was abandoned under mysterious circumstances in 1873, and what the visitor encounters to this day is a time capsule complete with unfinished floors, stairs leading to nowhere, tradesman's tools simply left where they were abandoned, and spectacular fireplaces built halfway up walls, seemingly floating in space. It is as if the people working on the site simply disappeared.

It was not until 1938 that some interest was again shown in the mansion when the estate was sold with the intention of converting it into a mental asylum. However, the advent of the Second World War saw American and Canadian troops using it as a base, and they even constructed pontoon bridges over the lake in preparation for D-Day. By the 1950s, the mansion had become a field study centre, but was not altered, and although emergency repairs have been carried out to the listed building, it is considered simply too expensive to completely refurbish and thus it remains unfinished, just as when it was abandoned.

Local legends associated with Woodchester Mansion and its grounds include an angel that haunts one of the lakes on the estate, a Roman centurion who patrols a gate on the entrance road, a ragged dwarf, a headless horseman, a floating coffin, and an old man in a ragged and torn night shirt. Legend also has it that a spectral black dog, a portent of death and doom pads silently along the entrance lane on dark nights following unsuspected travellers. The majority of ghostly sightings have surprisingly occurred not within the house itself but from the grounds and the lakes. Over the life of the estate it is rumoured, and probably true, that over twenty people died whilst either living there, or working there.

One of the main hauntings in the building is said to be that of a young girl, rumoured to be a servant, who can be heard talking or singing in the house. When I was visiting the place my guide at the time admitted that he had never seen the ghost, although he did assure me that he knew other guides that had either seen or heard her. In addition he told me of a black monk-like figure that reputedly sweeps noiselessly down one of the main corridors late at night. Quite a frightening apparition one would suspect and one I don't think I'd like to meet.

With this is in mind, and having met no spectral black dogs or Roman centurions whilst walking there, I entered the house only to be disappointed by the lack of anything paranormal whatsoever. I will admit, the building and architecture was superb and the history narrated by the guide second to none. However, spooky as it looked, it was just a large abandoned house. Or so I thought until I wandered away from the main group and downstairs into the dimly lit cellars.

The cellars consist of a long brick passageway with various small storerooms off to the sides. The doorways to the storerooms are dark and this blackness seems

to loom out as you pass by. The floor is dirt and building rubble, and the lighting makes it difficult to see what you are standing on. It is unnaturally cold in places, and somehow eerie in that the hairs stand up on the back of your neck, and you seem quite aware of your breathing as if the place is slightly suffocating.

Having said that, I still did not see anything ghostly, nor hear anything out of the ordinary. As for the cellars, well who is to say whether they are haunted or not? While I would not say that they are definitely haunted, I certainly would not discount it. As for the suffocating feeling and the sense of unease? I would suggest that, having arrived at Woodchester fresh in the knowledge that it was reputed to be haunted, I allowed myself to be taken in by the atmosphere of the place and thus felt what I expected to feel in that situation. In addition, cellars are underground and on a warm day, it would obviously be cooler than the upper area of the building.

Being that this is so, what about the rest of the house and why did I not feel the same whilst wandering around and marvelling at the structure? For one, I was in a group or at least with another person. Secondly, it was a beautiful spring day and the building was flooded with soft spring light in many areas.

And so what are we to make of Woodchester Mansion and its alleged hauntings? As for the grounds I cannot say, but the lane that twists and winds through the forest towards the mansion was, although stunningly beautiful in spring, not a place I would like to walk along at night, even with a group of people. As for the house itself, I most certainly would not want to spend a night alone in there. Sometimes I think it may be better to be safe than sorry. Legends may be legends, but they are usually based upon a grain of truth, and personally, I'm not sure I always want to meet that grain of truth.

But whereas Woodchester is an abandoned house in a spooky wood in the middle of nowhere, Dunster Castle, sitting serenely atop a hill above the quiet medieval town of Dunster, is anything but deserted.

Dunster sits in the English county of Somerset just within the northeastern boundary of the Exmore National Park. It began as a Saxon village with its name meaning "Dunn's torre" or "craggy hill." Later, a Norman by the name of William de Mohun built a castle on the rocky tor overlooking the town, at first a standard Norman motte and bailey, which was later demolished to make way for a much more substantial stone castle. The castle was remodelled, expanded, and modernised on numerous occasions by the Luttrell family, who were lords of the manor from the fourteenth to twentieth centuries. The medieval castle walls were mostly destroyed following the siege of the castle near the end of the English Civil War, when Parliament ordered the defences to be slighted so as to prevent further use as a military stronghold. Later, during the 1860s and 1870s, Anthony Salvin, an architect and expert of medieval buildings, remodelled the castle to fit the then-current Victorian tastes, extensively changing the appearance of the castle to make it appear more Gothic in design.

With the death of Alexander Luttrell in 1944, the family was unable to afford the death duties due on the estate. The castle and surrounding lands were sold off, although the family continued to live in the castle as tenants. Then, in 1954, the Luttrell family was able to buy back the castle, but in 1976, Colonel Walter Luttrell bequeathed the castle and most of its contents to the National Trust. Today it is a Grade I listed building and scheduled monument and operates as an extremely popular tourist attraction. It is, of course, reputed to be haunted with people reporting strange phenomena and even full apparitions on a regular basis.

There have been reports of ghostly sightings at Dunster Castle for many years with the most famous being a figure of a Grey Lady and that of a foot guard, who wears a tricorn hat. They have variously been reported as blurry indistinct shapes or faces to the occasional full-body apparition. Indeed, the Grey Lady has been seen so many times that volunteer staff have reputedly lost count of the number of reports and now consider her part of the furniture or family. Having said that, there are other ghostly presences that appear to be less distinct and who manifest themselves as noise, cold spots, a feeling of general unease or sickness, or sometimes as lights or floating orbs. When one wanders past the oubliette after entering through the magnificent gatehouse doors, it is hard not to forget that many people were imprisoned, forgotten, and starved to death in this place and the bodies simply left to rot. As such, one can believe that these spirits may still be restless.

The gatehouse, a magnificent structure that towers above you as you walk up the steep cobblestones from the old stables, dates back to 1420 and formed part of the barbican entrance. The oubliette itself is in the right hand tower and was some seven or so meters deep. Incredibly, excavations of the oubliette unearthed a male skeleton—not an ordinary skeleton but one that suggested the person was roughly seven feet tall. The skeleton was discovered manacled to the wall by his wrists and ankles and presumably had been left to starve to death like so many others. Legend suggests that his remains still lie in-situ at the bottom of the oubliette and, although it is now completely sealed and enclosed with a stone covering, people have reported hearing cries and whimpers from the dark empty space below them.

From the right hand tower and oubliette one makes their way up a flight of stone steps towards the castle. It has been said that on numerous occasions dogs have refused to enter the stairwell or to climb the stairs, although I would have to say that I found them in no way intimidating or frightening.

Exiting the stairs one is suddenly thrust into the light, made more glaring by the previous darkness of the stairwell, and there in front of you, with lush well-manicured lawns and crunchy gravel paths, sits the castle itself, a truly marvellous sight and one that temporarily takes your breath away. But it is not the incredible architecture that interests us here as we have other interests, including the alleged Grey Lady.

The Grey Lady, as we have previously mentioned, is Dunster Castle's most regularly seen phantom. She has been sighted in a number of rooms including the Billiard Room, the library, and the connecting corridor that flanks the two; however, she is most often reported on the main oak stairs that lead up from the entrance hall. It is said that the Luttrell family over the generations were regularly terrified by repeated encounters with the ghostly figure as she glided noiselessly up and

down the staircase before vanishing into a wall, leaving an icy chill in her wake. Although no one is sure, it is suggested that she may have been an abused servant girl who later died in the castle. Sightings of the Grey Lady continue to this day and although I caught no glimpse of her nor felt any tell-tale cold spots, many National Trust guides and visitors have witnessed her.

But the Grey Lady is not the only spirit that seems to haunt this incredible place as the King Charles bedroom is said to be the most haunted room in the castle. Named after Charles II, who as Prince of Wales slept here in 1645, the room definitely has a strange atmosphere that some describe as unpleasant, almost as if being watched. Many visitors have refused to enter the room claiming that it has a bad or malevolent feeling; however, once again, I felt nothing of the sort when inside the room. Having said that, it was a lovely sunny day, and the castle was filled with sightseers and tourists, which obviously lent itself to a genuinely pleasurable outing. Whether I would say the same if I were alone in the room at night is debatable, but I somehow doubt it.

Apart from this, the so-called Leather Gallery, which has leather hangings from its walls depicting the story of Antony and Cleopatra, is also said to be haunted. On numerous occasions the sounds of men shouting, heavy footsteps, and the slamming of doors have been reported by National Trust staff long after the castle has been closed and the visitors have left. Others, including visitors, have claimed to have been tapped on the shoulder only to turn and find no one there. As well, it is said that a distinct cold spot moves around the room, and in one case, a conservationist was working there when she suddenly became aware of a chill in the room. Feeling uncomfortable as if being watched she turned and was confronted by the ghostly figure of a man apparently dressed in Royalist uniform. Then, as quickly as it had all happened, it ceased and the figure vanished with the room temperature returned to normal. It is believed that during the Civil War, the Leather Gallery was used as a soldier's quarters. Perhaps some of them never left.

The old stable block, which we mentioned briefly, is also said to be haunted by a "Man in Green" while others have claimed to have seen floating green orbs at the far end of the stable block. The Man in Green has been witnessed on a number of occasions with a shop manager catching sight of him one afternoon walking past the entrance to the National Trust shop. Thinking he was a visitor who had not realised that they were now closed for the day, she followed him, but by the time she reached the shop doorway, the figure had disappeared. It must be noted here that the only way to reach the stables is past the shop entrance.

The Man in Green has also been seen at the far end of the stable block, and many have complained that it is unseasonably chilly, if not icy, in that area. I must admit that when I visited the stables I felt that it was distinctly cooler in that area than anywhere else. Having said that, the stables are extremely well insulated as they are built from thick stones walls and have a cobblestone floor and, when compared to the shop, which is heated, could explain the apparent drop in temperature. Still, others have reported seeing a man step out of the wall and then disappear at that particular place. As well, the storeroom is said to regularly suffer from what appears to be a poltergeist-like incident in that boxes, books, and stock are often found strewn around the floor when staff open up in the morning. It has also been suggested that a number of boxes of souvenirs and goods were damaged by mysterious green slime; however, this I find too fanciful to even contemplate.

But leaving both Woodchester Mansion and Dunster Castle alone, we are compelled to return to Avebury as it's not just the stately Avebury Manor that appears to be haunted. Indeed, the Red Lion Pub, probably the only pub in the world surrounded by a Neolithic stone circle, has been the scene of numerous ghostly apparitions and appearances over time and, at over 400 years old, it is not surprising that it is rated one of the most haunted pubs in the whole of the British Isles, if not the world.

Like most English pubs, the Red Lion seems to have a number of significant ghosts as well as some other, more nondescript hauntings. Having said that, the pub's most famous ghost is far from nondescript and even has a name: Florie.

Legend has it that Florie lived in the building sometime in the 1600s during the Civil War. And like the White Lady from Avebury Manor, her husband was also forced off to war. However, whilst he was gone she took a lover, which proved to be a tragic mistake as, when her husband unexpectedly returned, he shot her lover dead and then stabbed the unfaithful Florie to death. He disposed of her lifeless body in the village well.

The old village well is now a part of the pub and has been incorporated into the decor with a glass top that serves as a table. And it is from here that Florie's ghost has been seen rising before appearing around the room and, surprisingly, in the ladies toilets. As well as moving small items, rattling windows and chandeliers, it is said that she is attracted to men with beards, like the White Lady of the nearby manor. As such, one must wonder if the legend of Florie and the White Lady are one and the same or originated from the same source.

Whatever the case, while having a quick beer in the pub one fine spring afternoon, I braved an apprehensive peek into the dark depths of the well. Thankfully no ghostly woman rose up to greet me.

But whereas Florie is the most well-known of the Red Lion's ghosts, she is certainly not the only one known to drinkers and travellers alike. A previous owner of the building was believed to have been murdered in the seventeenth century after he was double crossed by outlaws, and it is said that his ghost now wanders the premises with a knife in his hand as if trying to protect himself from his attackers. Apart from this, outside the pub also seems to be quite busy with a ghostly horse-drawn carriage sometimes seen pulling up to the pub late at night in the mist or the fog, only to then disappear when the fog clears. And if ghostly carriages are not enough, then unearthly horse hooves often heard coming from the courtyard outside the pub are believed to be, like black dogs, harbingers of death and doom.

Upstairs in the pub is the Private Room, at some stage a guest room or bedroom but now used for other purposes, and it is in this room where people have reported seeing the ghost of two children cowering in a corner as if afraid of being beaten. Whatever it is that they are cowering from is unknown. In the same room, a woman is also seen but she appears completely oblivious to the children as if they are two completely unconnected events in the history of the room. To put it simply, these are ghosts from different periods of time, and there is no interaction between them whatsoever, which seems to suggest that, in some cases, ghosts are simply a replay of a historical event, and not necessarily an important historical event but, in this case, something rather mundane.

Some reports have the ghostly children and woman in the Avenue Room, another upstairs room in the pub, but it would seem that this room has its own separate ghosts and apparitions. And as with other haunted locations, things in the pub quite often go missing, turning up in strange places days later and numerous guests have complained that their rooms are extremely cold even in the middle of summer. In fact, it is not strange for guests to check out in the middle of the night vowing never to set foot in the room again. Whatever the case, the pub appears to be a hotbed of supernatural events and phenomenon. A notice board over a fireplace near the haunted well proclaims the following:

There have been reports of at least 5
different ghosts at the Red Lion.... A
ghostly horse drawn carriage has been seen
pulling up outside the pub & staff have heard
the phantom clattering of hooves in the
courtyard outside the pub...

Having said this, when I was there, I witnessed nothing more frightening than a friendly crow who was happily eating discarded chips on a wooden table in the beer garden.

One would think that a haunted manor house plus a haunted pub would be enough for one small village, and yet Avebury is no ordinary place. Set within a henge of stones that was constructed between 2400 and 2600 BC and contemporary in time with Stonehenge, it is a place of mystery and intrigue. Indeed, in the quiet stillness of the early morning one can truly believe in the numerous myths and legends that define this small village and the surrounding countryside.

Avebury has long been a place steeped in stories of ritual, ceremonies, burials, and magic, and the stones themselves seem to almost speak out. If one is to walk around the henge in its entirety and touch the massive megaliths one can almost feel the history of humanity in this area. What ghosts haunt this most ancient of places? What stories do the stones hold? Is it possible that these ancient stones hold answers to humanities past, answers that we have yet to form questions for? Are the stones somehow ancient recording devices that occasionally play back events from long ago?

Whatever the case, Avebury holds a fascination to all who have any semblance of interest in not only history and culture, but the supernatural as well. And if a haunted manor and an equally haunted pub are not enough, then one only has to step next door from the famed Red Lion to find another gem in the world of the supernatural.

The Lodge is a wonderful Grade II listed Georgian building, now an upmarket bed-and-breakfast, and was once owned by Sir John Lubbock, the inventor of the bank holiday. After he died in 1913, the Lodge was inherited by his wife who later sold it to Alexander Keiller along with the Avebury Henge and many village buildings. During the Second World War the Lodge was the village machine gun post and in the 1990s it was used as a recording studio and home. In 2003, it opened as an upmarket vegetarian bed-and-breakfast.

Situated in the middle of the stone circle next to the Red Lion Pub, it has been claimed that the Lodge is the most haunted house in England. However, given the innumerable haunted houses in England, and indeed across the whole of the United Kingdom, one would need to remain sceptical at this claim. Whatever the case, it does appear to have a lot of ghostly phenomena including a ghostly Georgian gentleman, eerie apparitions of children, a ghostly young woman, and spectral voices. In addition a ghostly coach drawn by four horses is said to occasionally pull up outside its front.

And if this is not enough, it is also known for strange noises, temperature changes, and most oddly for a vegetarian bed-and-breakfast, the smell of frying bacon, although one must note that smells from the nearby Red Lion Pub could easily permeate the Lodge. And it was in the Lodge that Kirsten and I had a strange and rather unexplainable incident that one could suggest was of a supernatural origin.

After a day of sightseeing, especially the incredible White Horse of Uffington, a Neolithic stylised representation of a horse carved into a hillside in nearby Oxfordshire not far from Avebury, we checked into the lodge for the night, fully knowing the haunted history of the building.

The Lodge itself is a wonderfully grand building with its white-washed walls, portico, and symmetric bay windows. Framed each side by large green trees that shade the building on hot summer days, it is as inviting as it is interesting. The old wooden door at the front has a sign requesting that visitors remove their footwear, and once inside one is taken by the huge creaky staircase that leads upstairs to the opulently finished bedrooms. From the top of the flight of stairs one can look out through an exquisite domed window at the ancient stone henge that surrounds the village. A more wonderful place to stay cannot be imagined.

But it is not the architecture of the place that is of interest to us in this case for, as previously revealed, the Lodge is haunted by a number of ghosts and apparitions.

The night was cool, and after dinner we retired to our room upstairs. The bed, a high and luxurious period four-poster, called out to us after a long and tiring day, and in the dim light of bedside lamps the room was dark with shadowy corners and a strange but not unfriendly ambience. The two of us lay in the bed and read some brochures about the local history of the area until Kirsten decided to turn the lamp off. As she reached for the switch *it turned itself off*, apparently by its own accord. As both of us knew about the history and ghost lore of the Lodge we looked at each other curiously and decided that, given the nature of the place, and a healthy dose of scepticism, that we should at least experiment with the lamp before jumping to conclusions.

At first we turned the lamp back on and replicated everything we had done. The lamp did not turn off. I checked the switch to see if it was faulty but found that if anything, it was stiff and difficult to turn on and off. We then tried moving it, bumping it, tapping it and generally knocking it around to see if we could get it to turn off without touching it or the switch but to no avail, the lamp steadfastly refused to turn off. After exploring all possibilities as to how the lamp had turned itself off, we could find no logical reasons as to how and why it had done what it had done.

Is it possible some sort of unseen entity had kindly helped Kirsten when she decided to turn the light off? Could the ghost of something somehow have read her mind and turned off the light even as she reached for the switch? Is it possible, given the nature and history of the building that the ghost of a servant reached out over the years and did what would have been expected of a servant, that being, to turn off the light? And if so, then one would have to concede that some ghosts have intelligence and can interact with the present.

Whatever the case, although we slept soundly in this luxurious bedroom, the event remained in the back of my mind and I made sure my arms weren't sticking out above the covers as the last thing I wanted to feel during the night was the ghostly touch of some unseen entity.

Of course, there was no ghostly touch, nor anything with any semblance of the supernatural, and the night passed without incident.

In the morning, Kirsten was in the bathroom when she called out saying that she could smell bacon cooking. I walked into the bathroom and without doubt a strong smell of bacon was evident. Could this have been the same ghostly smell that people have reported over the years or could it have been something more mundane as previously suggested, the Red Lion Pub cooking breakfast?

But if we thought this was the last we were to hear of ghosts and the supernatural in the Lodge, we were to be mistaken as, at breakfast, the hostess informed us that the room we were in, although haunted, was not the most haunted. After telling us of tales of keys, knives, forks, and other small items often being moved by unseen hands, she told us of her son's experience. Apparently, her son, while sleeping in another bedroom opposite to ours, had woken up early one morning and witnessed, to his horror, a tall hooded figure somewhat like a monk, walk out through the closed doors of the wardrobe and across the room before exiting straight through the wall.

Maybe the Lodge needs to add this monk to its already extensive list of ghosts although whether or not it has made any more appearances is unknown to me.

And yet for all the stories of this quaint Georgian Lodge, it all pales in comparison to the mystery and myth of the majestic and awe-inspiring standing stones of Avebury, the largest stone circle in Britain and the most popular megalithic tourist site after Stonehenge. However, for all its age and mystery, there appears to be few legends attached to the site. Having said this, such a place does not require legends or folklore to stimulate the interest of the visitor.

The circle was constructed roughly around the time of the first phase of Stonehenge, that is, the ditch and stone circles being built between 2400 and 2600 BC. Quite incredibly, it has been estimated that it may have taken as much as 1.5 million man hours to place the massive sarsen stones and to construct the bank and ditch.

For some reason unknown to archaeologists, the site was effectively abandoned by the Iron Age. Although there is some evidence of human activity during Roman times, it is thought that this activity was not significant, and certainly not for any military or religious reason. However, about 600 AD during the early Saxon Period, a village appeared around the monument and over time extended into it. Sadly, by the Late Medieval and Early Modern periods, locals had destroyed many of the standing stones around the henge for religious and practical reasons, that being to use in new buildings.

The henge, a large circular bank with an internal ditch, is not perfectly circular and has a diameter of about 420 metres with a ditch 21 metres wide and 11 metres deep. When one realises that the present day ditch has had thousands of years of erosion and infilling, one gets an idea of how massive these earthworks must have been.

With a past shrouded in the mists of time, Avebury remains a mystery. How and why it was constructed is still not fully understood, and when and why it was abandoned has never been fully explained. Having said this, the henge clearly forms an imposing boundary to the stone circle but appears to have no defensive purpose as do other hill fort earthworks found all over the British Isles today. Being a henge and stone circle site, astronomical alignments are a popular theory to explain the positioning of the stones but this theory is not supported by any real evidence.

Fascinatingly, there have been reports of small figures, possibly elves or something similar, between the stones at night. In addition, unexplained lights and ghostly visitations have been reported and yet, for all of these, legends and myths and supernatural events surrounding the site seem to be few and far between in comparison to the buildings in and around the henge.

But if the vast stone circle of Avebury appears to be somewhat bereft of ghosts and ghostly happenings, then what of other equally impressive, if not so grandiose Neolithic sites?

CHAPTER 3

†

CORNWALL AND OTHER NEOLITHIC SITES

From ghoulies and ghosties and long-leggety beasties
And things that go bump in the night, Good Lord, deliver us!

—(ANONYMOUS)

It is a cool and slightly overcast day as I stride across the field towards West Kennett Long Barrow. From the road where I previously parked my car, the barrow appears as a low mound on the horizon; in fact it appears anything but a site of great significance. I look around, behind me is Silbury Hill sitting like a severely eroded grass covered pyramid. It is part of the Stonehenge, Avebury, and Associated Sites, a UNESCO World Heritage Site, but unlike Stonehenge, no one has the faintest idea what it is or what it was used for.

At forty metres high, it is the tallest prehistoric man-made mound in Europe and one of the largest in the world, Indeed, as large as some of the smaller Egyptian pyramids, and is estimated to be over 4,000 years old. Legend has it that it was built by the devil to hide gold and that it is haunted by the ghost of King Sil, who was said to have been buried in the mound in a golden coffin. Archaeological records do not support this legend but this does not take away from the mystical evocations of the place.

But it is not Silbury that I have come to see, so I continue to tramp purposefully across the grass field towards the distant mound. Around me the wind whistles and grey clouds scurry across the sky. On a day like this one could imagine what life might have been like for Neolithic man in this ancient landscape.

West Kennett Long Barrow sits quietly on a chalk ridge roughly two kilometres south of Avebury. It is a chambered barrow with two pairs of opposing chambers and a single terminal chamber that was used for burials. It is a phenomenal 100 metres in length and is one of the largest barrows in Britain. The entrance is a stone facade made from huge grey stones somewhat like the stones at Stonehenge, which is understandable given that it was constructed around 3600 BC, just 400 years before the first building stage of Stonehenge.

As I approach the barrow I am impressed and somewhat overawed by its size. From the road it seemed just a low smudge in a field of cows but now, when confronted by its stone-flanked entrance and grassy banks, I can appreciate the work that was put in to create such a structure, and the importance it must have had for the local population. With some anticipation and a little trepidation, I climb down the slippery and muddy stone steps and enter the darkness of the ancient burial chamber.

Early excavations suggested that the mound was indeed a burial chamber, and between 1859 and 1956, at least forty-six burials were found within the barrow. These ranged from babies to elderly persons with a great number of the bones being strangely disarticulated and some of the skulls and long bones missing. Anthropologists have since suggested that this was probably due to pagan ceremonies where the bones of ancestors were periodically removed from their burial place and displayed to the local population.

Inside is dark and musty and the atmosphere slightly oppressive. It is a place where you feel that something is watching you or following you and you speak in reverent hushed whispers that echo into the depths of the chamber. The bones may be long gone but the spirits still seem to inhabit this holy prehistoric place. And yet, for all of this one must ask, is it haunted?

Well yes, according to local legend, which tells us that the barrow is visited by a ghostly priest and a large white hound at sunrise every midsummer's day. But this could be nothing more than a distant folk memory of a ritual event from a time that was significant in the use of the barrow. And yet even if this were the case, the barrow does have a strange atmosphere.

Some point to the fact that the barrow is used by modern-day pagans and occultists for various ceremonies, including satanic rituals, and that this somehow contributes to the manifestation of ghosts in and around its chambers. And yet, how can a simple ceremony bring about a ghost? Surely a ghost must already be present for it to manifest itself in any way, shape, or form? Or is there a deeper, darker secret at play?

Although firsthand accounts of ghosts at West Kennett Long Barrow are hard to come by, there is an interesting, if not slightly harrowing, story of a woman who visited the barrow one evening close to dusk, and was apparently touched by a large number of invisible hands when inside the actual structure.

But if the barrow is haunted, then today I am out of luck as nothing out of the ordinary occurs. I take a few photos of the area and the barrow itself and trudge back through the windy fields towards my car. If West Kennett Long Barrow has not thrown up anything of a supernatural nature, then surely my next stop will?

And with this I find myself driving further west as the weather begins to close in and a drizzle permeates the grey skies. Miles and miles of green tinged fields roll past the window of my vehicle as the rain patters softly on the windscreen. Through the drizzle I see the occasional ancient monument and desolate isolated farmhouses as the skies turn grey and a fog descends upon the land. This is not the England of childhood memories where the sun shines over rolling green fields and lush forests or where cows stand happily in the warm summer sun. This is no longer the world of Kenneth Grahame's *The Wind in the Willows* but something else more akin to a Grimm's brother's tale.

And sure enough, soon I am in a landscape that cries out its supernatural and mythological past. This is a place where people do not only fear the living but also the dead, and in the mist and rain one can understand why.

Bodmin Moor is a windswept, granite-strewn area covering over 200 square kilometres and dates back to Carboniferous period. It is a lonely and dramatic place punctuated by wind-eroded granite tors that sit silently in the thick rainy mist and tower over expanses of inhospitable open moorland. Marshland and ancient bogs on the high moors drain into shallow moorland valleys, and rivers cross onto softer shale-based ground carving themselves river valleys filled with ferns and oak woodlands. To the south is the legendary Dozmary Pool where Sir Bedivere reputedly threw the sword Excalibur into the lake, and prehistoric burial barrows dot the foreboding and isolated landscape.

Although the moor covers a relatively small area, the open, curving environment of the plateau creates a surprising sense of scale, remoteness, and isolation that seems to be enhanced or reinforced by an impression of timelessness that contributes to the moor's distinctive and challenging character. And although the moor is now crisscrossed with roads, it is still a place where the traveller can be faced with a natural environment in its most rudimentary form and the unwary or unprepared may easily become lost among the stones, bogs, and river valleys where the descending clouds and mist falls quickly creating an eerie and inhospitable setting.

It is a place where moss-encrusted tombstones and Celtic crosses lean wearily against the unforgiving weather, and mysterious stone circles huddle together in the mist as if protecting their long forgotten secrets. Abandoned mine buildings sit gaunt and stark against the skyline, their dark silhouettes giving off a menacing air in the misty atmosphere.

First farmed by Bronze Age settlers, and known for its wild and untamed beauty, it is a place that has engendered fear and awe, and as such has a rich history of folklore and legend. This is a place of ghosts, werewolves, devil dogs, and the Beast of Bodmin, as well as other creatures of legend and nightmare.

From the A30 motorway I glance across this vast expanse of largely uninhabited land. Now and then a granite tor looms prominent in the mist and a slight shiver runs up my spine. Today I am safe and warm in a motorcar, sheltered from the elements and the creatures of the moors, and yet, it was not that long ago that this place was a daunting obstacle for travellers with much of the ground falling away into featureless marshlands. With a lack of prominent landscape features and fickle and rapidly changing weather, including the aforementioned mist and rain, it would have been an easy place to become completely lost.

And once lost one would have been exposed not only to the creatures of the supernatural but to your fellow man and, although there are many small villages around the moor, large areas of it are completely isolated, the perfect hunting ground for robbers, murderers, and other malicious types who could work their dastardly deeds with impunity.

Whatever the case, the West Country is a particularly strange and foreboding place and as I drive across these lonely expanses I recall a peculiar and particularly frightening legend, that of the "hairy hands," which, although not from Bodmin Moor, were said to haunt a particular stretch of road on Dartmoor in Devon.

Since about 1910 the road between Postbridge and Two Bridges, now designated the B3212, has been the scene of many strange occurrences, and many motorists and cyclists have reported mysterious accidents where the driver has reported that their vehicle has swerved off the road as if something had taken hold of the steering wheel.

In most instances the victims of this apparent supernatural manifestation survived; however, in 1921, Dr. E. H. Helby, who worked at Dartmoor Prison, crashed his motorcycle and sidecar and died of a broken neck. Two young girls riding in the sidecar survived. And a few weeks after this event, a coach unaccountably drove off the road and some passengers were injured when flung from their seats. The driver later stated that he felt as if a pair of invisible hands had grabbed the steering wheel and wrenched it towards the ditch.

Later that year, in August, an Army captain reported that his motorcycle was forced off the road by a pair of invisible hands. In his statement he indicated that he felt a pair of hairy hands close over his hands and that, although he fought to regain control of his bike, they forced him to crash.

And strangely, not all the incidents involve vehicles. In 1924 a woman camping on the moor with her husband reported seeing a hairy hand clawing at a window of her caravan late one night. Apparently, the hand retreated only after she made some sort of religious sign, presumably the sign of the cross.

With the legend of the hairy hands appearing in the national press, investigations were carried out on the road and it was determined that the accidents were most likely due to the camber of the roads surface which, in places, apparently reached dangerous levels. These dangerous sections were duly repaired and locals simply blamed the accidents on people unfamiliar with the area and driving too fast. In any case, it seems that the hairy hands have been quiet in recent times.

And so with this story still strong in my mind, I pull into the carpark of the Jamaica Inn and scurry across its paved grounds into the warmth and safety of the old building. But if one expects sanctuary from the unknown world outside, then this isolated dwelling may not be the place to be.

The Jamaica Inn sits in an isolated part of Bodmin Moor in Cornwall. It was built in 1750 and was a haven for travellers and smugglers alike, and was also where Daphne du Maurier set her novel of the same name after she had become lost in thick fog and had to stay the night at the inn. Inside the inn is comfortable and warm with flintlock rifles, pistols, Toby mugs, and cutlasses hanging from low-slung beamed ceilings. And yet for all this, the inn is a place where ghostly legends and myths abound for the very stones of this place have witnessed much murder and foul deeds over the centuries.

On still moonlit nights locals will tell you of ghostly horse hooves and steel coach wheels being heard on the cobblestones outside the inn, while footsteps from an unseen person or persons are heard to pace the corridors late at night. In the main bar a strange, tall man in a black cape and tricorn hat often appears and then vanishes just as quickly through solid doors, and staff often hear whispered voices speaking in strange dialects.

Legend has it that in the late 1800s, a traveller was drinking ale when he was summoned outside, most probably to make some sort of shady deal. Leaving his ale he stepped outside into the chill and mist of the night and was never again seen alive. The next day his body was found on the moors. Today, when footsteps are heard pacing alongside the bar, it is believed that the man has returned to finish his ale. As well, there are numerous reports of a figure seen sitting on a wall outside the inn. Neither speaking nor moving his appearance is said to be that of the murdered traveller.

In addition there have been reports of the ghostly figure of a man hanging from a nearby tree and oddly, a ghostly flying cloak.

But it is not just the inn that is haunted, as in April 1844, eighteen-year-old Charlotte Dymond who worked for a widow and her son at Penhale Farm on the edge of Bodmin Moor, went for a walk with Matthew Weekes, a farmhand who also worked at Penhale. Charlotte was said to have been wearing her Sunday best, a green striped dress and a red shawl. Later that day, Matthew returned alone and told everyone that Charlotte had gone off on her own in a different direction and that he had no idea where she was. With Charlotte remaining missing after a few days, Weekes suggested that Charlotte had in fact left the region to find work elsewhere.

Tragically, several days after her disappearance, Charlotte's lifeless body was found in a stream with her throat savagely slashed. Matthew Weekes was tried for her murder. All the evidence pointed to Weekes being the culprit as it was thought that the dead woman was seeing another man and that he killed her while in a jealous rage. Weekes was later hanged in Bodmin Jail, although proclaiming his innocence until the very end.

Charlotte was buried in the churchyard at Davidstow, and a monument to her was erected at Roughtor where her lifeless body was found. However, in death she has never found peace, and on lonely nights, especially on the anniversary of her death, her ghost has been seen walking around the tor in a green striped dress and red shawl. It has also been suggested that sentry duty at a nearby military post was particularly unpopular due to the appearance of this frightening apparition.

But if the tragic tale of Charlotte Dymond is eerie enough, then what of the legend of Dozmary Pool and Jan Tregeagle?

Apparently, Tregeagle was a seventeenth-century steward of the Lanhydrock Estate near Bodmin. In life he was a cruel and heartless man who murdered his wife and children, mistreated the estates tenants, cheated an orphan out of his inheritance, and just to make sure no one had any doubts about his character, struck a bargain with the devil. After Tregeagle died, some of his victims went to court to try to get back what he had taken from them, but while the judge was summing up, the ghost of Tregeagle slowly materialised in the witness box and proceeded to answer the questions put to him.

Following this, Tregeagle somehow managed to escape being sent back to hell but instead was condemned to work for eternity on Bodmin Moor emptying Dozmary Pool with a broken limpet shell. So he cannot escape; he is watched over by the hounds of hell, who wait to drag him back to Hades should he try to escape.

Of course, Dozmary Pool is also well known for being the lake into which the dying Arthur instructed Sir Bedivere to cast Excalibur, and when one is surrounded by the awesome desolation of the pool one can truly believe in Arthurian legends of old as to walk this bleak expanse is to allow yourself to stray into a nether region, some sort of timeless limbo where the souls of previous ages mix with those of the present. The pool itself is a grim expanse of sullen water surrounded by rocky, reed-filled banks and low treeless hills, and it takes no imagination to see the ghostly image of a knight standing on the shores attempting to relieve himself of his king's great sword.

At Lanhydrock House an unknown entity is said to haunt the gallery and the drawing room, the only parts of the original house that still stand as a fire in the nineteenth century destroyed the rest of the house. The building is also said to be haunted by a man who was hanged by Royalists during the Civil War, and a little old lady dressed in grey has been seen sitting quietly in the Long Gallery. Some people, thinking she is a guide, have approached her only to see her vanish before their eyes. In addition, the nursery, complete with Victorian toys and books, seems particularly active and some people claim to have heard children giggling in this area. In the billiards room, where the gentlemen would retire after dinner, visitors have reported the smell of cigar smoke, remembering of course that smoking is strictly forbidden in National Trust properties.

Not that far away, at St. Nectan's Glen, the woodland has produced an abundance of ghostly sightings over the years, the majority of which appear to be ghostly hooded monks. In addition the ghostly figure of an old man has been observed standing by the water, and in a strange report from July 1981, a person witnessed a burning human skull in a tree after hearing whispering voices.

So what are we supposed to make of these strange tales? Are they just fanciful myths told around a roaring fire late at night when safe and warm inside a comfortable pub with an ale? Or do they indicate that something could really be happening in this desolate place? Without doubt, the ghostly stories of the Jamaica Inn and surrounding Bodmin Moor are really no different to those told all over England, it's just that the location of the inn seems to reinforce its eeriness. And of course, Bodmin Moor is also the home to the legendary Beast of Bodmin, a massive black feline creature that has been terrifying locals for centuries.

But it is not just the Moor and the Jamaica Inn that interests us on our supernatural quest as in these moist and clammy climes sits Bodmin Jail, now semi-ruined but open as a visitors centre, and reputedly haunted by many spectral figures. The ghost of Matthew Weekes, the convicted killer of Charlotte Dymond, is said to wander the corridors of this grim stone building, furious at the injustice dealt to him.

The jail itself seems to radiate an aura of unease from its crumbling walls and echoing corridors. At first glimpse the visitor is left in no doubt as to the sinister nature of the place for its grey bulk looms out of the mist, and a feeling of utter desolation and loneliness takes hold. And once inside one finds themselves in a nightmare world where the vestiges of a tortured past seems to linger in the very air itself, and the prospects of encountering something malevolent appear inevitable.

Constructed in the 1770s to hold Napoleonic prisoners of war, it was built using 20,000 tons of granite quarried on Bodmin Moor and remained open until 1927. Between 1785 and 1909, fifty-five people were executed in this grim and forbidding place, including, as we have seen, Matthew Weekes at whose execution an estimated 20,000 people turned up to witness his final throes.

Besides housing prisoners, the jail briefly housed some of Britain's greatest treasures. During the First World War the Crown Jewels and the Domesday Book, among other priceless artefacts, were locked up for safe keeping in the jail.

But this aside, what terrors must have gone through the minds of people like Weekes as they waited in their cells for the day of their death? Is it possible that these intense feelings and emotions are now part of the very building itself? Is this the reason that so many people who visit the site complain of being overcome by feelings of desolation and despondency as they explore its dark maze of dank mouldy corridors and claustrophobic cells? It is a place that seems to cry out in anguish as if the very stones are in pain.

Another former prisoner whose spirit seemingly cannot leave Bodmin Jail is that of Selina Wadge, who was arrested in 1878 for the murder of her youngest son, Harry. After her arrest she told a police constable that her lover, James Westwood, had urged her to murder him so that they could marry and be together. Westwood strenuously denied these claims and stated that he held no bad feelings towards the boy.

At her trial the jury found Selina guilty, and even though they recommended leniency on the grounds that she had taken good care of her children and that, in their opinion, the murder had not been premeditated, the judge disagreed and sentenced her to death.

On the morning of 15 August 1878, Selina Wadge was led from her cell clutching a white handkerchief and crying inconsolably. As she climbed the scaffold she uttered her last words, "Lord deliver me from this miserable world," and at 8:00 a.m., the executioner pulled the lever of the trap sending her to her death. Gruesomely her body, reputedly still holding the white handkerchief, was left dangling for an hour before being cut down and buried within the prison grounds. Her tormented ghost is now said to wander the prison grounds, a forlorn and tragic figure in a long dress, and although not malevolent, she is said to reach out for small children.

And so from the wilds of Bodmin Moor and the grey and confronting bleakness of Bodmin Jail, where else in this most ancient and mysterious of landscapes can we explore? What other features can we find in this landscape so steeped in myth and legend that the historical past has almost become indistinguishable from folklore? What other Arthurian legends exist and what are their contributions to this shady world of secretive half-truths and long forgotten tales. Indeed, if the still and soulful depths of Dozmary Pool is the resting place of King Arthur's sword, then what other places can we examine?

It is a cool, windy, and slightly overcast day as Kirst and I drive along the picturesque road from Boscastle, through Trethevy and into the small village of Tintagel. On our left we pass St. Paul's Catholic Church, oddly enough, for this part of the country, a mere forty-odd years old. A few hundred metres further and we pass the old post office, built out of stone in the fourteenth century and believed to be haunted by numerous ghosts. Now owned and run by the National Trust, it is a wonderfully ancient-looking building with a delightful wavy slate roof and sits nestled into the more modern parts of the village.

And yet it is not this fabulously old building that we have come to see because, not far from this building are the magical ruins of the legendary Tintagel Castle.

Tintagel Castle is a bleak but beautiful place as befits the legendary birth place of King Arthur. Sitting atop a windswept and barren plateau on the rugged North Cornwall coast, it offers dramatic views of the ocean from its fascinating ruins. Standing there on the stone walls looking across the ruins one can easily imagine the ghosts of past wandering aimlessly through the mist and ruined walls in this isolated and stunningly desolate place.

The castle itself is a medieval fortification located on the peninsula of Tintagel Island, just adjacent to the village of Tintagel. Due to a number of artefacts found at the site, it has been suggested that it was once occupied in the Romano-British period, although no distinct Roman era structure has been found to prove this.

What is certain, however, is that during the Early Medieval period it was settled, and was probably one of the seasonal residences of the regional kings of Dumnonia. In the later medieval period, around the thirteenth century, after Cornwall had become part of England, a castle was built on the site by Richard, Earl of Cornwall. Archaeological investigation into the site began in the nineteenth century, and the site soon became a tourist attraction with its long association with the Arthurian legends going back as far as the twelfth century when Geoffrey of Monmouth described Tintagel as the place of Arthur's conception in his largely mythical account of British history *The Historia Regum Britanniae*.

But it is not Arthurian legends that we are here to study, as interesting as they may be, as this little village in far north Cornwall has its own throng of spirits and ghosts.

After parking the car and dropping our bags at our accommodation, a quaint, vaguely Tudor-looking, two-storey bed-and-breakfast on Fore Street, we decide to take the path down to the castle. This track is initially hard to find considering that it goes to the most famous of Arthurian sites outside Glastonbury, and yet, when one finally finds the entrance and starts off on the track as it winds its way steeply through the Vale of Avalon past grassy fields and crystal clear streams, one is transported far from civilization to a land where legendary kings and queens and dragons and piskies all still exist. The grass is a peculiar emerald green and grey stones jut out from the landscape as they must have done a thousand years ago, and one would not really be surprised to see a goblin or elf or something similar sitting under a rocky crag cooking a meal.

The site itself is quite large with the major part of the ruin sitting on a peninsula that has, over time, eroded to the point that it is now almost an island. At the visitors centre one is bombarded with Arthurian legends from plastic dragons and knights and numerous books and booklets about King Arthur and the castle itself. Although interesting the lure of the actual ruin is too much to bear and so, vowing to stop back in after exploring the site, we continue on.

Below us is a pristine little beach sitting snugly between the eroded cliff face and covered mainly in smooth pebbles that are washed by the particularly cold green-blue seas that pound against the rocky cliff. Into this picture-postcard little cove falls a small waterfall, crystal clear and pristine after running through the grassy lands above the cliff. And also down here, next to the water, is the legendary Merlin's Cave where the actual wizard was reputed to live and whose ghost is said to still haunt.

The wind has picked up and it is slightly chilly when exposed to the elements but by now the sky is clear other than the occasional high cloud. We cross a narrow wooden bridge and then climb ancient stone steps that jut from the side of the cliff. Once at the top we enter a smallish courtyard through an arched wooden door. From the battlements one can almost touch the seas and sky simultaneously and it becomes evident why this place was chosen as a castle.

You then move on through the courtyard following a path that takes you past the remains of some Dark Age houses that date from about the fifth or sixth century. There is a choice of paths now that lead off into this magical place. The upper path leads up to a thirteenth century walled garden at the centre of the island while the lower path makes its way along the northeastern edge of the island towards the "Northern Ruins," like the early dwellings, dating from the fifth or sixth century AD.

The views from here are spectacular and the sheer size of the site becomes evident. If one is to wander around one soon finds a cave, possibly used as a medieval larder or cold store and, surprisingly, the visitor can walk down into it. Not far from this cave, almost in the centre of the plateau lies the well which would have been the only source of fresh water on the island.

As one continues on, the route starts to skirt the southern cliffs and the edge of the ruins falls off abruptly into the sea many tens of metres below. If one is to glance over these battlements, one can make out what looks like collapsed stones now sitting on the water's edge being slowly battered against the rocks. This side of the castle often collapses into the sea due to the never ending assault by the cold rough waters and as such must be a conservation and safety nightmare.

The path then passes a chapel, believed to have been built in the eleventh century but in a state of disrepair, like the rest of the island. The path soon drops down a number of well-worn steps back to the Courtyard, the exit from the Castle.

It appears that the castle is relatively free of ghosts and spirits, which seems odd given that this area is steeped with supernatural legends and myths. Given that historians have pretty much derided the Arthurian links to the castle, in 1998, the discovery of the carved inscription on a piece of stone, later dubbed the "Artognou Stone," sent waves of anticipation through the world of Arthurian legend.

The Artognou Stone was so called as its sixth century Latin inscription translates as *Artognou father of a descendent of Col made this*. It has been suggested that this stone was the foundation stone for a much older structure that once stood on the castle site and even if one doubts the link, the similarity between "Artognou" and "Arthur" is, to say the least, quite fascinating.

But this is a place where time appears to stand still and history and legend can comfortably exist side by side. This is a place where the magic of Merlin is very real and, when combined with the powerful and iconic imagery of Arthur, instills a sense of timeless wonder and beauty.

But as much as Tintagel remains a magnet for poets, dreamers, historians, and folklorists alike, it appears that the ghosts of the past remain hidden on this bleak rocky outcrop which, given the history of the region, seems somewhat surprising. Is this because the ghosts of this castle have now faded into the past like a long forgotten memory? Or maybe they choose to remain hidden from the prying eyes of the public? Or maybe they simply don't exist here?

Whatever the case, this is a place of exceptional rugged beauty and if one were to read of a particular ghost appearance at the castle, then one would not be surprised in any way. Having said that, if the castle seems to lack a ghostly presence then why it is so?

Surely this enigmatic place of mystery and legend must be haunted? Of course, there is the legend that Merlin himself haunts the dank seawater-sprayed cave in the small cove below Tintagel but as we have seen, Tintagel, for all its Arthurian connections most probably had nothing to do with the legendary king of old. And if this is so, then how could the ghost of Merlin, if he actually existed, haunt the cave?

Of course, he can't, and his ghost is no more than myth, somewhat like Jan Tregeagle emptying Dozmary Pool with a broken shell for eternity. And yet, if one is to enter Merlin's Cave one feels as if there is *something* in there, something that is not quite from this world. It is an ancient emotion, one that must have been felt by primitive man when hundreds of thousands of years ago he too entered strange dark caves where he left his mark through cave paintings of extreme beauty and wonder.

And it is this same emotion, something between fear, trepidation, and inquisitiveness that one feels in this dark cave. But there are no cave paintings here and it is doubtful that Cro-Magnon man ever sat in these caves. And as such, why does it feel the way it does? Do we, as modern day *Homo sapiens* somehow retain an evolutionary fear of the dark and of enclosed spaces given that our distant ancestors were creatures of the plains and the trees, not of dark musty caves.

True, over time we left the trees and roamed ancient African savannahs where we stood upright to enable us to better see danger. And as a consequence we soon found ourselves no longer suited to an arboreal life, therefore retreating to the relative safety of caves and rocky knolls and copses where we could at least defend ourselves from creatures of the night, leopards, lions, tigers, and other carnivores.

But who were these first beings to venture into the dark unknown of caves? Did they do it as a purposeful move or were they forced to do so by some calamity? True, caves afforded us shelter not only from the danger of animals but also from the weather. And in time we adapted to this new life. Indeed, what is a modern-day house but an artificial cave where we can sleep and live in safety?

And yet for all this, we still find caves somewhat frightening and we must ask why. Is it that we do have some sort of evolutionary memory from so many millennia ago or is it a simple fear of the dark, again, an evolutionary trait that we, as modern day humans, have still not quite managed to dispose of? And for good reason, as the dark still holds many secrets.

What superstitions and beliefs did ancient man hold? What did he talk about when safe in the knowledge that his fire which burned brightly at the entrance of a cave would ensure that he and his family would awake in the morning and not be dragged off into the night to meet a grisly end at the teeth and claws of a huge and ferocious carnivore. What would he have talked about in this flickering light?

The stars in the sky, the sun in the morning, and the moon at night? What were they? What purpose did they serve? And the darkness, what lived out there in the night? What horrors awaited the unwary? What creatures emitted the unearthly screams, grunts, and croaks? The fire and cave were insurance against these horrors.

Is this the time when man developed a sense of spirituality, and with it, the belief in the supernatural? In 1957, a grave dated at 60,000 BP to 80,000 BP containing the skeleton of a Neanderthal man was found in a cave in northeastern Iraq. Although crude and shallow, importantly, archaeologists discovered pollen. The man had been buried with flowers with the inevitable conclusion being that early man, both *Homo Erectus* and Neanderthal, had gained spirituality in that they were questioning what it was to live, and just as importantly, what happened when they died.

And with this newfound spirituality logical conclusions would have been drawn. Questions with no real answers that consisted of complex ideas regarding belief and ideals. What happened when you died? Where did you go after death? Did you become one of the stars in the skies above? Did you become the spirit of an animal? Was it possible that the rustling in the leaves outside was the spirit of your dead clansman?

Even today we see the residue of these ancient evolutionary traits. Every child can remember camping with friends and family when the night has fallen and the flames flicker with a hypnotic effect. And beyond these flames and safety is the dark, a void of unknown where creatures of the night exist, staying just out of sight but waiting for a chance to wreak their evilness upon the unwary. And every person today can remember that slightly panicky feeling when they ventured away from the campfire and into the bush where the strange noises and darkness sent an icy shiver up their spine, and one had to fight the urge to run when returning to the safety of the flames.

And when the fire has died down, and the embers pop and crackle and emit an eerie glow that barely lights the bush around the camp site, one only has to mention a ghost before everyone will come forward with their own ghost story.

Trees groan and creak, owls cry out in their haunting tones, various other animals scurry around in the undergrowth creating uncertainty in your mind as to what is making these sounds. And this uncertainty is amplified by the darkness so that, in the glowing light of a dying fire, the trees themselves seem to gather a life of their own and push forward towards you, as if to engulf you. It is little wonder that man has believed in goblins, fairies, elves, ghosts, and other creatures of the paranormal for in this highly-charged atmosphere they are very real.

These legends and myths are strong in the West Country and if not quite supernatural, they do have a supernatural air to them. But if we cannot find any real evidence of ghosts in such an ancient place as Tintagel then how can we be sure that ghosts exist in other places? Where should we now look having pretty much drawn a blank in this isolated but incredibly beautiful corner of the country? Should we follow the Arthurian trail and see where this leads us? Or should we follow the lead of Neolithic sites such as Avebury, Stonehenge, or any number of other mysterious prehistoric places and see what supernatural activity revels itself?

Given that Arthurian legends and castles are intricately entwined in both history and myth it would seem prudent that this is the path we should follow, at least, for a while. And as such we find ourselves at another site not only deeply ingrained in the Arthurian legend and significance, but also in supernatural events and activity. This place is Glastonbury.

CHAPTER 4

†

GLASTONBURY, THE BLOODY ASSIZES, AND A HANGING JUDGE

Ah, distinctly I remember it was in the bleak December,
And each separate dying ember wrought its ghost upon the floor.

—EDGAR ALLAN POE

Glastonbury Abbey, now a Grade 1 listed building and a Scheduled Ancient Monument, was founded in the seventh century, and by the fourteenth century had risen to become one of the richest and most powerful monasteries in England. From around the twelfth century the Glastonbury area was associated with the legend of King Arthur, a connection that was heavily promoted by medieval monks who proclaimed that Glastonbury was Avalon, the legendary resting place of Arthur. Christian legends have also claimed that the abbey was founded in the first century by none other than Joseph of Arimathea, the man who donated his own prepared tomb for Jesus' burial after his crucifixion.

Apart from this, it has also been suggested that the area around Glastonbury, then a swampy marshland, may have also been a site of religious importance in Celtic or pre-Celtic times, and the fact that these swampy marshlands surrounded Glastonbury Tor, where the abbey is situated, gave rise to the legend of Avalon being on a mysterious island surrounded by a misty body of foreboding water.

In 1184, a fire destroyed most of the monastic buildings and, although reconstruction began almost immediately, pilgrim visits to the abbey dropped. However, this was soon rectified by the fortunate discovery in 1191 of what was believed to be the final resting place of King Arthur as well as Queen Guinevere.

According to the chronicler, Giraldus Cambrensis, the Archdeacon of Brecon, the then Abbot, Henry de Sully, ordered a search and discovered, at the depth of sixteen feet, a massive hollowed oak trunk containing two skeletons. Above the trunk under a covering stone was a leaden cross with the specific inscription *Hic jacet sepultus inclitus rex Arthurus in insula Avalonia* which translates to *"Here lies interred the famous King Arthur on the Isle of Avalon."*

Of course, after this miraculous discovery pilgrim visits again became more frequent. Whether the coffin was planted by the monks is not known, but it is almost certain that the whole thing was a hoax designed to entice pilgrims back to the monastery.

In 1536, at the start of the Dissolution of the Monasteries, it was believed that there were over 800 monasteries, nunneries, and friaries in England. However, by 1541, there were none. More than 15,000 monks and nuns were dispersed, and the buildings seized by the Crown to be sold off or leased. Glastonbury Abbey, having significant amounts of silver and gold as well as its attached lands, was ripe for picking. In September 1539, the abbey was visited on the orders of Thomas Cromwell, First Earl of Essex, and the abbey was stripped of its valuables. The abbot at the time, Richard Whyting, who had been a signatory to the Act of Supremacy that made Henry VIII the head of the church, resisted and as such was hanged, drawn, and quartered as a traitor on Glastonbury Tor in November 1539.

Today, the Abbey is nothing more than a ruin. However, this is not to take away from the place as it possesses a somewhat evocative beauty that seems to have transcended time itself. Along with the ruins of Tintern Abbey in Wales, immortalised by the words of Wordsworth and others, it is the archetypal ruined English monastery. It is a place of legend, romance, grand history, and in our case, ghosts.

But what sort of ghosts would one expect in such a place? Do eerie dark shadows of hooded monks lurk in the now open corridors of the ruins? Does the tragic figure of Richard Whyting make his presence known to those who dare to wander alone at night through the remnants of this once great institution? Is it possible, however remotely so, that the ghost of King Arthur himself appears to the unwary, now a tragic figure betrayed by his comrades and loved ones and defeated in battle?

There is a legend that suggests that Arthur did not die on the Isle of Avalon, and that he is simply waiting for a time when his country once again needs him when he will rise like some biblical messianic being to right the wrongs of the country and restore it to justice. A number of locations have been suggested from where Arthur would actually return from with the earliest recorded place being none other than Avalon. The medieval chronicler Geoffrey of Monmouth stated that Arthur had been mortally wounded at Camlann but was then carried by boat to the Isle of Avalon where he was be to be cured of his wounds.

Another tradition, first referenced by Gervase of Tilbury, an aristocratic thirteenth-century canon lawyer, statesman, and writer, in his treatise *Otia Imperialia* (c. 1211), indicated that Arthur was waiting to return from beneath a mountain or hill. This legend was maintained into the nineteenth century in British folklore, and many subsequent writers have interpreted it as Arthur residing in some sort of otherworldly underground.

Other notions suggest that Arthur is simply absent as he is leading the Wild Hunt, an ancient folk myth prevalent across northern, western, and central Europe which tells of a ghostly group of huntsmen complete with

horses, bugles, and hounds in mad pursuit across the skies or along the ground. The hunters may be the dead or fairies or even unidentified lost souls, deities, spirits, historical figures, or mythical figures such as Woden, or as we have seen, Arthur himself.

Other legends suggest, somewhat mundanely when compared to being the leader of the Wild Hunt, that Arthur had simply been turned into a crow or raven.

The romantic idea of Arthur's eventual return in times of dilemma or unrest has become popular with a number of modern writers. John Masefield in his poem *Midsummer Night* from 1928 used the idea of Arthur sleeping under a hill as the central theme while C. S. Lewis, writer of the *The Chronicles of Narnia*, among other works, was also was inspired by this aspect of Arthur's legend in his novel *That Hideous Strength* (1945) in which King Arthur was said to be living in the land of Abhalljin, oddly enough, on the planet Venus.

Of course, C. S. Lewis, novelist, literary critic, poet, academic, medievalist, essayist, theologian, as well as close friend of J. R. R. Tolkien, wove both Arthurian and Christian motifs into his works, which dealt quite implicitly with Christian themes such as sin, humanity's fall from grace, and redemption. And given that the modern (French) construct of Arthur is based upon strong Christian beliefs, it is little wonder that Lewis chose this path as a background to underpin his writings.

But what does this have to do with ghosts? And especially those that are reputed to haunt the ruins of the abbey as well as the tor that sits high about the town? And to find out, maybe we should delve a little more into what a ghost is, or at least, is suspected or reputed to be.

What is a ghost is a question that I am asked many times. After my book *A Case for Ghosts*, people began actively seek me out to explain my views on ghosts and hauntings. I even fronted a number of talk-back radio programs where I would listen to the audience who would phone in and tell me their experiences, to which I would put forward my theories as to what may have happened, or be happening.

And so, what exactly is a ghost?

Well firstly, I should say what a ghost isn't, as when we speak of ghosts people generally assume that they are the spirit of a dead person who for some reason or another, is destined to haunt this world forever, unable to be truly dead, or alive, stuck in some sort of limbo where they don't understand that they have to move on to somewhere else, be that heaven or hell or something we have yet to name. Although this is a popular opinion about what ghosts are, it is not supported by the evidence. Indeed, ghosts it would seem *can be* the spirits of dead people or lost souls, but most obviously, not all ghosts react or act the same; therefore, how can all be simply long-dead people from previous historical eras?

And to demonstrate this I shall start with an easily understood working definition which would suggest that a ghost is a human, or sometimes animal figure or shape that cannot be logically physically present and has been witnessed by a person or persons. As such we can then define a haunting as being a series of unexplained events or experiences in a certain specific location due to the suspected presence of a ghost or spirit.

Of course, these definitions are extremely broad and, as we shall see in the final chapter of this book, do not quite cover the complete spectrum of ghosts and hauntings, either in a traditional or modern sense. And so we must ask, what are ghosts really like?

In a very basic sense it appears that ghosts can appear at any time of day or night, during any time of the year, in any weather, environment, or atmospheric conditions. There is no definite rise in sightings on certain special days such as Christmas, Easter, Halloween, Samhain, or Beltane, and they are reported in many different places and cultures. However, ghosts are seemingly more concentrated in areas where people currently work or live, or once worked or lived. Contrary to popular belief, ghosts are rarely sighted in graveyards. After all, graveyards are where bodies are taken after death, and not the actual place of death.

Surprisingly, as ghosts are suspected to be spirits of the dead, they almost always are seen wearing clothes, although one must note that some ghosts appear as shadowy forms and the witness cannot distinguish clothes or any other features. They can sometimes appear as if they are slightly blurred, and are not usually accompanied by any background of a historical nature, for instance, a background from the ghost's actual past like a castle wall or gallows.

Oddly enough, most ghost reports suggest that they usually look like normal people. Indeed, there are numerous ghost sightings where people have reported what appears to be a real person, albeit, usually in odd clothing, only to find that they have inexplicably disappeared. And, contrary to popular belief, ghosts rarely glow and are rarely transparent, although in some cases this is so. If we now throw in the phenomena known as a poltergeist, we can see that ghosts are not as simple to describe as we first may have thought so.

And just to ensure the reader knows what we are talking about here I shall give a quick rundown on the poltergeist phenomena, something that has been reported for thousands of years.

Poltergeists have been described as being noisy, mischievous, and occasionally malevolent spirits who manifest their presence by making noises, moving objects, turning electrical equipment on and off, and even assaulting people. The term poltergeist comes from the German words *poltern* which means "to knock," and *geist* meaning "spirit."

Poltergeist activity ranges from the non-threatening to the inexplicable and can include moving and hiding keys to throwing stones and smashing glass or pottery. Reports of large furniture being moved around rooms, and even levitation of people has also been reported in some circumstances. In the most severe cases people have allegedly been attacked and have shown bites and scratch marks on their bodies.

In general, poltergeist activity starts and stops abruptly although the duration of the occurrences may last up to several hours spread randomly over a period of up to a few years. The activity almost always occurs at night when someone is present. Strangely, poltergeist activity is usually associated with a person who seems to serve as a focus for the activity, more often than not, a prepubescent female.

It has been suggested by some researchers that most poltergeist occurrences are not caused by spirits or ghosts, but by a person suffering from intense repressed anger, hostility, and sexual tension, which makes perfect sense in the case of the presence of a teenage girl. It is also suggested that the activity is a way for the child to express hostility without the fear of punishment.

Whether a poltergeist is a ghost or not is an interesting question and one we shall look at further in this book. However we can say, without doubt, that poltergeist activity falls well within the scope of ghostly or supernatural occurrences. And as such, the reader starts to get the idea that ghosts come in many different shapes and forms.

The word ghost is the most common and most popular collective term for paranormal phenomena. And as a result pretty much everything supernatural can be attributed to ghosts and ghostly behaviour. However, we have seen that poltergeists act very differently, using psychokinesis, the ability to use the mind to move matter, while other ghosts generally use simple phenomena such as noises and flickering lights as evidence of their existence. Of course, the spectrum is so wide that it is difficult to generalise, suffice to say the two are very different, especially as poltergeist activity appears to be intelligence driven and somewhat frighteningly, can interact with people.

Although I am greatly simplifying the argument, common or standard hauntings or ghostly phenomena tend to be more sedate. They are heard, smelt, seen, felt, and sensed but generally do not appear to be able to, or want to, cause harm. If anything, most are something like a tape recording of a historical event, a holographic image if you wish, and adhere to the stone tape theory of hauntings.

In his book *Ghost and Ghoul* (1961), Thomas Lethbridge proposed the theory that ghosts may be recordings of past events stored in some way by the physical environment in which they occur. This hypothesis about residual hauntings has since been called the stone tape theory.

The theory notes that often ghosts or apparitions behave like recordings in that they repeat their actions over a long period of time without ever deviating away from the original sighting, while at the time showing no knowledge or even acknowledgement of the surroundings, environment, or even people around it. Indeed, it was noted that, at times, they appeared to be in a completely different building to the one that now existed, for example, the ghost may have walked through a wall where a door used to exist but no longer did, or appeared only from the waist up as if walking on a section of floor that was once lower than the current surface.

The stone tape theory puts forward the idea that, just like a magnetic recording tape, stones can hold magnetically stored information. As such, when we replay a music tape we hear music, and when we replay a stone, we see an event being replayed from history. This theory also applies to buildings and other sites. Simply put, the theory suggests that a place can somehow record certain snippets of history and replay them at a later date.

But apart from poltergeists and stone tape theory ghosts we also have reports of apparitions, another form of supernatural manifestation, but one that may not actually be a ghost.

Some researchers have suggested that there exists a part of our brain that survives the death of our physical body and that this part of the brain can be artificially activated in sleep or in periods of great stress. Somehow this creates a vision or apparition of the person that is visible to others at certain specific times.

Apparitions have been reported all over the world in many cultures over many hundreds of years, and usually involve a person receiving a visitation from a friend or a family member even though that person is known to be many miles away at the time. Generally the apparition appears to a person then fades away, with the viewer finding out at a later stage that the person who appeared to them in the apparition has died at exactly the time when the apparition appeared.

These apparitions can be broken down into four separate categories: "dead" apparitions, "crisis" apparitions, "collective" apparitions, and "deathbed" apparitions. All could be considered as being a reciprocal apparition in that the apparition and the person experiencing the apparition can converse.

Whereas the categories are similar all have distinct differences, for instance, dead apparitions usually appear to someone who was very close to them in life and try to communicate comfort, love, or information in times of grief. It has been reported that these apparitions relay vital information to people, such as the location of a will or something similar to help a loved one through life after they have died. In simple terms, this apparition appears to be, in pretty much every way, an intelligent ghost.

In a crisis apparition the purpose it seems is to convey to a close friend or relative that the apparition, or at least the person who the apparition pertains to, is in great peril, or trauma. Most visions of this sort involve a person who has just recently died or is about to die. Again, these apparitions show intelligence and people have reported having conversations with them before they fade away. As these visions can be either of living or dead people they are undoubtedly different to the dead apparitions discussed previously.

Collective apparitions are similar to both dead and crisis apparitions except that the apparition itself is viewed by a group of people, not just the individual, which either validates the phenomena or suggests mass hallucination on the part of those experiencing the apparition. Of course, it could be argued that this apparition is simply the same as the first two, just experienced by more people.

Deathbed apparitions, the last of our apparitions, are interesting in that it is the dying person that reports seeing ghostly visions. Generally these occurrences happen when a person is very close to death, and they report seeing dead loved ones and friends, angels, holy beings, and even Unidentified Flying Objects (UFOs). While UFOs are beyond the scope of this book, it could be suggested that this is very similar to near death experiences.

Apart from the aforementioned ghosts, there is also a school of thought amongst paranormal investigators that suggests that a place can somehow absorb energy or emotions, either positive or negative, from people who have inhabited a place for a long period of time, and that energy can somehow manifest itself later as an apparition. It is not the ghost of a single dead person, more so a build-up of emotions or residual energy over time. This could explain why places such as prisons have an oppressive and dark atmosphere given the desperation of the men who would have once inhabited the confines of the walls.

But is this a ghost? In the traditional sense, that being a dead person whose soul is unable to leave the mortal world, we would have to say no. However, is it really that different from the traditional ghost of literature and screen? And in saying that, surely one could experience this combined residual energy just as one experiences a "normal" ghost. Of course, this would suggest that ghosts can not only be spirits of the dead, but collective memories or emotions of living people. Indeed, if we are to follow this line of reasoning, one could even go as far as suggesting that a person may haunt two places at once given that it is likely that a ghost is a sort of energy source attached to a place. And as we have seen earlier, this is quite possible.

While we are on the subject of energy sources and different types of ghosts we should explore the phenomena of orbs, a seemingly supernatural occurrence that has become more and more popular in the present day due to the advent of digital cameras.

Orbs are an interesting phenomenon. I have taken a number of photos that appear to show orbs and yet I am not convinced that there is anything supernatural or paranormal about them. Having said that we shall still explore the phenomena simply because there is a growing school of thought that they are ghostly or supernatural energy sources.

So what are orbs? Orbs are a new sort of supernatural occurrence; in fact, one could say an internet phenomenon. When I was child I immersed myself in books about ghosts and hauntings and surprisingly, not one of them mentioned orbs. And yet, if the internet is to be believed, orbs would seem to be the most prevalent form of ghost encountered these days. It appears that the term orb first came into circulation around the early 1990s to explain any anomalies including dust and pollen, as well as supernatural incongruities, which were captured on film and digital cameras. Over time this term was appropriated by ghost hunters, both serious and amateur, and now appears to only have a supernatural meaning.

Many in the ghost hunting fraternity believe orbs to be ghosts or spirits in the form of a ball of energy or light. As such they are supposedly the life form of a once alive person and have willingly stayed behind because they feel duty bound for some strange reason. There is a theory that the entities that form these orbs do so by choice as it would take less energy to form a small ball of light than it would to appear as a full-blown apparition.

Orbs are the most photographed incongruity caught on film or video by ghost hunters. They can be transparent or solid and seem to appear more often than not in old buildings and cemeteries. They also seem to appear mainly at night.

Having said this, in my opinion they are simply specks of dust reflecting whatever light exists and is being caught in the camera lens or by the camera flash. Others are simply camera lens flares or flaws or even weather conditions such as rain, humidity, or moisture close to the lens at the time of the flash. I will admit that there exists reports of orbs being seen and photographed or videotaped that have behaved in extremely bizarre and sometimes apparently intelligent fashions. However, I am somewhat dismissive of the orb phenomena, and from where I stand it would appear that too many people are too quick to jump on the supernatural bandwagon every time they take a photo with a spot of light in it and, rather than dismiss it as something completely natural or normal, use it as definitive proof of ghosts, which frankly is a preposterous way of doing things.

In light of this, where do we stand in relation to a place like Glastonbury? Without doubt one suspects that Glastonbury has all the vital aspects a place needs to be haunted. With suggestions that it may have been a site of religious importance in Celtic or pre-Celtic, through to the Romano-British period and beyond, it has seen war, such as the Battle of Peonnum in 658, the Norman Conquest in 1066, destruction in 1184 when it burnt to the ground, as well as the Dissolution of the Monasteries in 1536.

Like Tintagel Castle, Glastonbury is a place of evocative beauty. On spring mornings a mist hangs heavy over the green carpet of grass that surrounds the abbey and one cannot but be overcome by its mysterious and secretive demeanour. And, because its origins are so deeply rooted in legend and mysticism, it has an almost supernatural ambience that suggests some sort of other-worldliness. Apart from the Tor, which sits high on a hilltop near the town, it is the abbey which contributes greatest to this other-world sentimentality.

Strangely, it has been said that the most famous ghost that haunts the abbey is not that of a long forgotten monk or a dead abbot. Instead, it is a dark armoured knight complete with demonic glowing red eyes whose mission it has been said is to destroy all record of King Arthur and his life. Over the years a number of researchers have witnessed this figure in the abbey grounds although nobody knows why he is trying to destroy the memory of Arthur.

The legend of the ghostly knight is said to be over 400 years old, but he is not the only supernatural figure that stalks these ancient hallowed grounds. During the 1970s it was reported that a local ghost club was investigating the Lady's Chapel when one investigator walked into the Chapel and became aware of a white-robed figure ahead of him. Thinking he was witnessing a recreation or ceremony of some sort he exited quickly to the centre of the chapel where he saw, to his surprise, a column of figures walking towards the exit. Although he could not determine whether they were nuns or monks in white habits he was in no doubt as to what he had seen. As he excitedly made his way out of the abbey he reported that he began to feel slightly peculiar and he lost sight of the figures.

On numerous occasions visitors have reported having their clothes grabbed and something unseen touching them on the shoulder. As well, the ghost of a high ranking monk whose life was constantly blighted by blackmail due to an illegitimate child, is said to also wander the grounds, his presence being felt in a wave of desperate unhappiness that floods over visitors.

In the orchard a mad, but harmless spectre of a monk has been seen hunched and downtrodden and mumbling to himself in a foreign tongue. It is though he was accidentally poisoned when he drank a lethal cocktail designed to do away with someone else.

Richard Whyting, who we have already spoken about, is said to haunt Dod Lane. "Dod" is an old word for ley-lines, which are alleged alignments of geographical places such as ancient monuments and megaliths, natural ridge-tops, and water features. This suggests that the apparitions represent, or use some sort of natural earth energy to exist. It does appear that certain geophysical features may affect the human mind and as such, could possibly lead us to imagine that we have seen something strange or unworldly.

Whatever the case, what cannot be denied is that Glastonbury is a truly mystical and wondrous place. It is a place where one cannot be anything but overawed when the ethereal early morning mists rise from the fields smothering the surrounding district and highlighting the domed bulk of Glastonbury Tor that rises above it, creating the illusion of an island as it was hundreds and hundreds of years before today. In a place like this one can truly believe in the legends and supernatural stories of the area. But if the abbey is haunted then what of the town?

The George and Pilgrims Hotel, a quaint fifteenth-century stone building with mullioned windows, sits quietly on High Street. Originally constructed to accommodate the many wealthy pilgrims and other visitors to the abbey, it is one of the oldest purpose-built pubs in the southwest of England and is believed to be haunted by at least two ghosts, if not more, especially with its low-beamed rooms, narrow corridors, and old winding stone staircase.

It is widely believed that in the years leading up to the Dissolution of the Monasteries, lots of clandestine matters were expedited in an underground passage that used to run from the abbey gatehouse to the cellar of the hotel.

Legend has it that a monk used the tunnel for an illicit affair, and when found out, he was punished by being bricked into the tunnel alive. The figure of a ghostly monk often seen in the hotel is believed to be the tormented soul of this man.

Staff and guests at the hotel often report strange experiences with some guests checking out of the hotel at night after witnessing unnerving events or hearing disembodied voices and footsteps. Over the years one particular ghost has been reported on numerous occasions, this being a man in historical clothes, who looks for all purposes as flesh and blood, and who walks through the bar and then simply disappears.

In addition, the smell of cigar smoke drifts around some rooms even though smoking has been banned in hotels in England for a number of years now. Moving lights and sudden bangs often occur, startling visitors and staff alike. Oddly, some hear what sounds like a violent argument coming from a small lounge but when the room is checked it is invariably empty.

A spectral monk has been seen silently gliding down a passage but those who have seen this apparition maintain that it does not seem to mean any harm. However one of the bedrooms apparently holds a much more frightening and malevolent presence that leaves visitors literally paralysed with fear. One guest, upon hurriedly leaving the hotel, commented that he "felt a great pressure above me but not touching me. It was large and it was as if my life force was completely immobilised. I was paralysed. I could not move a muscle, nor could I make a sound."

Glastonbury itself has been dubbed the occult capital of England due to its attraction for new-agers, modern-day druids, and present-day pilgrims. As well, tens of thousands of revellers flock to the area for its annual music festival as well as for the summer solstice on Midsummer's Day.

But it is not this that we are interested in as the town itself is as haunted as anywhere in the country.

Indeed, the *New York Times* of 7 August 1910 stated that the strangest ghost story on record comes from Glastonbury in that the supernatural manifestations *take place in broad daylight on the busiest streets of the town.* The article then goes on to describe the Glastonbury ghost as something that *does not make its presence known by being seen of felt, but it makes itself smelt.* Sceptically, the article does conclude that heat or dampness draws a heavy aromatic scent from old wood permeated with the smoke of centuries of incense burning, and this is supported by the fact that a lot of the places where the ghostly scent is encountered is near houses either partly or wholly constructed of timbers and beams from the old abbey or have been occupied at some time by the abbots.

Glastonbury was also involved, if only in a small way, in the Battle of Sedgemoor in 1685. Of the twenty-nine local men who joined the Duke of Monmouth's ill-fated rebellion against the Crown, six were hanged from the sign of the White Hart Inn. Locals believe that the tortured souls of these lonely hanging bodies can be felt up to the present day.

Continuing the war time theme, locals talk of a ghostly echo of marching troops that is occasionally heard along Glastonbury High Street, a cadence that makes the ground shake for no visible reason. It is believed that they are the footsteps of men marching to their death in the First World War.

Interestingly, the Sedgemoor battlefield is widely regarded as one of the most haunted places in the country. Fought on 6 July 1685 at Westonzoyland in Somerset, it was the final battle of the Monmouth Rebellion, and followed a series of skirmishes around southwest England between the forces of James Scott, the First Duke of Monmouth and the Crown, his uncle James II of England. Predictably, the Crown was victorious and about 500 of the Duke's troops were captured.

Monmouth himself managed to escape the battlefield but was later captured and executed on Tower Hill in July 1685. Various accounts of his death exist with some suggesting that it took eight blows before his head was removed from his body. The Tower of London fact sheet, however, lists the number of blows at five. Gruesomely, even after all the blows the Duke's head remained attached to his twitching body. Finally the head was separated from the body with a knife, on the order of the sheriff.

Sedgemoor appears to be one of England's most distressing battle sites. Two huge trees silently tower over a poignant memorial stone commemorating the men of both sides who died horrifically in the battle that was fought on the lonely site in the early hours of the morning of 6 July 1685.

It was on that tragic summer morning, as the first warm rays of the dawn sun rose slowly over the blood spattered landscape, that the hopes and dreams of the Duke of Monmouth were trampled into the mud of Sedgemoor field, along with the bodies of his horrifically slaughtered followers.

The raw and bloody emotion of the battle, the crushed hopes and inconceivable suffering and pain from that long ago conflict seem to have left their mark on this poignant place and it is with little wonder that there are many stories of ghosts, spirits, and other traditions attached to the area. As well, it would seem that the events of the battle and its bloody aftermath have left a deep mark upon the locals.

Farmers tending their animals talk of seeing galloping horsemen racing across the swampy expanses, or tell of eerie, disembodied voices that call out to them from across the River Carey. Ruth Tongue, in her book *Somerset Folklore*, records the local legend of a researcher in the eighteenth century being told by a farmer that one foggy night near the battlefield he had distinctly heard the sound of someone shouting, "Come over and fight." This was widely believed to have been the battle cry of Monmouth's men who, while being mown down by musket fire, desperately tried to get their enemies to join their cause. Tongue also dryly records that the farmer believed that the voice must have been from a drunk wandering through the area. Having said that, others have heard the same ghostly voice.

Witnesses also speak of the seeing the quivering figure of Monmouth who cowardly ran away from the battlefield when all was lost. Indeed, it is said that he even outran his colleagues such was his panic to escape. His ghost is said to appear on the battlefield on the anniversary of the battle.

One heartrending tale tells of a young girl whose tragic ghost haunts the now tranquil fields. She had a lover who, in the battle, was captured by the Royalist troops. They promised to spare his life if he could keep pace with a galloping horse. With nothing to lose the young man, apparently quite fleet of foot, managed to keep up with a horse at full gallop; however, the soldiers had cruelly used the lad for their own warped amusement and reneged on their promise. He was gunned down with the girl watching on.

In her sorrow, the devastated girl flung herself into the River Carey and drowned. Her ghost is said to intermittently return to the site where she died, gliding silently along the route of her lovers last run. But if this is not enough, the thundering of an invisible horse is often said to accompany her distressed vigil, and the desperate panting of the murdered lad can also be heard.

The cowardly Monmouth, as we have seen, was captured and executed, however, this was not the end of the bloodshed. His execution was soon followed by what was called the Bloody Assizes where many of Monmouth's supporters and soldiers were tried and executed or even transported abroad in a frenzy of bloody revenge.

The Bloody Assizes were a series of trials that were held in Winchester in August 1685 after the battle of Sedgemoor. Over 1,000 rebels were held in prison awaiting the trials which started in August 1685. The first notable trial was that of an elderly woman who the jury reluctantly found guilty of treason and she was sentenced to be burned. Somewhat lucky for her, this was later commuted to beheading which was usually the preserve of the rich or royal. She was executed in early September.

The trials were preceded over by five eminent judges including the Lord Chief Justice George Jeffreys, commonly known as the Hanging Judge. Over the period of the trials more than 1,400 prisoners were punished and although most were sentenced to death, surprisingly, less than 300 were hanged, or hanged, drawn, and quartered. This was a particularly nasty type of execution where the guilty were fastened to a wooden yoke, and drawn along the ground by a horse to the place of execution. There they were hanged until nearly dead, emasculated, disembowelled, beheaded, and quartered, that is, chopped into four pieces. The heads of the victims were then displayed in public places such as London Bridge as a warning to others who dared rebel against the monarchy.

The Taunton Assize was held in the Great Hall of Taunton Castle with the prisoners brought before the court in September. As a result of these trials 144 were hanged and their bodies displayed around the county. Apart from this, over 800 men were transported to the West Indies as a source of cheap labour while many more perished due to the unsanitary conditions common in most English gaols at the time.

After the Assizes, Jeffreys returned to London to report to the King. As a reward for his service to the Crown he was made Lord Chancellor and was given the infamous nickname of the Hanging Judge.

Inevitably, given its grisly past, Taunton Castle is now considered haunted with the echoes of marching feet being heard in the lonely corridors as well as a man dressed in period costume and a wig carrying a sword and pistol who is seen on a landing. It is also reputed to suffer from regular poltergeist activity. However, it is not Taunton Castle that interests us at this stage, interesting as it may be, as Jeffreys, the so called Hanging Judge, appears to haunt not one place, but a number, and in one of these in what one could only describe as a bizarre guise.

Lydford Castle in Devon is an ancient castle that was designed to help control the inhabitants of Devon. Built in the late 1060s, it now appears as if it has somehow sunken into the green mound on which it stands. The tower is roofless, yet for some reason the air is chilly within the thick stone walls. Even on a hot summer day, as you climb down into the now underground level, one gets an inkling as to what a formidable and intimidating place this once must have been. Indeed, during the reign of Henry VIII it was described as being one of the "most heinous, contagious and detestable places within the realm." Today the castle still induces cold shivers and a sense of unease in visitors.

Is it a wonder that such an odious place like Lydford Castle be haunted? Who knows how many souls suffered deep within these walls? Oddly enough the castle's main spectral inhabitant is said to be the spirit of Judge Jeffreys but not in a form expected of such a man. Jeffreys held court in many Devonshire towns, and although legend suggests that he was at his cruellest at Lydford, there is a distinct lack of historical evidence to suggest that he ever visited the village. Having said that, the legend of his ghost is strong in these parts, even though he is bizarrely said to appear as a huge black pig, snuffling and snorting around the castle and village.

Another ghostly figure is also reported to exist in the dark, deep recesses of the castle dungeon. This is a terrifying apparition that takes the shape of a dark misty outline of a tall man. In addition, and strangely much like the Tower of London, the ghostly figure of a bear has also been reported in the castle grounds. Apparently, it has been seen walking along before disappearing through a stone archway and leaving an icy chill wherever it has been.

Next to this ancient and forbidding piece of medieval history is the Castle Inn. Built in 1550, its delightful pink exterior tantalisingly offers a clue to what awaits the visitor inside as the place drips with character and charm. Within the interior are low beamed ceilings, a slate floor, open fire and other curios that hark back to a simpler time. Although now a hotel, it once served as the gaoler's quarters so it is no wonder that it is often visited by the ghost of a man described as being broad and muscular and attired in workman's clothing. It is believed he appears most often along the corridor adjoining the bar before simply vanishing. Apart from this, other supernatural events that occur at the inn include an opaque mist that suddenly forms and floats around before disappearing.

Not surprisingly in such an ancient village, there also exists another reputedly haunted area, this time a low, grassy mound marked on Ordinance Maps as a tumulus. Quite possibly it is a Bronze Age barrow, but whatever the case it is known as Gallows Hill for reasons that do not need explaining. On quiet nights when the wind has stopped and the mist rises from the ground, tortured moans and shrieks are said to come from the area as the spirits of those hanged relive their agonising and terrifying last moments.

About a kilometre from the village is the famous Lydford Gorge, a lush oak forested river gorge with exceptional natural beauty and numerous local legends from elves and pixies to ghosts. The river plunges and tumbles along its merry way as it travels through the gorge where it forms the spectacular thirty-metre-high Whitelady Waterfall and the Devil's cauldron, a reminder as to how strong legends about the devil are in these parts. However, it is not the falls or the Devil's Cauldron that interest us as, by a pool known as Kit Steps, lurks the ghost of "Old Kitty" or "The Red Lady" who has been described as staring into the cascading river. Whether this is the restless soul of a woman drowned in the river is unknown but witnesses have reported her as wearing a red shawl. Who knows, maybe she is the long lost lover of one of the men put to death by the Hanging Judge?

But if Old Kitty has no real connection to the Hanging Judge of the Bloody Assizes then what can we make of Wapping in the once less salubrious area of the London Docklands? Why would locals warn tourists who venture out into the dark of night after a few pints to beware of the Hanging Judge, indeed the same Hanging Judge whose ghostly presence is seen and felt in the form of a large black pig at Lydford Castle?

Lord Chief Justice George Jeffreys, commonly known as the Hanging Judge, died in 1689 but locals swear that his ghost lurks around the banks of the Thames near what was once Execution Dock. Frighteningly, he is said to have a grim smile on his lips as if he is satisfied with what he sees, or has seen.

Jeffreys was one of Britain's more unusual and cruel judges, and had a macabre and ghoulish pleasure in that he enjoyed watching criminals hang, especially those he himself had sentenced to death. As we have seen with the Assizes, he seemed to have had no qualms in sentencing people to death.

It appears he was a man of custom and was said to have never passed up the opportunity of a cool and refreshing ale on a warm day, regularly visiting a pub on the Thames called the Prospect of Whitby. Gruesomely, in between his pints he would wander up to Execution Dock, a mere 100 metres or so upstream, where he could watch sailors convicted of capital offences being hanged, a horrific death even for those days as the men were hanged at low tide with a short rope. As a result their bodies would twitch and jerk uncontrollably for hours and hours. They would then be left to hang until three high tides had washed over them.

After each hanging the elated judge would then head back to the Prospect of Whitby for another ale before retiring home for the night. However, Jeffreys' enjoyment of macabre entertainment could not last forever as in 1688 King James was finally overthrown by the supporters of William of Orange, who quickly installed him as King of England. Whereas King James fled to France, Jeffreys realised too late that his support of the deposed King could lead to tragic consequences.

By the time it had all sunk in it was too late, and as he tried to sneak out of the country ironically dressed as a sailor, he was recognised. Rightly fearing his life he fled to another nearby pub, the Town of Ramsgate where he quickly ordered a pint to sooth his nerves. However, legend has it that he only had time to drink the one before an angry mob arrived. Somewhat fortuitously, or maybe not, he was saved by the army, who arrested him and took him to the Tower of London, ostensibly for his own protection, where he died of kidney failure four months later.

Chillingly, a sign on the wall of the Prospect of Whitby proclaims the following:

> The infamous "Hanging Judge Jeffreys" was a local and a regular patron here.
>
> It is said that he would enjoy his lunch on this balcony while watching the hangings at the place known as Execution Dock.
>
> It was at Execution Dock that the famous pirate Captain Kidd met his end in 1701.
>
> The noose below this point reminds us of this gruesome man who later died in the Tower of London.

The Town of Ramsgate pub is also said to be haunted by the ghostly figure of the judge; apparently his spirit remains trapped on the stairs. As well he has been reportedly seen by river police in recent years. As we will later see, he is also reported to haunt the Skirrid Mountain Inn in Wales. However, the Town of Ramsgate pub, not unusual for an old pub on the Thames, has a colourful past, and was once known as the Red Cow. Legend has it that it was named so in honour of an ill-tempered barmaid with flaming red hair who once worked there.

Of course, for such an old pub one would suspect that the Prospect of Whitby is also haunted by more than a single soul, and indeed it is reported that highway woman Moll Cutpurse also lurks in the dark, wood-panelled interior of this traditional English pub. Moll Cutpurse, also known as Mary Frith or "The Roaring Girl," was a notorious pickpocket and fence of the English underworld in the early 1600s. She was known for cross dressing and working as a pimp, among other less savoury exploits. She died in July 1659 of dropsy.

But it is not female pimps from the 1600s that we are concerned with, no matter how interesting their life may have been. And with that we shall move onto another pub, also in London, and like the Prospect of Whitby and the Town of Ramsgate, is also haunted by a number of ghosts, including one of an important, yet infamous historical figure.

CHAPTER 5

†

Highwaymen, Multiple Sightings, and Haunted Pubs

The murdered do haunt their murderers, I believe.
I know that ghosts have wandered on earth.

—Emily Bronte

The Spaniards Inn is an historic pub located between Hampstead and Highgate in London. Built in 1585, the inn formed the entrance to the Bishop of London's estate, and is a quaint, oak-panelled building with an excellent beer garden and superb grounds. Indeed, it has been suggested, though never proven, that John Keats wrote an *Ode to a Nightingale* in the very gardens that one can now sit and enjoy a good ale and a hearty meal. But this is not surprising as the inn has a great literary heritage, being mentioned in Charles Dickens's *The Pickwick Papers* and Bram Stoker's Gothic horror novel *Dracula*.

However, it is not the literary heritage that we seek, even though Stoker's *Dracula* is completely based in folklore and the supernatural, for it is here that the ghost of Dick Turpin is believed to reside.

Local legend suggests that the infamous highwayman Dick Turpin was born in the inn but this is now widely discredited. Having said this, on dark winter evenings the warm and comfortable upstairs rooms have been known to turn unnaturally chilly and a dark figure has been seen as drifting through the walls.

Downstairs in the main bar the otherworldly hand of Black Dick, a money lender who was run over and killed by a coach outside the inn, has been known to grab people by the arm or to tug their shirt sleeves as they drink; while in the car-park people have been shocked by the appearance of a ghostly horse. Elsewhere, in the gardens, a woman in a long white dress has been witnessed, as has the ghost of Dick Turpin.

In his early life, Turpin was believed to have been a butcher like his father, but by the early 1730s he had joined a gang of deer thieves and soon became a poacher, horse thief, highwayman, and murderer.

In 1735, following the arrest of most of his gang, Turpin disappeared. He reappeared once again in 1737 with two new collaborators, one of whom Turpin is believed to have accidentally shot and killed. After this latest episode Turpin fled and in the process killed a man who attempted to detain him. In disguise and under the alias John Palmer he made his way to Yorkshire where, although apparently having no means of living, he stayed at an inn. Before long local magistrates became suspicious of him and suspected he was a horse thief. As a result he was imprisoned in York Castle as he awaited trial.

Turpin's identity was soon revealed when a letter he wrote to his brother-in-law was intercepted by authorities. As a result he was tried in late March 1739 and found guilty on two charges of horse theft. He was sentenced to death and executed in April of the same year. Not surprisingly, given his exploits, he became the subject of legend and was romanticised as a dashing hero in English ballads and popular theatre of the eighteenth and nineteenth centuries.

But back to the Spaniards Inn itself. Whether or not Turpin was born at the inn is irrelevant to this book but it is known that he used the place as a hideout from where he could plan and execute his many gruesome highway robberies, and it is said that the woods and heaths that border the road to the inn contain the lost souls of many of his victims.

The woods that lie to the side of Spaniards Road in Hampstead are dark and foreboding, especially late in the evening when the long shadows of the twilight start to disappear, and the darkness of the woods becomes all pervading. There is no footpath along the road so one must walk along the grassy verge ducking low branches and stepping around saplings while attempting to avoid small, muddy puddles.

In the dark with the wind whistling softly through the tall deciduous trees one can believe that the place is haunted. Mixed in with the wind and other sounds of the early night you can almost hear the screams of Turpin's victims and as you walk along in the darkness the hairs on the back of your neck rise with each step. If one stops and allows their mind to wander, they can imagine all sorts of ghostly apparitions and lonely spirits haunting this small piece of forest. Indeed, if a large black devil dog were to emerge one would not be surprised.

Perhaps Turpin's victims were restless this cool spring night? Or were there other, unknown spirits in those dark woods? And if so, then who could they be? The Spaniards Inn sits on the edge of Hampstead Heath, which in itself is reputed to be haunted by a number of ghosts. Or maybe I simply had a heightened sense of awareness due to the reputation of the inn? Whatever the case, I would not have stepped alone into those woods that night, or any night.

But it is not just these spooky woods and the Spaniards Inn that Dirk Turpin is supposed to haunt as surprisingly one of his best-known haunts is at Hounslow Heath, the site of Heathrow Airport. His ghost was reported on the site of the airport before it was built. As well, it was reported in *The Sun* as recently as January 2013 that Harry Styles, singer from the boy-band One Direction, had bought a four-bedroom property that backed on to a pub frequented by Turpin and his gang in the 1700s. According to Styles, the outlaw's ghost has been seen inside the house, and the sound of his famous horse Black Bess heard outside.

In late 2003, the production crew from *Most Haunted*, a television program hosted by Yvette Fielding that investigates ghosts and haunted places, had to be rescued from the dark of Epping Forest during a live nighttime broadcast after they became lost. The crew, who went into the forest with a psychic medium, believed that they had tracked down the ghost of Dick Turpin.

The director of programming, Richard Woolfe, said of the event, "The psychic medium was basically trying to show Yvette Fielding the spirit of Dick Turpin, which actually presented itself in the undergrowth and this was why they went off the footpath and deeper into the forest." He dolefully added that, "they suddenly realised they had no idea where they were. They hadn't got a clue." Luckily for the television crew they were able to radio for help and the head forest keeper was able to locate them and lead them to safety. Whether or not they managed to see and film Turpin's ghost is debatable.

But these are not the only haunts of Dick Turpin, as in Woughton on the Green in Buckinghamshire, now a relatively modern 1960s town, Turpin's ghost is also seen. Of course, one could question why an eighteenth-century highwayman would turn up in a late twentieth-century town until it is realised that Woughton on the Green is one of the oldest villages in Buckinghamshire, being mentioned in the *Domesday Book*. Even with the 1960s revamp, remnants of past days remain, such as a medieval church and other buildings that date back hundreds of years. And all of these building overlook the village green which is the place where a phantom rider, believed to be Turpin, lurks.

The ghost in question is usually only glimpsed for a few seconds. Mounted on a large dark horse, the man appears to be dressed in dark clothes and wears a tricorn hat although one report from the mid 1980s suggested that he was wearing a cloak over a fancy waistcoat with thigh high boots of black leather. Whatever the case, he is not seen for long as the spirit generally rides out of sight behind a hedge or round a corner.

The locals at Woughton on the Green believe this apparition to be Dick Turpin with the reason being that Watling Street, now better known as the A5, runs close to the village on its way from London to Chester. Rich merchants who used the road would have made easy pickings for men such as Turpin, and it is known that he used to operate in this area and held up more than one coach on Watling Street.

But how can anyone be sure that this phantom-like figure is Turpin? After all, he already appears to haunt the Spaniards Inn, Hampstead Heath, Heathrow Airport, and Epping Forest. Is it possible that ghosts, apart from being the souls of the dead, are also something else, perhaps a remnant emotion or some sort of residual energy source?

Dick Turpin's ghost, like that of Anne Boleyn who is seen at the Tower of London, Blickling Hall, and Hever Castle, would suggest that ghosts can and regularly do appear in various places. Another case of multiple location sightings is the spirit of no less than Sir Francis Drake who we have already seen is reported to ride at the head of a pack of hounds or devil dogs seeking out the souls of the unwary or unbaptised on the rugged and eerie moorlands of Dartmoor in central Devon. And yet Sir Francis Drake died at sea of dysentery in 1596 while anchored off the coast of Portobello in Panama.

Another case is that of Sir Walter Raleigh whose spirit is often reported in the Tower of London grounds but who was executed many miles away. Likewise Thomas à Becket's ghost is the same. It would seem that we can suggest that ghosts are not just the souls of the dead, and in some cases are more akin to energy sources or raw emotion that have somehow been absorbed over a period of time by a place or site. And if this is so, then the classic pub ghosts of British Isles become more believable, after all, pubs are places of intense emotions, love, hate, rage, and indifference. They are also the place of joyous celebrations, muted half-whispered conversations, shady deals, and even murder. It is little wonder that most pubs have a ghost story or two to relate to visitors and passers-by.

We have already looked at the Red Lion in Avebury as well as the wonderful Spaniards Inn in Hampstead. But what of others?

As pubs go, the Royal Standard of England on Forty Green Road in Beaconsfield near Amersham is truly wonderful. Originally known as The Ship and dating from 1213, it is believed to be the oldest free house in England, and when one enters through the warped and slightly askew front door one can immediately see why, with its heavy black beams, twisted uneven floor, sagging ceilings, helmets, banners, rickety chairs, and old stained tables that would have seen thousands and thousands of drinkers. If one could bottle character this would be the place to set up shop. It would seem almost impossible that it were not haunted by at least one spirit, which it is. In fact, it is reputed to have at least two.

Since 1663, the inn has been known as The Royal Standard of England as the restored monarch King Charles II allowed its name to change as a reward because the place had offered safe haven to his father's supporters during the English Civil War. Indeed, it is believed that King Charles II is thought to have stayed there with one of his mistresses.

During the Civil War the pub was used as a mustering place for the Royalists under King Charles who raised his personal standard to draw royalist supporters to fight the Parliamentarians or Roundheads. The pub also had connections with Irish Catholic mercenaries who decided to fight on the royalist side. However, in November 1642, they were part of a Cavalier army that was heavily defeated at Turnham Green by the greater Roundhead army. The pub fell under the Parliamentarian control and a dozen cavaliers were executed with their heads displayed on pikes outside the door of the pub. Included in these was a twelve-year-old drummer boy. His ghost is believed to haunt the pub, and the sound of a beating drum is often said be heard in the car park, the original rallying point for the soldiers.

Another ghost is also widely seen in the main bar but its origins are less well known than those of the tragic drummer boy. There are two interpretations for this phantom that appears to be a shadowy male figure that strides across the room and then disappears in the wall next to an old fireplace in the Candle Room. He is believed to be either the spirit of an executed cavalier, not a bad guess one would think, or that of a traveller accidentally killed by the Earl of Barrymore in 1788. Apparently, Barrymore belonged to a clandestine club called the Four Horse Club where young regency men would bribe coachmen to give them the reins and then drive at breakneck speed through the lanes and streets of the town. The traveller was tragically crushed outside the pub by a speeding coach driven by Barrymore and his bloodied and broken body was brought into the pub where the landlord was bribed to stay quiet about the whole incident. Ever since, his ghost has haunted the bar.

The Earl himself also died a somewhat gruesome and unexpected death when, in March 1793, while escorting sixteen French prisoners of war between Folkestone and Dover as an officer with the Royal Berkshire Militia, a loaded gun on a carriage seat accidentally discharged and shot him through the eye.

It also seems that the ghostly figure of a woman haunts the ladies bathroom although it is unknown who she may have been in life. Who knows, perhaps she was the wife or lover of one of the executed cavaliers?

Sadly, I was suffering from a serious bout of jetlag when I managed to visit the pub in the spring of 2009, and after two pints I was ready to fall asleep. However, while I was there I did hear a story from a local that on some nights, when a clammy fog is swirling around this ancient building and the night is deathly quiet, one can sometimes make out the ghostly decapitated heads of the royalist soldiers as they sit silently with unseeing eyes on bloodied pikes. Whether or not this is true is unknown, but who am I to doubt such a story? Maybe next time I am in the area I will visit the pub and wait quietly hoping for a fog to form, as who knows what things the eye and mind can conjure up in circumstances such as these?

Luckily, in the early spring of 2015, I was able to revisit the quirky old pub and this time without the effects of jetlag, and as I walked from the gravel carpark towards the pub it seemed somewhat smaller than I remembered it. The day was cold and overcast and a thin drizzle hung in the air chilling your bones and reminding you that, for all this is a beautiful place when the sun shines, it can also be just as miserable when it wishes.

And so I walk towards the pub huddled beneath my jacket, my hands shoved deeply in my pockets and my head bowed against the incessant rain. The flagstone paving is wet and slippery and I wonder how many people have slipped on these medieval stones over the years. Reaching the front door I am again surprised by how small it is, not much taller than me. I reach for the ancient latch and let myself in. Inside the wall of hallway that leads to the bar bulges like the belly of a whale on its side and I have to walk around it to enter the bar. To the left are small dark dining rooms and ahead is the bar sitting under heavy black beams that I suspect are oak.

To my right, looking down the bar, the ceiling appears to get higher as the floor slides away as if this side of the building has sunken into the soil during its centuries of use. At the far end of the bar I look up and notice the high-beamed ceiling and wonder if it one time supported a second storey. Sitting on the huge beams above the bar are copper urns, other indistinguishable artefacts, and a stuffed badger. Beyond here the room widens into another section which harbours the main fireplace, a darkened brick structure adorned by a lion statue built into the mantelpiece. To the sides are old, dusty, and faded lounges, and the walls behind the lounges have turtle shells embedded in them. To the left of the fireplace the wall also contains a carved block of stone proclaiming:

The kiss of the sun for pardon
the song of the bird for mirth
one is nearer to God in a garden
than anywhere else on earth.

I smile, nice sentiments, but on a day like today, inside is where one wants to be complete with a pint and a warm fire.

Cavalier and Roundhouse helmets, armour, and weapons adorn the beams above the tables and the place emanates a feeling of incredible age. Outside the rain begins to fall heavier and soon beats on the lead-soldered windows as it has done for the past 900 or so years. I sit with my pint and contemplate this place. How many people have sat in this pub over the years, indeed, how many people have sat in the very place I am now sitting? What deals were struck within these walls? How many lives were broken, taken, started, destroyed, set on paths to wealth, fame, and even death? This we can never know, but whatever the case, one can believe that within these walls something supernatural exists.

Interestingly, in 1944, an American B17 Flying Fortress, *Tomahawk Warrior*, crashed over the road from the pub killing all crew. Whether the ghosts of these men haunt the adjoining field is unknown.

But if the Royal Standard has a slightly bloody past and is haunted, then what of the Skirrid Mountain Inn in Llanfihangel Crucorney, Wales?

The Skirrid Mountain Inn lies at the foot of the Skirrid Mountain in the small village of Llanfihangel Crucorney. It is believed to be Wales' oldest pub and is among one of the oldest in the United Kingdom, believed to have been serving patrons since at least 1104, and possibly earlier. It is also reputed to be one of the most haunted places in the whole of the British Isles.

The inn itself is very much the same as it was 900 years ago with exposed oak beams, said to have been fashioned from medieval ship timbers, original wooden window frames and doors, and a dining room with authentic medieval wooden panelling. And with such a past one would expect that it possesses an absorbing history, indeed, it is believed that in the early 1400s, Owain Glyndwr, the last native Welshman to hold the title Prince of Wales and a fierce opponent of English rule, used the inn as a rallying point for his troops.

As well, between the 1100s and the 1600s, it served as a court room and, as was the case in those days, harsh sentences, including the death penalty, were given to murderers and petty criminals alike. It is thought that over 180 people were executed by hanging at the inn during its days as a courtroom. The first floor of the inn is believed to have housed the courtroom and a holding cell for prisoners was located halfway up the stairs.

Even more interesting was the fact that, after the Monmouth Rebellion, which we have already looked at previously, 180 rebels were hanged on the word of the Lord Chief Justice George Jeffreys, who we have already met as the Hanging Judge. As in the Bloody Assizes that were held in Winchester in August 1685, James II sent the judge to Wales to punish the supporters of the Duke of Monmouth after his ill-fated and doomed rebellion. The rebels were duly hanged from a beam beneath the inn's staircase. The beam on which the prisoners were hanged exists to the present day, still with a grisly reminder of the past, rope burn marks.

And like Lydford Castle in Devon, there appears little documentary evidence to suggest that Jeffreys ever attended the courtroom in the Skirrid. However, as we have seen, the ghost of the Hanging Judge doesn't seem happy haunting one location alone and is rumoured to stalk the upper floors of the inn, most probably looking for someone to hang so he could get his perverse pleasure from the sight.

Visitors to the inn, sometimes quite unaware of its history of supernatural occurrences, have reported a variety of disquieting phenomena including the terrifying feeling of being strangled or feeling a rope around their neck. Some have even presented with what appears welt marks on their neck after the phenomena. Others have complained of dizziness, nausea, or fear on the stairs under the hanging beam while others have reported being bumped into, or feeling an invisible presence, also on the stairs.

Recently, a number of late night drinkers witnessed the bizarre sight of pound notes weighed down by coins, a common practice in pubs, levitating. Allegedly the notes hovered briefly in mid-air before crashing to the ground spreading the coins far and wide. The inn also experiences peculiar knocking sounds with doors either slamming shut spontaneously or shaking violently before flying open as if pushed by some violent unseen hand. Disembodied footsteps are also heard all over the inn and numerous cold spots can be felt, sometimes in the heat of summer when there is absolutely no logical cause or source for a draft of freezing air.

But not all the spirits in the inn are unfriendly or malevolent. A local clergyman, Father Henry Vaughn, is believed to haunt the building and his presence is said to be welcoming and harmless, if not just a little unnerving. The ghost of Fanny Price, a girl who was employed by the inn during the mid-eighteenth century is also said to be very active. She is thought to have died of consumption in 1873 at the age of thirty-five.

Other ghostly manifestations include the sound of soldiers in the courtyard, the rustling of an unseen woman's dress, a White Lady accompanied by a powerful scent of perfume, and glasses that occasionally leap unaided off the bar.

Like all hauntings we must ask, are there rational, logical, and utterly conventional explanations for the extraordinary events that are reported to happen in the Skirrid Mountain Inn? Is it possible that the hotel's bloody history has somehow been permanently imprinted within the very fabric of the building, that is, the wooden beams, stone walls, and associated material? And are these events spontaneously replayed in no particular order or sequence over the years? And if so, then how and why? Maybe we shall never know.

However, although stories attached to the Royal Standard and the Skirrid Mountain Inn are somewhat startling, they seem positively benign when compared to our next haunted pub where murder, Satanism, torture, and child sacrifice are just some of the activities supposed to have taken place at the site. Indeed, this ramshackle twelfth-century building, reputedly built on a pagan burial ground, is said to experience inexplicable freezing temperatures and an evil, oppressive atmosphere that has scared even the most hardened of sceptics and ghost-hunters. Certainly it was so for a television crew member who, after shooting an episode of *Most Haunted*, wrote in the guest book, "Never been to a scarier place."

Whatever the case, the Ancient Ram Inn in Wotten-under-Edge, Gloucestershire is a spooky and unnerving place, no matter what time of the day or night. Built in 1145, the former hostelry sits half submerged into the landscape beside the road as if it is sinking into a bog or slowly being reclaimed by the earth. It is a mass of rough, uneven stone walls, strange angles and decaying wooden window frames that seem to protect some dark, unknown secret that lies within its walls. Many years ago priests used the inn as a keeping house for slaves and workers who helped construct the nearby St. Mary Church. In 1930, it was sold and has since been private property, no longer used as an inn. The current owner, John, has lived there since 1968 when he purchased the property off a brewer. In addition the land on which the inn sits is reputed to be the intersection of two powerful ley lines.

But the presence of so called ley lines doesn't seem to help the ambience of the place as the current owner believes it to be haunted by both an incubus and a succubus, demonic creatures that reputedly have sex with their victims at night and suck the life force from them much in the way a fictional vampire does with blood. In addition, there is a ghostly witch, strange glowing lights, orbs, and other paranormal phenomena. Oddly enough, it is widely believed in the area that the redirecting of water on the Ancient Ram property caused a portal for dark energy to open up, and now it acts as some sort of magnet for dark, malevolent forces.

It is a coolish, slightly overcast morning when Kirsten and I visit Wotten-under-Edge with the view of simply taking a photo of the old building. I park the car on a side street in the medieval town and head for a local coffee shop located just off the main street. The shop is warm and inviting and provides a haven from the gusty wind and cold as well as good coffee and fantastic scones. While there I happen to mention the Ancient Ram Inn to the wife of the proprietor

who informs me that her husband has attended many ghost hunting vigils in the area. Before long I am chatting to him about all manner of ghostly occurrences and theories regarding the supernatural.

After a period of time he says goodbye and leaves to tend to another customer but before he goes he tells me where I can find the old inn and adds that I should knock on the door and ask the owner for a tour of the house and to tell him that he sent me. I thank him for his help and, as a sign of appreciation, leave him a copy of one of my books. And with that, we leave to find this apparent most haunted house in England.

We walk along old streets past wooden-framed buildings of all shapes and sizes and ages. In places the cobblestones are slippery under our feet and the wind still blows. The streets in this town are generally quiet as we wind our way downhill past the old church with its moss-encrusted tombstones that sit at strange angles in the slightly unkempt lush green grass. The church itself is not remarkable, well, certainly not for this country, but is interesting all the same. According to the proprietor of the coffee shop we previously frequented, it is also haunted.

Still, we find no evidence of this and soon exit the graveyard and walk down along a small thin walkway lined by a stone wall of indeterminate age. From there we turn a corner and are surprised to be standing across the street from the legendary inn.

The inn, now a private house, is smaller than I expected. One side, I suspect a barn at some stage of its life, seems to have sunken into the earth as if the ground is reclaiming it. We walk along the side of the house; it is truly magnificent in a way that a grand stately house can never be in that it is so incredibly old, almost decrepit one could say, and yet, it is still standing and will probably do for another 500 years. Reaching the end of the barn-like structure at the end of the building we walk into a gravel yard which is obviously used as a carpark. Sitting there in a van are two tradesmen who are doing some work around the property. I chat to them for a moment and one of them advises me that there is no way known that he would stay in the building overnight, and that he refuses to enter the building on his own. We have a laugh about this, and I find that I have to agree—it is a spooky and unkempt looking building that seems to sit there brooding and somewhat goading you. Still, this is what I have come to see so I stride towards what I hope is the main entrance.

Knocking on a door I happen to look up at a third-floor window and am surprised to see an old man with a grizzled grey beard and a shock of grey hair waving furiously at us. I step back and wait for what seems to be long minutes before the ancient wooden door creaks open to reveal the old man and a dark, crowded interior. John, the owner of the inn, is sprightly, if somewhat dishevelled, and is dressed in tight jeans and a motorcycle jacket. He says hello and invites us in.

Once inside I am struck by how dark the place is. John tells us stories of his days in the RAAF and his life as a train driver before explaining that he saved the building from demolition. He then goes on to detail the ghosts that apparently haunt this incredibly old building.

The inn, apart from being a hideout for highwaymen, is believed to have been a place of ritual child sacrifice, black magic rituals, suicide, witchcraft, and murder. Chillingly, the current owner has found ample evidence of devil worship and ritual sacrifice and, under the staircase, discovered the skeletal remains of children with daggers embedded in them.

One widespread legend surrounding the building is that of the witch burned at the stake in the 1500s. Although essentially the execution of a wise woman or herbalist by followers of the ever powerful Christian church, it is believed that she took refuge in the building to escape her persecutors before she was found and killed. John believes her spirit still haunts one of the rooms in the house today, not surprisingly called The Witch's Room. Oddly enough for such a strange place, in this room it is reputed that a spectral cat urinates on the bedspread and that the stain can never be removed.

Another room in the building is dubbed the Men's Kitchen and is reputed to sit on top of an ancient pagan burial ground. John tells us that the bodies of four children, ritually sacrificed, lie beneath our feet and witnesses have often claimed to hear the cry of a distressed baby from within this room while people ascending the steep staircase up to the first floor have been pushed or thrown up the stairs by invisible hands. Interestingly, a photograph taken here in June 1999 seems to show a white mist, roughly the height of a person, which appears to be ascending the staircase.

John leads us up the rickety, thin staircase where we find ourselves outside the Bishop's Room, reputedly the most haunted of all rooms in the old inn. John invites us inside and then exits the room, closing the door. People who have visited here before have suggested that inside this room the atmosphere is oppressive and somewhat disturbing, as if something bad has happened here, or indeed, is about to happen. A psychic medium, while exploring the hauntings of the inn, was once said to have pushed open the door to the room and was lifted off the ground and thrown violently across the corridor.

In addition to this unseen assailant, a ghostly cavalier has been known to materialize next to a dressing table before striding across the room to the opposite wall where he simply disappears, while in a corner two monks have been seen. Witnesses have also been terrified by the bloodcurdling screams of a man who was reputedly killed in this room by having his head thrust into the fire. And if this is not enough to turn people off, a phantom shepherd and his dog have been seen near the door, and those who spend the night in the room have commented that they have been accosted, apparently by an incubus or a succubus.

However, the room, dark and bathed in an eerie red light from the red velvet curtains that hang across a small window, feels calm and benign. Kirsten and I spend a good ten minutes in the room, sitting on the beds, walking around and looking at the old furniture, fittings, and artefacts. We remain quiet, listening intently. Nothing happens; the room is peaceful and we exit only to find there is no sign of our host. Instead, we are greeted by his daughter, Caroline, who has decided to visit. We chat with her for a moment and then continue our journey through the house, marvelling at its age and odd angles. The Priest's Room, we decide, although peaceful during the day, is not somewhere we'd like to stay for a night.

In the attic, where the innkeeper's daughter is said to have been murdered in the early 1500s, there is an intense feeling of sadness and melancholy. Up here the heavy, dark rafters hang low and one needs to crouch so as not to bang your head. People sleeping in the Bishop's Room directly below this space have often reported hearing the distinct sound of something heavy being dragged across the floor above their heads. Is this as claimed, the ghost of the girl's body being dragged away from the murder scene by an invisible killer?

With its dark, chilly rooms filled with eerie antiques, memorabilia, old and weathered furniture, and menacing stuffed animals, the Ancient Ram Inn looks and feels every bit a haunted house, and judging on the reports it would seem that there is little doubt that the spirits and demons that are reputed to live within the building are very active. Later, after we have finished looking around the house, we sit in the garden with John and Caroline and talk about ghosts and all sorts of things. Caroline explains that she lived in the house for many years but never experienced anything too untoward except for a piece of furniture, a chest of drawers, being thrown down the stairs by invisible hands and then having its contents scattered all around. There was no one in the room at the time, she explains. Having said that, she also explains that she was often so scared of the house that she slept in a caravan in the yard, and that tradesmen have often left the building quite white faced vowing never to return. Interestingly, after we leave, Kirsten tells me that, while in the Bishop's room, she felt uneasy and quite nauseous, whereas she felt fine in the rest of the place.

Haunted pubs are a dime a dozen in the British Isles. Indeed, it is actually harder to find an unhaunted pub than it is to find one that is alleged to have at least one spirit. But this is not surprising given that pubs are places where people have congregated for many hundreds of years. Deals have been made, hearts have been broken, sweethearts found, friends feted and lost. Pubs are a vital and inherent part of community life and have been for countless generations. And so, like castles, prisons, and other haunted places, we see that any place where people congregate over long periods of time can be haunted.

The city of York in the north of England is reputed to be extremely haunted. As such, it comes as no surprise that one of its oldest pubs, the Golden Fleece, is haunted.

Although not a great deal is known about its history, it is suspected that it has been standing since before 1503 when it was first mentioned in the York City Archives. Designated a Grade II listed building by English Heritage in 1983, it certainly looks its age and overlooks the medieval shops and narrow street of "the Shambles," one of York's oldest and most picturesque rows of shops. It is instantly recognisable by the large sheep effigy hanging above its front door and, while it has an extremely narrow frontage, is quite deep and spacious with a front bar, a corridor containing staircases and toilets that lead to a second bar and past that a dining space. Upstairs it has another small dining area and four bedrooms, which can be rented for the night.

Remarkably, there are thought to be fifteen ghosts that haunt the pub, although the most well-known is Lady Alice Peckett, wife of John Peckett, who once was the Mayor of York as well as the owner of the pub. Numerous patrons have reported seeing her ghost wandering along the darkened corridors of the hotel, moving furniture, and walking up and down staircases late at night.

Another well-know spirit that seems to appear regularly is that of a man known as One-Eyed Jack who is often seen in the bottom bar of the pub wearing a sixteenth-seventeenth-century red coat, a tri-corner hat, and carrying a pistol. He paces up and down and although no one knows his identity, it is believed that he died in the bar. Also in the same bar is the ghost of a grumpy old man who mumbles to himself, while in the top bar the ghost of a young boy from Victorian times who was trampled to death by horses is regularly seen.

Another of the pub's ethereal residents is a Canadian airman by the name of Geoff Monroe, who, after a night of heavy drinking, either fell or was pushed from one of the upper windows during World War II. Guests have reported being awoken in the dead of night and seeing a dark figure in a military uniform standing over them.

Roman soldiers have also been seen in the cellar of the hotel, which was once used to incarcerate criminals on their way to be sentenced at the nearby prison. Those sentenced to hanging were hung at Baile Hill and their bodies then stored in the cellar of the pub until their families came to collect them. As such, it is not hard to see why this quaint little pub is considered haunted and, therefore, a perfect place for me to stop and have a meal and a pint or two of beer.

It is a cold, wet, and exceptionally windy day when Kirsten and I walk from the Jorvik Viking Centre, and the cobblestone streets and alleys are slippery from the rain. We soon find ourselves outside the Shambles and, after taking a few photographs of this amazing place, spend a good hour exploring its quaint little shops and nooks and crannies after which we head to the Golden Fleece. The pub itself is warm, and a number of people have sought refuge from the cold and wet and are sitting around drinking pints and talking. We find a seat near a wall and are surprised when we notice a skull, that of a woman by the name of Elizabeth Johns who was executed for forgery in 1800. We order a meal and a couple of pints and I manage to convince the barman to allow me to go upstairs and have a look at the rooms, explaining to him that I am a writer and that I am researching for this book. He explains that the rooms are currently empty or are being cleaned and that I can spend as much time as I want looking around. I take the opportunity to climb the strangely angled staircase up towards the haunted bedrooms.

Upstairs is particularly cold, especially in one of the bedrooms that has a large dark wooden four poster bed. I later note that this room is called the

Shambles as it overlooks the medieval street. The stairs are extremely narrow and steep and certainly would not comply with any building regulations of today. I quickly have a look at the other rooms, St. Catherine's room, Lady Peckett's room and the Minster Suite, which also houses a king-sized four poster double bed. Sadly, I see no ghosts nor hear or experience anything supernatural, so I head back downstairs where I find Kirsten about to tuck into a vegetarian meal. I sit back down and write a few notes in my notebook and look around this most ancient building, noting its strange angles and imprecise measurements. Later, I speak again to the barman who tells me that staff at the pub often claim to feel their necks tighten while working behind the bar, and have seen glasses mysteriously flung off the shelves. He points upwards towards a false ceiling above the bar and explains that there is a hook where a landlord once supposedly hanged himself.

I thank him for his time and retire back to my seat. Apparently, during a ghost hunt in 2002, a number of people saw a man dressed in seventeenth-century clothing walk through the wall of the front of the bar, stopping at one stage to stare at the horrified onlookers before walking off through another wall. However, on this occasion all I see is happy tourists eating meals and drinking pints.

The Mermaid Inn, a Grade II listed historical inn in the medieval town of Rye was established in the twelfth century and has a long and turbulent history due to a strong connection with the notorious Hawkhurst Gang of smugglers, who used it in the 1730s and 1740s as one of their strongholds. The current building dates from 1420 and has sixteenth-century additions in the Tudor style, although the cellars are much older and are believed to date from 1156.

The picturesque black-and-white timber-framed and tiled building has thirty-one rooms, each of a different design and spread over a number of floors. The upper story is jettied, and a section to the west spreads over the entrance to the inner courtyard and what was once the stable area. This extension is supported on wooden columns and adds to the overall feel that this is a building of substance and one that has seen many a winter and many a soul. The ceilings have thick, dark teak beams while the windows are made of lead frames. Diamond-paned windows are situated at the back, and the wooden floors creak with age.

As well, small wood-lined passages wind their way through the inn now refurbished as fire escapes but once the secret tunnels of smugglers. Painstakingly conserved, it is packed with original furnishings, features, and paintings, including sombre portraits with eyes that seem to unnervingly follow you around. It is a place that has stood the test of time and has seen countless generations come and go through its ancient wooden doors. But maybe, just maybe, some of these souls never left.

The Mermaid, like a number of its contemporaries, such as the Red Lion in Avebury, is reputed to be one of the most haunted pubs in England. Of course, this is not surprising given its connection to the Hawkhurst Gang, which was believed to have been founded by George Gray, and was a notorious criminal organisation involved in smuggling, stand-over tactics, extortion, beatings, and murder throughout southeast England from 1735 until 1749. So brazen were they that they successfully raided the customs house at Poole, a large coastal town and seaport in Dorset and quite a hike from the Mermaid Inn. The gang was finally stopped in a battle with the Goudhurst Militia in 1747, and two of their leaders, Arthur Gray and Thomas Kingsmill, were executed in 1748 and 1749 respectively. Others in the gang were tried at Chichester Assizes and sentenced to hang. One of them died in gaol before the sentence could be carried out, and the rest were hanged as a warning to anyone else who wished to follow in their footsteps.

Room 17 of the Inn, the Kingsmill Room, named after one of the smugglers who inhabited the inn, is said to be haunted by the ghost of a woman who is believed to be the wife of the Hawkhurst Gang founder George Gray. She is said to haunt a rocking chair in the room, and guests often report waking in the early hours of the morning to see the chair rocking back and forth on its own. In the end, the chair was removed by the owner of inn because it was causing too many disturbances to guests.

The Elizabethan Room, Room 16, is reputedly haunted by a most extraordinary sight in that it is the scene of a duel involving two men described as wearing sixteenth-century clothing. Bizarrely, after the spectral swordsman have fought their way through some nearby rooms, one of them is mortally wounded and then is dragged by his ghostly adversary through a hidden smuggler's door and thrown down the stairwell. Visitors have reported and recorded strange light anomalies in the room, and the ghost of a maid, a former girlfriend of one of the smugglers who was murdered as they feared she knew too much and would talk to the authorities, is also believed present.

But these are only a few of the ghosts that haunt this ancient building. In Room 1, the James Room, a lady in white or grey has been reported sitting in a chair next to the fireplace. Eerily, guests have reported waking up in the morning and finding their clothes on the chair wet, despite no windows or plumbing being near the chair. In Room 10, romantically titled the Fleur-de-Lys, the ghost of a man terrifies guests by walking through the bathroom wall into the main room, while in the Nutcracker Suite, Room 5, the ghost of a white lady has been reported walking across the room, stopping at the bed before continuing and disappearing. In Room 19, the ominously named Hawkhurst Suite, a gentleman in old-fashioned clothes appears to startled guests. An amusing story of this ghost is that one night an American visitor, after seeing his apparition at the end of her bed, spent the night in an adjacent room with a mattress pulled over her head.

Judith Blincow, who part owns the inn and has worked there since 1980 has stated that: "Although I have not personally seen ghosts, I certainly have met some very convinced and frightened guests."

CHAPTER 6

†

Witches and Things that Go Bump in the Night

A thousand ages were blank if books had not evoked their ghosts, and kept the pale unbodied shades to warn us from fleshless lips.

—François Fenelon

The Pendle witch trials are among the most famous witch trials in English history and tell a sorry tale of seventeenth-century persecution against a number of women who lived in the area around Pendle Hill in Lancashire who were accused of practicing witchcraft. All but two were tried in August 1612 in a series of trials that are now known as the Lancashire witch trials. Of the eleven individuals who went to trial, nine women and two men, ten were found guilty and executed by hanging. Only one was found not guilty.

The accused all lived near Pendle Hill in Lancashire, a wild and lawless region known for its theft, violence, and lack of sexual inhibitions—and a place that the church generally ignored.

With the dissolution of the nearby Cistercian abbey at Whalley in 1537, the people of Pendle generally remained faithful to Roman Catholic beliefs. However, when the protestant Elizabeth I came to the throne in 1558, Catholic priests once again had to go into hiding.

Elizabeth died in 1603 and was succeeded by James I who was obsessively interested in Protestant theology and focused much of his interest on witchcraft. After attending some witch trials in Denmark in the early 1590s, he became convinced that Scottish witches were plotting against him, and a year after he was crowned King of England, he enacted a law that imposed the death penalty in cases where it could be proven that harm had been caused by the use of magic or if corpses had been exhumed for magical purposes.

With the King's new decree regarding witchcraft and witches, local magistrates saw an avenue in which they could find favour with the King through a zealous pursuit of supposed witches to the point that trials were a farce with torture used to gain false confessions from those accused.

The Pendle witch trials were no different, although pretty much all involved confessed and even openly bragged about their affiliation to the devil and witchcraft.

It is generally thought that the beginnings of this sorry tale began when Alizon Device, was out walking one day when she came across John Law, a peddler. Alizon, coming from a desperately poor family begged for some food, but Law slapped her and told her to leave. According to legend, a large black dog suddenly appeared and asked Alizon, "if he should strike the man down." Alizon agreed and Law collapsed, paralysed down his left side.

After many hours he was stretchered to Colne where his family was called. When his son arrived, Law told him that he had been cursed, and that the witch who did it must be found and taken to a magistrate. Alizon was soon apprehended, but rather than deny the charges, she boasted about it and claimed that her mother, Demdike, and Anne Whittle, alias Chattox, were also witches. Alizon confessed that she had sold her soul to the devil and that she had summoned the devil to injure John Law. As a result all three were arrested and imprisoned at Lancaster City Gaol.

A couple of days later, a number of witches gathered in protest at Malkin Tower and proceeded to make some sort of potion in a bubbling cauldron with the intention of blowing off the doors of the gaol to free the imprisoned women. This gathering soon came to the attention of the local magistrate, who concluded that they too must be witches and within days many of those present were also arrested.

Further incriminating statements and reports of witchcraft were soon made by others, which saw more people sentenced under the terms of the 1604 Witchcraft Act. Demdike died in Lancaster Gaol awaiting trial while all the others accused were found guilty of witchcraft. On 20 August 1612, they were taken to the moors above the town and hanged.

It is believed that members of the Demdike and Chattox families made false accusations against each other as a result of competition in making a livelihood out of witchcraft so as to remove a competitor and ensure some sort of financial stability. It is also thought that there may have been some sort of family feud between the Demdike and Chattox families. However, being that as it may, it must also be remembered that these women were highly uneducated and probably did not think of themselves as witches; instead, they would have thought of themselves as village healers who practiced magic, probably in return for payment.

Such men and women were common in sixteenth century rural England and were an accepted part of village life. As such, it is easy to see why someone as poor and unimportant as Alizon Device was happy to be credited as a witch, and by default, powerful enough to summon up the Devil. Interestingly, the appellation "Demdike" is derived from "demon woman."

But if the Pendle witch trials were a result of paranoia on behalf of the anti-Catholic James I and a basic family feud for control in the Pendle area, then why are we examining it in a book about ghosts? This is because the area has been long believed to be haunted by the spirits of the slain witches themselves.

Pendle Hill is a hypnotic but bleak outcrop not far from Clitheroe in Lancashire. Set among rolling countryside and beautiful little villages, and nestled between green fields and sheep farming country, it seems somewhat idyllic, even benign, on a warm summer day. However, on a dark moonless or stormy night it takes on a different atmosphere, and the lonely mountain becomes dour and depressing—an ugly scar on the landscape and a place that one could easily believe is haunted by the tormented souls of long dead witches.

The name "Pendle Hill" is apparently from three different languages, all meaning "hill." In the 1200s, it was called *Pennul* or *Penhul*, apparently from the Cumbric *pen* and Old English *hyll*, both meaning "hill." The modern English "hill" was added later, which gives us a name that means "Hill Hill Hill," although locals still refer to it as just "Pendle."

Whatever the case, it is an important and significant place containing a Bronze Age burial site near the summit of the hill, and was also visited in 1652 by George Fox, a founder of the Religious Society of Friends, commonly known as the Quakers or Friends. While there, Fox claimed to have a vision and wrote in his autobiography: "As we travelled, we came near a very great hill, called Pendle Hill, and I was moved of the Lord to go up to the top of it, which I did with difficulty, it was so very steep and high. When I was come to the top, I saw the sea bordering upon Lancashire. From the top of this hill the Lord let me see in what places he had a great people to be gathered."

But if Pendle Hill itself is said to be haunted by the ghosts of dead witches from the early seventeenth century, then what of other places in the area, places that may have also been visited by the women?

Tynedale Farm is located in the Pendle Hill area, and although the current building was built in 1750, records exist dating the previous building that stood on the site back to at least 1600. The current building and surrounding areas are very well known due to the witch trials and, quite incredibly, the building is still owned to this day by the Nutter family, Alice Nutter being one of the women found guilty and later hanged for being a witch. Tynedale, like many haunted buildings, has a long and tortured history, and its current rundown state gives it a somewhat ominous presence.

It is said that the Nutter family refuse to come here, and if they are coaxed by guests into visiting the building, refuse to enter. A number of ghostly phenomena and apparitions have been witnessed in the building over the years ranging from the ghostly figure of a woman in the downstairs corridor, to heavy footsteps, groans, high-pitched screams, and the feeling of strangulation and bewilderment on the top floor. Another odd thing is that the electrical meter for the house continues to work even though there are no appliances working in the building. Do the entities of the house somehow consume energy? Or does the energy fuel the paranormal events that are said to happen?

Mediums have reported feeling the presence of a woman in the basement making clay effigies, presumably of her intended victims. Many years ago these dolls would have then been later stabbed or burnt to inflict pain or death. Is it possible that this woman is Elizabeth Demdike, or even Alice Nutter? Has the fabric of Tynedale Farm somehow absorbed the energy of these women?

But this is not the only legend of a ghostly witch as Wookey Hole Caves near Wells in Somerset is also well-known for the appearance of a spectral witch.

Going back some 50,000 years, Wookey Hole Caves has been inhabited or used since prehistoric times. It is apparently a perfect place to mature cheddar cheese but is better known for being a tourist attraction with circus shows, kids' play areas, a mirror maze, and a penny arcade. Apart from that, it was the abode of a witch.

The legend of the Witch of Wookey Hole Caves varies, although the basic legend remains the same in that many years ago a woman who had been wronged by life decided to take her anger out on the females of the village and cursed the romance of a certain couple. The romance failed due to the curse and heartbroken, the man became a monk. However, while a monk, he secretly plotted revenge upon the witch who had destroyed his happiness.

At a later time he entered the cave, and blessed the waters of a spring that bubbles up in the depths of the caves. He then started splashing holy water around so as to ward off evil and, in doing so, accidentally splashed some on the witch who was immediately petrified. She remains in the cave to this day and can be seen as a pillar of stone deep within the dark recesses of the cave.

A variation of the legend tells of a monk from Glastonbury who entered the cave and confronted the witch before throwing holy water on her, which also resulted in her being turned to stone.

Whatever the case, the Witch of Wookey Hole is actually a stalagmite and can be found in the first chamber of the caves. Over the years, erosion formed the rock until it took on a human like form and as such, the legend was born. However, there is other evidence that suggest that the story of the witch of Wookey Hole may just be true.

In 1912, a cave explorer found evidence that suggested someone may have been living in the caves hundreds of years previous. To his surprise, deep with the depths, he found a milking pot, a ball made from a stalagmite, tools, and even human remains begging the question, is it possible that a real, flesh and blood person once lived own here? And so, was she considered a witch by those who knew of her?

This we will never know, but it should be noted that the site is also said to be haunted by the ghost of a potholer who drowned in the caves as well as the ghostly spirit of a child who died at the site. And so we must ask, is the ghost of the witch of Wookey Hole simply a folklore memory of an old woman who made the cave her home? Or are the caves somewhat like Tynedale Farm, and have somehow absorbed the energy of people over the years in a way that somehow inexplicably manifests itself in the form of an apparition, witch or not?

Of course, we can never know the answers to these questions, and yet, if we look at the majority of ghost reports and hauntings we see the same situation in

which a specific place sees a significant event in history which later seems to manifest itself in a replay of the event, or at the very least, hints at a reply of the event.

Having said this, the stone tape theory style of haunting only accounts for some ghostly reports. For instance, what do we think of reports of poltergeists, a completely different supernatural phenomena and one that is regularly reported? And for good reason given that we are no longer speaking of benign figures that do not appear to possess intelligence or the ability to interact with the present day living?

And so, where do we start when we talk about poltergeists? Do we study the origins of the word, and then examine classic historical poltergeist events such as the Enfield poltergeist that terrorised an English family in the early 1970s? Or do we look at the incredible Humpty Doo poltergeist in Queensland, Australia, in the late 1990s, a case that was equally as frightening as well as perplexing?

As we are concentrating on the British Isles for this book we shall stay away from the Humpty Doo poltergeist although we will point out that it was an exceptionally strange case, and seemed to indicate that the ghost of a dead person may have been responsible for the attacks. Having said that, in the case of Humpty Doo, there didn't appear to be a certain unique connection that is generally thought as an integral part of poltergeist experiences, that being the presence of a young prepubescent girl. As such we shall quickly look at poltergeists, their definition and their general modus operandi.

Poltergeists are generally described as being noisy, mischievous, and occasionally malevolent spirits who manifest their presence by making noises, moving objects, turning electrical equipment on and off, and even attacking people by various means. The term poltergeist comes from the German words *poltern,* which means to knock, and *geist* meaning spirit, therefore a "knocking spirit."

Poltergeist activity has been reported as ranging from the benign—such as knocking, and items being moved or hidden—to the bizarre—with anything from moving large pieces of furniture to throwing stones, and smashing glass or pottery. Reports of levitation of people and beds have also been reported in some cases. In the most severe cases people have allegedly been attacked and have later displayed distinct bite and scratch marks on their bodies.

In general, the duration of poltergeist activity may last up to several hours spread randomly over a period of up to a few years although it has been observed that in these occurrences it generally starts and stops abruptly. The activity almost always, but not at all times, occurs at night when someone is present, although this could be a result of people simply being in the vicinity of the activity more at night than during the day. Bizarrely, poltergeist activity is usually associated with a person who seems to serve as a focus for the activity. Strangely, this person is more often than not a prepubescent female.

It has been suggested by some researchers that poltergeist behaviour is not from some unseen entity or ghost but is a manifestation from a person, such as a prepubescent girl suffering from intense repressed anger, hostility, and sexual tension. It is also suggested that the poltergeist activity is a way for the child to express hostility without the fear of punishment as the blame can be placed upon the unseen entity. It often appears that the person is unaware that they are the cause of the activities.

Having said this, there are numerous poltergeist reports that seem to suggest that poltergeists are indeed a ghost or spirit, however different from stone tape theory ghosts, and that they invariably are connected with a young girl. This of course begs the question as to what is it and why?

Whether a poltergeist is a ghost in the true sense or not is beyond this study. However, we can certainly say that it falls well within the scope of ghostly or supernatural occurrences and is, therefore, worthy of our attention. As such we shall look at a celebrated case that occurred in the 1970s in a council house in the Borough of Enfield.

The Borough of Enfield is a fairly unremarkable place. It borders the boroughs of Barnet, Haringey, and Waltham Forest as well as the Hertfordshire districts of Broxbourne and Welwyn Hatfield and the Essex district of Epping Forest. It was recorded in the *Domesday Book* of 1086. In Old English it means "field where lambs are reared," and in Roman times it was connected to Londinium by Ermine Street, the major Roman road which ran all the way up to York. In 790, King Offa reputedly gave the lands to St. Albans Abbey, and the area became strategically important as East Anglia was taken over by the Danes.

After the Norman Conquest of 1066, Enfield had roughly 400 inhabitants and was a parc, a heavily forested area for hunting. This parc was instrumental in Enfield's existence throughout the Middle Ages as wealthy Londoners came to Enfield to hunt, and then later to build houses. And it was in this unremarkable corner of London, in a council house on Green Street, that one of the world's most remarkable poltergeist happenings was observed and documented.

Late one night in August 1977, Peggy Hodgson, a single mother of four, claimed to have witnessed many unexplainable manifestations that seemed to centre on her two oldest daughters, and more specifically, Janet. The family consisted of the mother, Peggy, Margaret aged 12, a younger sister Janet aged 11, Johnny aged 10, and Billy aged 7.

At least twenty-six unexplained events were observed and recorded, and investigators insisted that these could not have been hoaxed, or if they had been, then the hoaxes were extremely sophisticated. These occurrences included the movement of small and large objects, beds being moved and bedclothes ruffled, unexplained pools of water on the floor, various physical assaults, apparitions, equipment malfunctions, strange inexplicable graffiti, spontaneous combustion, disappearance and reappearance of objects, and levitations.

On the first night Hodgson told investigators that she watched as a chest of drawers in the girl's bedroom slid across the room of its own accord before stopping in front of the stunned children. After moving the piece of furniture back to its original position, Hodgson was again shocked to watch as the chest repeated the movement. When she attempted to move it back again, it seemed to be held by some invisible weight. In addition, while this was happening she became aware of a disembodied knocking sound. This knocking and rapping would continue almost continuously for the next fourteen months.

Alarmed, Hodgson contacted the local police who dispatched two officers to the home. The two officers initially suspected a prank but were astounded when, upon arriving, one of the officers, WPC Carolyn Heeps, witnessed a living room chair slide five feet across the floor apparently of its own accord. In an attempt to make sense of this she placed a marble on the floor to see if it would roll away, which it didn't. Heeps also checked for wires or ropes under cushions that may have explained the movement of the chair but found nothing. Not having any idea of what to do, the officers suggested that Hodgson call the local media.

Soon after Hodgson contacted the *Daily Mirror* in hopes of being able to find someone who could help her unravel the mysterious happenings, and as a result two journalists, Graham Morris and Douglas Bence, were sent to cover the story. When they arrived they found the family nervous and somewhat overwhelmed but also reported that the poltergeist activity seemed to have stopped. The group sat around in the living room and discussed the events of the previous night with no hint of anything supernatural or untoward happening. However, as the journalists began to pack their equipment in their car in preparation to leave, they were stopped by a hysterical Hodgson. When they re-entered the house they were astounded at what they saw.

To their surprise small, inanimate objects were flying around the room, crashing into walls and people. Morris ran back to his car to get a camera and when he returned he immediately began taking photographs. He described the scene as "frantic" and reported that he was hit just above the eyebrow with a Lego brick. Unfortunately, when developed, the photos failed to show what any of the witnesses claimed to have happened. Sadly, this lack of tangible evidence was to prove a common happening in the Enfield incident and gave sceptics everywhere a major debating point over the genuineness of the claims.

Soon after, the Society for Paranormal Research was contacted, and two members, Morris Grosse and Guy Lyon Playfair, decided to investigate. After visiting the house and listening to the testimonies of those involved, they concluded that something genuinely paranormal was taking place as, over time, the knocking, banging, and scratching plus movements of furniture continued. Grosse soon believed that they were dealing with a poltergeist that was manifesting itself by feeding off psychokinetic energy.

In October, Grosse witnessed the aftermath of the destruction of a fireplace in the girls' room. Hearing a loud banging and then feeling a shaking in the floor, he ran into the bedroom to find the fireplace had been completely torn from the wall ripping a solid metal pipe in half. The two girls, Margaret and Janet, both who claimed to be sleeping at the time, were the only ones in the room. That the girls faked it is highly improbable given that the fireplace weighed around 120 kilograms.

Desperate to prove that something supernatural was at foot, the University of London was contacted and a student in experimental physics went to the house hoping to test the girls for telekinetic ability. Within a short period of time Janet managed to bend a spoon completely in half apparently without touching the object. Due to this, the student suggested that the activity was centred on Janet, who suspiciously appeared to become less frightened of the strange events as they continued to occur.

However, even with this, there were doubts as to the veracity of the events being reported, especially in the minds of some of the Society for Paranormal Research members. Indeed, even Grosse and Playfair openly admitted that on more than one occasion the two girls had been caught using simple hoaxes to try and trick them. As well, Janet's behaviour had become more suspicious and questions were raised as to the whole thing being an elaborate hoax.

In late November, however, after three months of investigation, the ghostly knocking became so persistent that it could just about be considered intelligent. Grosse tried to communicate with it by asking it to answer questions by knocking on the wall once or twice. Quite startlingly, and somewhat chillingly, the response that followed the questions was a succession of more than fifty distinct knocks, all recorded on a tape recorder. It was if the unseen entity was attempting to prove that it existed.

About this time Janet started to fall into disquieting trance-like states and is said to have developed phenomenal strength while in these states. She also started to become somewhat violent, not only to others, but to herself as well and as a result was restrained and sedated. Interestingly, considering the suspicions of hoaxing, on the twenty-sixth of November, Janet was sedated with ten milligrams of valium, which should have rendered her nearly unconscious but half an hour later was found in her bedroom on top of a dresser, kneeling on a wide clock radio with her head hanging towards the ground and her legs in the air.

Graham Morris, a photographer from *The Daily Mirror*, suspecting that something was taking control of the girl's body, set up a remote control camera in the bedroom that could be operated from anywhere in the house. Once activated, the camera could take a photograph every four seconds until stopped. Some of the subsequent photos captured appear to show Janet being vigorously pulled out of her bed and thrown across the room.

Not long after these events, things took an even more worrying turn when Janet began to speak in a deep, gruff voice. Grosse suspected that she had become some sort of conduit for whatever was haunting the house. As a result he asked her a series of questions; however, to ensure that it was not a hoax her mouth was filled with water and taped closed. Surprisingly, the gruff voice continued without impediment.

During Grosse's questioning it became apparent that Janet referred to herself as being a man by the name of Bill, a previous resident of the house who had died in a chair on the first floor. Months later, Grosse was surprised when he was contacted by a Terry Wilkins who claimed that his father, Bill, had lived in the house and had died of a brain haemorrhage in his favourite chair on the first floor.

By July 1978, Janet was admitted to hospital for psychiatric testing. However, after two months she was discharged with a clean bill of health and returned home. Noticeably, during her absence, the house experienced much less poltergeist-like behaviour, which suggests that she was mainly responsible for a hoax, or that the poltergeist had given up or had simply moved on. Of course, we must also remember that poltergeists are generally known for attaching themselves to prepubescent girls, and if Janet had been removed from the house, then surely the poltergeist would move on as well?

Whatever the reason, the unbelievable nature and subsequent media coverage of the Enfield poltergeist case made it one of the most famous, if not the most famous poltergeist case known. However, due to admissions of some fraud by the girls, some confusing evidence, and some less than convincing photographs, one must remain sceptical about the events

Having noted this, many people witnessed strange phenomena where there was no obvious hoax or method to apply a hoax. Indeed, Margaret, the eldest of the sisters later stated that it was, "ridiculous to suggest that either my sister or I could have been responsible for the strange activity that went on in our house."

In his book, *Will Storr Versus the Supernatural*, Storr takes a retrospective look at the case, and his conclusions, while not sceptical, throw some doubt upon Maurice Grosse who, after the death of a family member, seemed almost fanatical in his search for life after death. As such Storr suggests that Grosse may have unwittingly let his beliefs cloud his judgement. Conversely, there is absolutely no doubt that Grosse was methodical in his reporting and recording of the case, which simply clouds the issue more.

But the Enfield poltergeist case, sensational as it was, is not the only well-known case in the British Isles. As such we shall examine more of this phenomena in the next chapter.

CHAPTER 7

†

ASSORTED POLTERGEISTS AND A HAUNTED SCOTTISH GRAVEYARD

The consequences of our crimes long survive their commission, and, like the ghosts of the murdered, forever haunt the steps of the malefactor.

—SIR WALTER SCOTT

The Enfield poltergeist case is possibly the best known poltergeist case in England, due mainly to the extensive reporting in the press and the diligence, or some may say, pig-headedness of Maurice Grosse. Either way, it attracted the public's attention to the fact that these things could possibly exist. However, as sensational as it was, it is not the only well-known case in England as, in August 1972 in the south London district of Thornton Heath, Croydon, a family suffered from the same sort of paranormal symptoms as were experienced by the Hodgson family.

The supposed entity was first experienced late one night when the family was woken by a bedside radio that had somehow turned itself on, tuned itself to a foreign-language station, and turned itself up to full volume. This inexplicable event was the beginning of a string of strange happenings that lasted nearly four years.

Over this time a particular lampshade repeatedly fell to the floor as if pushed by some unseen force, and at Christmas 1972, an ornament was hurled across the room, crashing violently into the husband's forehead. As he flopped back in the armchair stunned, the Christmas tree began to violently shake, which scared the family. On New Year's Eve disembodied footsteps were heard in a bedroom, and one night the couple's son apparently awoke to find a man in old-fashioned dress staring threateningly at him.

At this stage one would suspect that the happenings had all the hallmarks of what could be thought of as a standard haunting with objects being moved or occasionally thrown and the ghostly figure of a man appearing. However, things escalated one night when, while entertaining friends, there was a loud knock at the front door, the living room door was violently flung open, and all the house's lights came on.

Now worried, the family contacted the local church who duly sent a priest to bless their home. Sadly, this appeared to have little effect as the phenomena continued unabated with objects flying through the air, and loud noises being heard. On occasion, the family would hear a large crashing noise, which suggested a large piece of furniture crashing to the floor. However, upon investigation, nothing would be disturbed.

A psychic medium was then consulted and was able to relay to the family that she believed the house to be haunted by the ghost of a farmer by the name of Chatterton, who now considered the family to be trespassing on his property. A subsequent investigation soon established that the man had indeed lived in the house in the mid-eighteenth century. But if the family thought that revealing the identity of the culprit would lead to a settling down of the phenomena, they were wrong as Chatterton's ghostly wife was reputed to have joined in the mayhem. Often the tenant's wife would be followed up the stairs at night by an elderly lady with her grey hair tied back in a bun and wearing a pinafore. When challenged or looked at, she would simply disappear. The family even reported seeing the Chatterton's image appear on their television screen seemingly wearing a black jacket with pointed lapels, a high-necked shirt, and black cravat.

Not surprisingly, the family soon moved out and the poltergeist activity reportedly ceased. Remarkably, or maybe not, new residents in the house have not reported anything amiss.

In 1938, Nandor Fodor, a parapsychologist and pioneer in linking the psychic with the psychological, studied a similar case also in Thornton Heath known as the Thornton Heath poltergeist. Fodor was influenced by Freudian theory and later became a psychoanalyst, and put forward the theory that poltergeists are external manifestations of conflicts within the individual subconscious mind rather than autonomous entities existing of their own volition, that is, poltergeist activity is caused by human agents with hostile or disagreeable emotions such as feelings of repressed hostility, anger, and sexual tension.

The 1938 Thornton Heath case was interesting in that Fodor believed that it validated his views. When the case came to Fodor's attention he had an inclination to attribute the activity to natural means and through observation concluded that this case and others like it needed further study in the fields of the psychological in parapsychological research.

Mrs. Forbes, the woman at the centre of the phenomena, did not present as your typical poltergeist victim in that she was no longer a prepubescent girl. She was the mistress of London's Thornton Heath House and was thirty-five, married with a son. The first time Fodor observed her and the poltergeist phenomena, he decided to have her studied in his laboratory at the International Institute for Psychical Research where he was the director of research. He believed that he and his colleagues needed to scrutinize her actions to validate, or at least try and understand, what was happening. To ensure that there was no outward influences and trickery, she was required to undress for examinations and wear special clothing that would reveal any hoaxing.

When in laboratory Forbes seemed to have a paranormal effect on numerous objects in that dishes moved and crashed on the floor, glasses flew out of her hands, and objects seemingly appeared out of nowhere, ostensibly having being aported from Thornton Heath. Fodor was convinced that Forbes was producing the phenomena by physical means but could not quite prove it until he had her x-rayed, which revealed that she had secreted two objects that later mysteriously appeared in her hands.

She later claimed that a ghost tried to choke her with a necklace and showed Fodor marks on her neck that looked like burns. She also claimed that a vampire had bitten her and as proof showed Fodor two neat puncture marks in her neck. Bizarrely, she also reported that she was clawed by a tiger and produced five wounds on her arm as proof.

Fodor rightly concluded that Forbes was neurotic and had a troubled and disorganized psyche. She showed signs of dissociation and separating emotions as well as having thoughts or experiences that were completely dissociated from each other either consciously or subconsciously. In addition, she had hysterical reactions and auditory and visual hallucinations that seemingly produced symptoms, such as swelling in her abdomen. Fodor also believed that the ghost, vampire, and tiger injuries were subconscious attempts at harming herself, a criterion for borderline personality disorder.

The case further convinced Fodor that mental processes involved in psychic phenomena, psi, and parapsychological research had to be studied even if the phenomena was obviously a hoax. He believed that the events surrounding Forbes indicated the subconscious nature of the alleged poltergeist activity, and that to understand the nature of Forbes' actions was to understand the nature of a poltergeist.

And yet, while there have been numerous well-documented cases of human agent poltergeists, it was apparent to Fodor that Forbes was not a true agent and produced the phenomena by deception, even if it was unsure that she even realized that she was doing so. Through this case he theorised that there was a need to understand the psychological processes that go hand and hand with apparent psychic phenomena, no matter how much the phenomena is hoaxed. He suggested that the anguish and distress that she undoubtedly suffered was real, and that it all seemed to point to an unconscious action.

It should be pointed out that Fodor, along with famed ghost hunter Harry Price, had earlier investigated an exceptionally odd story about a talking mongoose or poltergeist, which we will briefly look at in the next chapter. However, at this stage we are not interested in talking mongooses and shall continue to look at some more poltergeist-like behaviours and activities, in particular the strange case of Eleonore Zugun.

Eleonore Zugun was born in Talpa, Romania, on 24 May 1913. In February 1923, when she was eleven years old, she went to visit her grandmother's house at Buhai, a few miles away from her village. Later, it was reported, she found some money lying on the road in her village with which she used to buy some candy. Upon hearing about this, her grandmother, who was reputed to be a witch, flew into a rage claiming that the money was left by evil spirits and that it would only bring her bad luck.

The next day, and seemingly coincidentally, poltergeist like activity began, firstly with a shower of stones that was hurled at her grandparent's cottage. The phenomena continued and soon became so frequent that the grandmother sought out a local priest in the hope that he could help her. While at the house investigating the stone throwing, the priest witnessed a stone smash through a window and land on the kitchen table. The stone was wet, which suggested it had been lying in a stream only a few yards from the house. The priest marked the stone with a cross and threw it back out of the window. However, seconds later the same stone was thrown back, complete with the cross marking.

The superstitious grandmother was convinced that the girl was possessed by the Devil, and sent home to Talpa. Over the following days and weeks reports of poltergeist activities, such as dishes breaking, iron pieces exploding, and objects flying through the air were commonplace, and all had one thing in common, Eleonore was present when it happened. Indeed, a school teacher reported seeing a jug of water at one end of a bench float a few feet into the air and do a half-circle rotation before floating to the other side of the bench where it promptly landed, all without spilling a drop of water. Other events included a trunk shaking violently and a porridge bowl flying at a visitor, hitting him on the back of the head and causing a painful wound.

After enduring months of this, Eleonore's father sent her to the Convent of Gorovei where it was hoped she could be cured, or at least, whatever it was that seemed to beset her could be removed. Priests there said prayers and held masses to help the unfortunate girl, but nothing seemed to stop the poltergeist-like phenomena that accompanied her. At one stage an exorcism was performed but also to no avail, and as a result she was sent to a local asylum.

Before long the local press picked up on this extremely strange story and it was soon all over the newspapers. Upon reading about the situation, Fritz Grunewald, a Berlin-based engineer and a psychic researcher convinced Eleonore's father to get her released from the asylum so he could observe her symptoms. Grunewald managed to observe and document numerous unexplained phenomena in a controlled environment, but before he could do more he died of a heart attack.

In his papers, published after his death, Grunewald described phenomena, such as the slow movement of a large pot on the oven to the sometimes violent throwing of things at, or close to, people. In addition, he noted that objects also appeared seemingly from nowhere, and there were occasional knocks and raps on walls and ceilings. Once or twice, matches were mysteriously set alight. More alarmingly, however, the unseen entity also began slapping the girl.

With the death of Grunewald, Eleonore was once again left in the care of her apparently unconcerned family. However, later that year she found another protector, this time an attractive young Viennese woman by the name of the Countess Zoe Wassiliko-Serecki, a part Romanian who had an interest in psychoanalysis. When she visited Eleonore at the monastery of Gorovei in September 1925, she found an uncared for, confused, and very frightened girl.

While at the monastery the Countess saw for herself a number of bizarre paranormal occurrences. As a result she wrote a short book about her experiences, later published as *Der Spuk von Talpo*. Realising that the girl was terrified by what was happening to her, she managed to negotiate her release and brought her to Vienna to live with her in her flat.

In Vienna, Eleonore was happy and healthy, and as a result the Countess had her trained as a hairdresser. At this stage it is reported that, although she was emotionally stable, happy and healthy, the poltergeist activity continued as before. The Countess kept a diary of these occurrences and made some intriguing and significant observations including the following: "Once I entered my room and looked at the window. Eleonore was standing behind me. Suddenly I saw a shadow, which glided down slowly in front of the window and not straight, but in a zigzag line. Then I heard a low sound of something falling. I looked and saw a little iron box filled with dominoes. The box was closed but some of the dominoes lay next to it on the floor."

Another time she noted that: "she was sitting with Mr. Klein at the round table while Eleonore stood with a cat in her arms at the bookstand. Mr. Klein unintentionally looked at the girl, and on this occasion noticed a dark grey shadow come from behind her, pass along her right side and fall under our table upon the cushions at our feet. It was a tin box which had before stood on the washstand on the other side of the room."

Occasionally raps and taps on furniture were heard in Eleonore's presence, and sometimes disembodied voices. Cherished possessions often disappeared and were sometimes never seen again or if they were returned, were broken or damaged. However, as annoying as this could be, the most significant development at this time was the occurrence of what appeared to be physical assaults on the girl's body, apparently by a malicious spirit called "Dracu."

Objects were violently thrown at her, she was slapped, thrown to the ground, tossed out of bed, had her hair pulled out, and her shoes filled with water. However, this wasn't the end of it, and by late March 1926, the situation was dire with her hands and fingers constantly pricked as if by needles. Indeed, sometimes real needles were found embedded in her flesh.

Harry Price, the well-known and controversial English psychical researcher, arrived in Vienna in late April 1926. Having heard of Eleonore's case, he was very much interested in observing and recording whatever it was that was happening. In all he visited the Countess' flat on three occasions and while there witnessed object movements, such as a steel letter-opener fly across

the room, a small mirror float over the partition of a room, and a cushion move off a chair. On each occasion he had both the Countess and Eleonore in view. He also observed bite and scratch marks appear on Eleonore's arm and chest.

Price was fascinated and was soon convinced that some of the telekinetic phenomena could not be explained by normal means. As such he decided to bring the Countess and Eleonore to London for study at the National Laboratory of Psychical Research, an institution largely created and administered by Price himself.

The group arrived in London in September 1926 and stayed until mid-October. While there, Eleonore spent many hours at the laboratory. On occasions she was alone and at other times with the Countess. However, whatever the circumstances, it appeared that the girl was still under attack as physical lacerations in the form of bite and scratch marks occurred in ordinary daylight even when she was under close observation. Indeed, Price even managed to photograph some stigmatic-like markings.

Interesting as this was, Price was more impressed by the object movements that occurred in the vicinity of the young Romanian girl, and although he recorded two possible attempts at cheating, he was convinced that the psychic phenomena were real. Indeed, the validity of the phenomena was attested to by various prominent observers.

In the laboratory was a notice board that had small metallic letters. The spare letters, which were rarely if ever used, were kept in a locked cupboard. However, on one occasion there was a need to use the letter C which, to the surprise of Price and his colleagues, was missing. Eleven days later the letter was found by a Professor Tillyard; however, it was not as if it were simply mislaid as the small metallic letter was somehow fastened tightly around the metal rim of his pocket knife case, sealing it shut. Professor Tillyard had used the knife more than once that day and he swore that the metallic letter was not there when he did. Hoax was immediately ruled out as close control and observation of Eleonore and the Countess was followed in the laboratory at all times. This bizarre and unexplainable incident helped to convince many of the scientists and doctors that they had witnessed genuine paranormal phenomena.

Eleonore's visit produced great interest in the British press with large headlines, innumerable articles, photographs, and cartoons being dedicated to her. Meanwhile, in the laboratory, Price and the Laboratory Council continued their experiments and concluded that Eleonore had indeed shown "that under scientific test conditions, movements of small objects without physical contact undoubtedly took place." Put simply, Price and his fellow researchers agreed that the girl possessed what could only be described as psychic abilities.

In late October, Eleonore and the Countess said goodbye to London and headed back to Berlin. Although Eleonore's psychic and telekinetic ability appeared to be fading, the biting and scratching continued. However, unlike before, there was a new and quite baffling aspect to the attacks in that her skin appeared to be covered in large amounts of saliva.

Samples of the saliva-like material were taken from Eleonore's arm and face and analysed by a Dr. Walther Kroner. Remarkably they were found to be full of micro-organisms not from Eleonore or the Countess. Bewildered, and somewhat perplexed, Kroner decided to test whether the marks on Eleonore's body were caused from outside of her body, something he was sure was happening. As such, he smeared her face and arms with greasepaint and soon discovered that when scratches appeared, the greasepaint had been pushed aside, clearly demonstrating that the scratches and bites were created externally.

Dr. Hans Rosenbusch, a Munich doctor, soon invited Eleonore and the Countess to his home so that he could also observe the phenomena. However, after a number of sittings he was convinced that Eleonore was a fake and that together with the Countess they had hoaxed the entire poltergeist-like events. Price replied that, although he agreed that the girl sometimes cheated, all of his experiments were held under the strictest of control and that there was no conceivable way that she or the Countess could have faked anything. As such, Price was still convinced that he had found genuine and unexplained phenomena. It must be noted, however, that Rosenbusch based his findings completely on what he had witnessed and not on the previous studies of the phenomena, which occurred with no trace of fraud. Indeed, later analysis of a documentary film taken in Munich also showed no indication of fraud.

Whatever the case, the controversy raised by the case soon became irrelevant in the early summer of 1927, when Eleonore's abilities seemed to cease completely. At this stage she was fourteen years of age and had started to experience menstruation. The fact that the phenomenon stopped after her menstrual cycle began gives much credence to the theory that there exists a strong connection between prepubescent children and psychokinetic abilities.

And so what are we to make of this strange tale and how does it relate to ghosts? As far as the Countess Wassiliko-Serecki was concerned, Eleonore's unconscious mind was responsible for the attacks. Influenced by Freud, the Countess believed that Eleonore had developed strong sexual urges, possibly centred on her father, and the "attacks" were a form of self-punishment for these feelings. It has also been suggested that Eleonore confessed to the Countess of some sort of incestuous event or affair in her younger days, and if this were so, then we can suggest that Eleonore was in a confused state of mind, which somehow led to the phenomena happening. Price agreed with the Countess to some degree, although he compared the bites and scratches to the stigmata often found on some intensely religious people.

It has been suggested that tests revealed that Eleonore had an underdeveloped mind and at the age of thirteen she was developmentally the age of an eight year old. As such sexual feelings would have been extremely confusing and even frightening to the girl.

Having said this, how did Eleonore gain this strange power? It would seem that the threats of her grandmother, an alleged witch, and the peasants of her village, could have taken a strong hold on her young and impressionable mind, and then somehow manifested itself in the phenomena later witnessed. But even if this is possible, how does one gain the ability to move objects without touching them, that is, through telekinesis? And even more so, why and how did objects apparently apport from one room to another, or even from one building to another? And how did she generate the energy to harm herself, seemingly by her own mind and nothing else?

Of course, there is another aspect we must think about and that concerns the reports of foreign saliva being found on her arms and face. Is it possible that in her tumultuous and distressed state the young girl unwittingly allowed some sort of malevolent presence to enter her life, or to attach itself to her being? Or did she equally unwittingly invite this being into her soul, or whatever you want to call the life force that exists within a person? And was this spirit or entity something similar to what we would call a ghost?

We do know from early reports of the girl that sometimes a grey shape was seen to move around or past her during her poltergeist episodes. Is this the creature that was responsible for the phenomena? Is this the creature that scratched and tore at the girls face? If so, there are some extremely dark secrets out there that we know absolutely nothing about.

No convincing explanation has ever been presented in regard to Eleonore Zugun. However, much like in the Enfield case, the fact that she was sometimes caught cheating created enough doubt to have her labelled a fraud. And yet for all this many respected witnesses, including medical doctors, testified that what they saw was completely unexplainable. And if this is so, then is it possible that prepubescent girls that have experienced traumatic and/or psychologically scarring events can unwillingly manifest this phenomenon?

Whatever the case, the Eleonore Zugun poltergeist phenomena, although still well known in the present day, ceased for good, and when last heard of she was running a hair-dressing business in Czernowitz, Romania in the 1930s.

But if the Zugun case was unusual and posed genuine questions to believers and sceptics alike, then what of the next case reported in the *Sun* newspaper on 22 January 2013?

Under the slightly sensational headline, "Poltergeist wrecks house in Coventry and kills the dog," the paper reported that a family residing in a Coventry council house were living in fear due to a poltergeist, which they claimed killed their dog.

The family, consisting of thirty-four-year-old mother Lisa Manning, her eleven-year-old daughter Ellie, and six-year-old son Jaydon, said the phenomena started around two weeks after they moved into the house. Manning told the newspaper that: "lights would flicker, or I'd hear footsteps when there was no one upstairs," and that chairs would fly across the room and crash into walls, cupboard doors would open by their own accord and then violently bang shut, often ripping them off their hinges, and that two family dogs were pushed down stairs, one being so badly injured that it had to be put down.

According to Manning, their twelve-year-old Staffordshire bull terrier, Phoenix, fell down the stairs suffering terrible injuries while another pet, a six-month-old bull terrier called Rocky, suffered two broken legs after falling on the same stairs.

Manning added: "It's like a horror movie. We've had so many incidents in the kitchen and Ellie's room. She's too scared to sleep there. The poltergeist has smashed her Nintendo and her TV."

A Church of England priest was called and later carried out a blessing. For two weeks the poltergeist was apparently quiet but then returned. A little later, the family claimed they were watching television when the living room door slammed shut. Six-year-old Jaydon tried opening it, but it would not move. Lisa Manning said, "We climbed out of a window and ran."

In addition, the family managed to film footage of a cupboard door opening and a pink chair mysteriously moving across a room; however, like so many similar videos, it is sadly inconclusive. Interestingly, Lisa Manning had recently asked her housing association to move her to another house, which one can look at in two ways: she was genuinely afraid of the reported phenomena, or she hoaxed the whole thing in order to have an excuse to move. Both theories are as strong as the other.

But poltergeist behaviour, like ghosts and hauntings, is not a new phenomenon, and the number of reports would suggest that, if not exactly commonplace, then poltergeist activity is not unusual in frequency. And this can be observed in historical reports.

In 1877, in Derrygonnelly, Ireland, Sir William Barrett, a respected physicist and parapsychologist, investigated a report of poltergeist activity at a small farm inhabited by a widower and his five children. The family claimed they were hearing knocking and rapping sounds at all hours and had witnessed objects that apparently moved by themselves. As with every poltergeist-like report there was the possibility that it was being hoaxed by one, or more of the children. However, in the course of his investigation Barrett performed one test that couldn't be faked: he simply asked the spirit to knock the number he was thinking of, which, to Barrett's surprise, it did. Stunned by this, Barrett performed the same test on a number of occasions, and each time the disembodied knocking apparently gave the correct answer.

Barrett first became interested in the paranormal in the 1860s after an experience with mesmerism. He believed that he had witnessed genuine thought transference, and by the 1870s, he was actively investigating poltergeists and like behaviour. In September 1876, he published a paper outlining the result of his investigations, and by 1881, he had published preliminary accounts of additional experiments about thought transference. With the publication causing controversy, Barrett decided to found the Society for Psychical Research for like-minded individuals.

Similar to the Derrygonelly episode, an incident in 1883 in Nottinghamshire, England, was witnessed by no less than a police constable and a family doctor, both, one would agree, being respected witnesses. The aggrieved person complained of poltergeist activity was a man by the name of Joseph White, and he reported the odd goings-on to the doctor and the constable who agreed to visit his house to see what was happening.

White and his family described the poltergeist activity that they had witnessed to the constable and the doctor, both of whom were, quite understandably, doubtful about what they were hearing. However, when they were left alone for a moment in the parlour, the two men observed a ceramic bowl rise by itself in the middle of the room. To their surprise the bowl continued to rise all the way to the ceiling then fell to the floor where it was smashed into tiny pieces.

Likewise, in 1894 in Durweston in England, a Mr. Newman answered panicked cries from his neighbour, a Mrs. Best, who claimed she had heard scraping and rapping sounds and had seen objects flying around a room in her house. Mrs. Best, in a panic, pointed to a boot that she claimed had flown toward the back door. Nearly hysterical, she picked up the boot and threw it into the garden. Mr. Newman, quite disbelieving one would suspect, walked out into the garden and stood on the boot, reportedly saying: "I defy anything to move this boot." When he lifted his foot, the boot suddenly flew up into the air and kicked his hat off his head.

As we have seen, poltergeist activity is generally irritating, frightening, and sometimes destructive, and considering the damage and destruction that sometime occurs with the incidents, it is somewhat surprising that more people have not been injured. There are, however, exceptions to this and there have been a number of reports where the poltergeist seems intent on causing actual physical harm. There have been numerous reports of poltergeists attacking people by hurling objects at them or, as in the Zugun case, scratching and biting the victim. And this appears to be the case in the celebrated Mackenzie Poltergeist of Edinburgh.

Greyfriars Kirkyard is the graveyard that surrounds Greyfriars Kirk in Edinburgh and has seen burials since the late sixteenth century. It is associated with Greyfriars Bobby, the loyal dog who guarded his master's grave after his death, although recent research seems to suggest that the legend of the little dog is a myth. It is also the place of many notable burials, including the poet, William McGonagall, who won notoriety as an exceptionally bad poet who showed no concern for peer opinions of his work. Indeed, his infamous "The Tay Bridge Disaster" is widely regarded as some of the worst writing in the history of English literature.

Whatever the case, legend has it that, in 1998, a rain-drenched homeless tramp, obviously seeking shelter for the night, broke into one of the old mausoleums in the Covenanters' Prison section. Once inside the vault he decided, for whatever reason, to explore the surroundings, possibly to see if there was anything of monetary value that he could steal. He removed an iron grate in the floor and descended a short, twisting, stone staircase where he came across a second chamber. In this chamber he came across four wooden coffins, and hoping to steal grave goods, he began to smash them open. However, as he did so, a hole suddenly opened up in the floor beneath his feet and he fell through the wooden surface into a third chamber, one that had not previously been known about. Unluckily for the man this chamber had formerly been used for dumping plague victims and, despite being hundreds of years old, the bodies of the dead were not skeletal and mummified but still putrid and rotting and covered in an evil-smelling greenish-grey slime.

The man frantically fled and a security guard and his dog, having heard strange noises coming from the Covenanters' Prison, quickly went to explore the source of the noise. They were met with the bedraggled figure of a man covered in rotting slime and congealed blood running from a crypt towards them. Not surprising, the security guard also fled. It is believed that the security guard quit his job the very next day.

What happened to the homeless tramp is unknown; however, it is widely agreed that of all the tombs to break into, this was the worse. Called the Black Mausoleum, it houses the remains of the most notorious resident of Greyfriars Kirkyard, the seventeenth century judge and Lord Advocate Sir George MacKenzie.

MacKenzie was, without doubt, a harsh and brutal man. Made Lord Advocate in August 1677 by King Charles II, he organised a bloody prosecution of the Presbyterian Covenanters in retaliation for their refusal to replace Scotland's Presbyterian Church with the Episcopalian Church that had been introduced in England. And it is said, he did this with a particularly cruel enthusiasm.

In the summer of 1679, the Covenanters were defeated at the Battle of Bothwell Bridge and some 2,000 were captured. MacKenzie transported them to Greyfriars where he sentenced some to be hanged and others to be beheaded. He then displayed their rotting skulls on the walls around the city as a warning to others. Numerous other Covenanters were publicly tortured while thousands were imprisoned in a section of land adjacent to Greyfriars Kirkyard in what was essentially an open-air prison somewhat like a latter-day concentration camp. By mid-November, most of the 1,200 detainees had died from starvation, disease, or exposure.

In all, it has been estimated that MacKenzie was responsible for the deaths of over 18,000 Covenanters during a reign of terror now referred to as "The Killing Time," a dark period of conflict in Scottish history that occurred roughly from 1680 to 1688. However, as interesting as this is, it is the chance 1998 incidence that curiously seems to have been the catalyst for one of the most frightening ghost/poltergeist-like hauntings ever recorded.

As strange as it seems, it appears that the bedraggled tramp's unwelcome entry into the tomb seemed to awaken a spirit or entity of some sort as almost immediately afterwards mysterious and disturbing activity was reported in the graveyard itself. The day after the break-in a woman who was peering through the iron grate set into the vault's door, reported that she was "blasted back off its steps by a cold force."

Soon after, another woman was found sprawled on the ground near the tomb; chillingly, her neck was ringed with heavy bruising. She later claimed that "invisible hands had tried to strangle her." Similar injuries were found on another victim, this time a young man who was discovered lying opposite the vault.

With an apparent outbreak of paranormal assaults, the Edinburgh City Council locked the Black Mausoleum's doors and declared the location to be out of bounds. However, local author and amateur historian Jan-Andrew Henderson asked the council for permission to conduct tours to the mausoleum, and the site now is exceptionally popular to ghost hunters, psychics, and the like.

Having said this, the attacks have apparently increased in number. Since 1998, there have been over 450 reported attacks in which some 180 people have lost consciousness. Strange cold spots abound, inexplicable fires have broken out, and an unusually high number of dead wildlife has been found in the vicinity of the vault. People have complained of their fingers be broken by unknown assailants, hair pulled, and a sensation of being punched or kicked. In addition, people frequently report and document unexplained bruises, scratches, burns, nausea, dizziness, and numbness while in the area. And similar to other haunted sites, cameras and other electrical equipment often malfunction.

A schoolboy, hiding in the vault to escape a master at George Heriot's School, reputedly found himself trapped inside and lost his mind on being confronted by a ghost. Even more interesting, a number of unexplained deaths have taken place in the Kirkyard itself.

And it is not just frightening physical attacks that happen either, as at times the aroma of smelling salts and sulphur have been reported, while inexplicable laughing and growling has been heard. To add to this, strange knocking sounds that seem to come from beneath ground level are also reported. Indeed, a tour member once commented that, "we had not been in the Black Mausoleum long when we started hearing knocking noises coming from beneath us, which steadily grew louder and seemed to move up and round the walls."

Somewhat baffling, although attacks are often immediately reported, the physical signs of some assaults often go unnoticed until people get home or return to their hotels for the night when they find, to their surprise, unexplained injuries. Whereas some of the scratches and burns heal quickly, other injuries have been reported to last for months, and even years. Even more bizarrely, people often report that the phenomenon doesn't stop after the tour and that it appears to follow them home, something that is rare, but not unheard of in ghosts and hauntings.

And so, what is it that seemingly haunts the Black Mausoleum and Greyfriars Kirkyard? Historians like to point out that, even before the mass burials of the Covenanters, the graveyard was literally full. Established in 1562, it was originally in a depression roughly twenty feet deep, although today, thanks to some 500,000 or so recorded burials, it has become a hill, some fifteen feet high. And with such a concentration of burials it is not uncommon today, especially after rain, to find the bones of long dead people rising to the surface. As things go, it is the perfect location for ghosts and the supernatural as surely; if ghosts were to exist then this place would be uppermost in haunted localities. Indeed, there have been many reported sightings of unidentifiable misty shapes, ashen figures, eerie wraithlike children, and grey shadows lurking between the headstones.

Respected historian and ghost hunter Richard Felix of television's *Most Haunted* fame has spent countless years researching ghosts and hauntings and has stated that an old English, or possibly Anglo-Saxon legend exists whereby the first person to be buried in a graveyard is doomed to haunt that graveyard for eternity. Is this the case with Greyfriars? Sadly, even with such a long and rich history, we will never know.

Despite the innumerable spooky happenings, it is hard to say whether or not the perpetrator is of the ghostly kind or a poltergeist. For sure the attacks, knocking, rapping, and disembodied voices all suggest poltergeist-like behaviour but the sightings suggest a ghost, or a multitude of ghosts. However, as we have seen, poltergeist-like activity is usually centred on a person, generally a prepubescent female who seems to serve as a focus for the activity. Having said this, no one lives within the grounds of the Kirkyard, therefore, no one can act as a hub to the activity. In addition, poltergeist activity generally ceases within a few months or at most a year or two, whereas the MacKenzie Black Mausoleum has been displaying these traits since 1998. Is it possible that the place is haunted by ghosts as well as a malevolent poltergeist?

Of course, there could also be some quite rational, if somewhat sensational reasons for the phenomenon. To the rear of the mausoleum is Edinburgh University's Artificial Intelligence Unit where high voltage machinery is housed. These machines give off massive amounts of electromagnetic energy, which some scientists believe can create an atmosphere in which hallucinations can be induced and therefore could be construed as being paranormal. Of course, if this is so then one must ask, why don't we see more ghosts under high-tension electrical wires? And equally, it doesn't explain the physical attacks that visitors sometimes suffer.

An even more bizarre explanation is attributed to the sandstone that forms much of the rock underneath the Greyfriars area. It is suggested that if the pores of the sandstone were to become saturated with mineral electrolytes, it would in effect create thousands of tiny batteries and given the right conditions the stored energy could be discharged, which in turn could create an electrical field above the ground affecting a person by causing a tiny seizure in the temporal lobes of their brain. These seizures could be viewed by that person as something akin to a supernatural experience.

Of course, with explanations like these it is somehow easier to believe that the spirits of the dead might just conceivably walk the earth.

Perhaps the electrical theory provides the most rational explanation although hysteria and suggestion whipped up by the theatrics of the tour guides cannot be discounted. After all, who can rightly say that at some time in their life they have not been alone and afraid of the dark? Fear is contagious and standing in the dead of night in an ancient graveyard reputed to be haunted by a malevolent and spiteful spirit is enough to frighten most people, even without melodramatic tales of ghostly attacks from beyond the grave.

Whatever the case, on 2 July 2003 it was reported in *The Scotsman* that the mausoleum containing the remains of George MacKenzie was broken open by vandals and his skull was stolen. The attack on the mausoleum was only stopped when a group of people on a ghost tour passed through the churchyard and disrupted the vandalism. *The Scotsman* also reported that tour guide Jan Henderson, who runs the ghost tour, said that the attack would enrage the spirit of MacKenzie.

Henderson was reported as saying: "No doubt the ghost will be angry. The legend of the poltergeist is that it appeared three years ago when there was some damage to the graveyard and someone broke into his tomb. God knows what will happen now."

Luckily, the skull was quickly recovered by police, so we'll never really know if MacKenzie was particularly annoyed. Of course, the continued reported attacks on people would suggest that maybe, just maybe, he was although, during my visit he appeared to remain quiet. Having said that, a friend of mine, while visiting the site explained to me that she experienced an unsavoury and frightening attack while she visited the Kirkyard, specifically in MacKenzie's vault, where she was scratched and pushed by an unseen entity.

But the Kirkyard is not the only haunted place in plain view to the visitor when they emerge from the city's railway station for up on the hill that overlooks the station and the Kirkyard, is the forbidding Edinburgh Castle, a truly wondrous sight and one that has existed for centuries as one of the most important strategic strongholds in the entire United Kingdom. Situated on Castle Rock, a volcanic protrusion that formed some 340 million years ago, the original castle was built during the twelfth century by David I, son of St. Margaret of Scotland, although it is suspected that the site has been used for human habitation since the Iron Age.

During the War of Independence the Scots and English struggled for control of the castle, and in 1314 it was recaptured from the English in an audacious night raid led by Thomas Randolph, nephew of King Robert the Bruce. As one of the most important strongholds in Scotland, the castle was involved in many conflicts from the Wars of Scottish Independence to the Jacobite Rising of 1745. It has been besieged by various people on a number of occasions, both successfully and unsuccessfully. However, from the 1400s the castle's role as a place of residence declined, although it did continue to be a royal residence until the Union of the Crowns in 1603 with the accession of James VI, King of Scots to the thrones of England and Ireland. By the 1600s, it was principally used as military barracks supporting a large garrison.

Over its centuries the castle has protected many Scottish monarchs, including Queen Margaret, later St. Margaret, who died there in 1093, and Mary Queen of Scots, who gave birth to James VI in the Royal Palace in 1566. Her great-great-great grandson Charles Edward Stuart, Bonnie Prince Charlie later captured the city of Edinburgh but was unable to take the castle during the Jacobite Rising of 1745/1746.

Although very few of the present buildings predate the Lang Siege of the 1570s when the medieval defences were destroyed by artillery bombardment, there does exist earlier structures including St. Margaret's Chapel from the early 1100s and which is regarded as the oldest building in Edinburgh. The Royal Palace and the Great Hall date from the early 1500s.

The castle also houses the Honours of Scotland, in essence the Scottish Crown Jewels, and is also the site of the Scottish National War Memorial, a hugely impressive structure within the actual walls of the castle. It also houses a regimental cavalry museum.

From the early 1800s its importance as a part of Scotland's national heritage has been increasingly recognised, and numerous projects to restore the buildings have been instituted. These days it is the most prominent of tourist attractions in Edinburgh, if not the whole of Scotland and tourists can scale the heights and marvel at the incredible view from the ancient stone battlements. Interestingly, there is no public carpark at the castle. Instead, one must park in the rough cobble streets that lie beneath the impressive rocky outcrop on which the complex sits. As such, when I visit I find myself being turned back by the attendants at the castle and have to park in an adjoining street a few hundred metres away. Leaving the car and rugging up we head for the castle entrance.

It is overcast and wet and a blustery wind blows coldly through the ancient streets as we make our way up Johnstone Terrace and turn left onto Castle Hill over slippery cobble stones. Above us the grim walls reach into a grey sky and one gets an idea of how difficult this place must have been to take with its towering walls and unclimbable rocks cliffs acting as a natural barrier. After stopping for a cup of coffee to warm our fingers we soon find ourselves crossing the famous parade ground and entering the castle itself.

To say that the castle is magnificent would be a lie as it is much more than that; however, as much as I have come to see this impressive piece of Scottish history, I have also come to find out about its ghostly stories and tales as this is a place of mystery, murder, violence, and intrigue and reputed to be one of the most haunted places in Scotland, including the legend of the Lone Piper who, as the story goes, vanished a few hundred years ago in some deep underground tunnels running from the castle. Apparently, the tunnels were discovered and the piper boy was sent down to investigate, all the while playing his pipes so that those above ground could track his progress. However, the pipes suddenly stopped and when a search party ventured into the tunnel they could find no evidence of him. These days his ghostly pipes can be heard playing in the castle.

Apart from the piper, the castle also boasts a ghostly dog that wanders around the pet cemetery, a headless drummer who only appears when the castle is about to be attacked, something he allegedly did before Cromwell's attack on the castle in 1650, spirits of French prisoners from the Seven Years War, colonial prisoners from the American Revolutionary War, and the spirit of Janet Douglas, a woman unfortunately accused of witchcraft and burnt at the stake. Douglas, Lady of Glamis, was imprisoned in Edinburgh Castle in the sixteenth century and accused of witchcraft and conspiracy to murder King James V. Evidence was obtained by the torturing of her servants, and she was burned at the stake on 17 July 1537 with her son forced to watch from the battlements. Her restless spirit is now said to still haunt parts of the castle. As well, in 1960, it was reported that a sentry standing guard heard strange drumming and went to investigate. On the battlements, he saw a headless figure that turned towards him before vanishing into thin air.

As previously mentioned, the castle, in some parts, is extremely old, indeed, up to 900 years, and so one has to admit that it has seen its fair share of history. The cells of its ancient dungeon, the site of innumerable deaths, are also believed to hold a number of ghostly apparitions. In April 2001, as a part of the Edinburgh International Science Festival, Dr. Richard Wiseman, a psychologist from Hertfordshire University, enlisted the help of 240 volunteers to explore the allegedly haunted sites in a ten-day study.

As part of the experiment volunteers were led in groups of ten through the spooky, dark, damp cellars, chambers, and vaults while Wiseman's team was equipped with equipment such as thermal imaging cameras, geo-magnetic sensors, night vision equipment, EMF metres, temperature probes, and digital cameras. Although the volunteers were carefully screened previous to the study, it was reported that nearly half of them reported phenomena that they simply could not explain. These experiences included sudden unexplained drops in temperature, seeing shadowy figures, feelings of being watched, the sensation of something tugging at clothes, being touched on the face by an unseen entity, and, most impressively, one person reported sighting a ghostly figure in a leather apron, a ghost that had been seen before at the same location on several occasions. Wiseman, an avowed sceptic admitted to being surprised at the results and commented that the "events that have been taking place over the last ten days are much more extreme than we expected."

In one experiment a young woman was enclosed in a vault alone so that she could record whatever she saw, felt, or heard. Almost immediately after being placed in the vault Wiseman noted that "she reported hearing breathing from a corner of the room, which was getting louder. She thought she saw a flash or some sort of light in the corner, but didn't want to look back."

Having said that, the only "hard" evidence was a few digital photographs that featured odd anomalies, such as dense spots of light and strange misty shapes. In addition, two photos showed a green glob that no one could explain.

But as we have previously discussed with Greyfriars Kirkyard, Edinburgh is considered one of the most haunted cities in the British Isles and for good reason given its age, history, and turbulent past. Indeed, Brodie's Close, only a short walk from the castle itself, is reputed to be haunted by the ghost of William Brodie, a lock maker who it was said would unscrupulously copy his customer's keys so he could later rob their premises. However, he was eventually caught and sentenced to hang. His ghost has been seen carrying a set of keys walking down the Close. Oddly enough, he is often accompanied by a fire-breathing dark horse.

At the Niddry Street vaults at South Bridge, another haunted part of underground Edinburgh, a hooded figure has been seen as has what has been described as an alien-like face. The vaults are built into the structure of the South Street Bridge and have been subject to several paranormal investigations over the years. As well as the former, the vaults are also thought to be haunted by *"hauf hangit"* Maggie Dickson, a woman sentenced to hang for infanticide but who miraculously survived. It is said that the vaults contain a cursed witches' circle and during the 1990s the area was reportedly the site of poltergeist activity, a phenomena we will revisit somewhat in the next chapter.

Leeds Castle. Just south east of Maidstone in Kent and sitting on two small islands in a large but shallow lake, it has survived for nearly a thousand years and is one of the most significant and historically important buildings in English history. (*Photo: JG Montgomery*)

Hever Castle. Does the forlorn spirit of Anne Boelyn haunt the lonely corridors and grounds of this pretty medieval building?
(*Photo: JG Montgomery*)

The Tower of London. Reputedly the most haunted building in England, if not the entire world. (*Photo: JG Montgomery*)

Traitor's Gate, where so many people were previously brought by boat to meet their fate at the hand of a gleaming executioner's axe. In the drizzle of a grey London day it is a grim and thought-provoking sight. (*Photo: JG Montgomery*)

Avebury Manor. Believed to have been built around 1551. Does the broken spirit of Sir John Stawell haunt the rooms and grounds of this stunning country house?

(Photo: JG Montgomery)

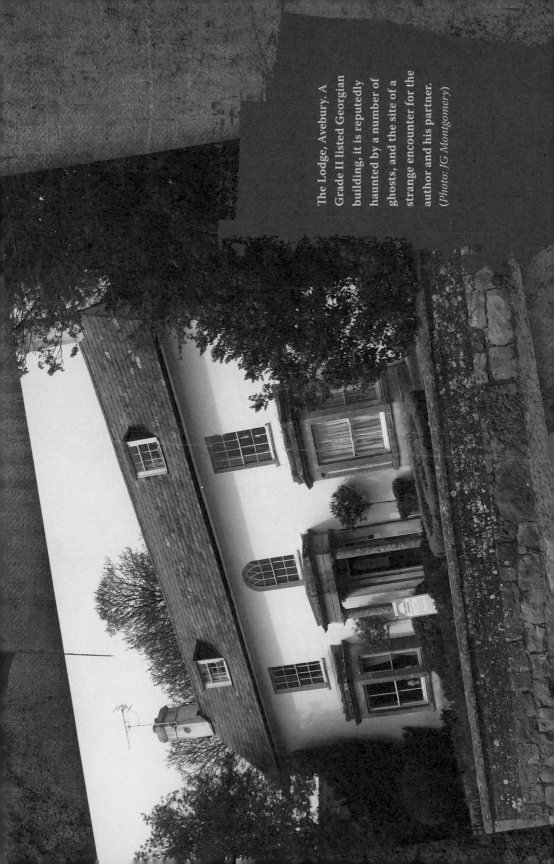

The Lodge, Avebury. A Grade II listed Georgian building, it is reputedly haunted by a number of ghosts, and the site of a strange encounter for the author and his partner. (*Photo: JG Montgomery*)

The Red Lion Pub in Avebury, the only pub in the world situated inside a Neolithic stone circle and at over 400 years old, is said to be haunted by a myriad of ghosts, including the infamous Florie, reputedly murdered in the 1600s by her jealous soldier husband. (*Photo: JG Montgomery*)

A noticeboard in the Red Lion Pub proclaiming; "There have been reports of at least five different ghosts at the Red Lion. A ghostly horse drawn carriage has been seen pulling up outside the pub and staff have heard the phantom clattering of hooves in the courtyard outside the pub." (*Photo: JG Montgomery*)

Avebury, at over 5,000 years old, has long been steeped in stories of ritual, ceremonies, burials, and magic. What spirits haunt this ancient stone ring? (*Photo: KW Willcox*)

The author at West Kennett Long Barrow in 2009, a Neolithic burial mound just south of Avebury and the site of some strange supernatural reports. (*Photo: KW Willcox*)

The entrance to West Kennett Long Barrow. The photo appears to show what could be construed as an orb but is probably just a light anomaly. (*Photo: JG Montgomery*)

The Spaniard's Inn, built in 1585 and reputedly haunted by the ghost of none other than the notorious highwayman Dick Turpin. (*Photo: JG Montgomery*)

The Royal Standard of England. On foggy nights it is said that one can sometimes make out the ghostly decapitated heads of the royalist soldiers as they sit silently with unseeing eyes on bloodied pikes. (*Photo: JG Montgomery*)

The interior of the Royal Standard of England. The ghost of a long dead cavalier has been seen near the bar and the ghostly figure of a woman haunts the ladies' bathroom. (*Photo: JG Montgomery*)

The Prospect of Whitby. This quaint little pub in the Wapping area is believed to be haunted by, among others, the Lord Chief Justice George Jeffreys, commonly known as the Hanging Judge, who died in 1689. (*Photo: JG Montgomery*)

The infamous "Hanging Judge Jeffries" was a local and a regular patron here.

It is said that he would enjoy his lunch on this balcony whilst watching the hangings at the place known as Execution Dock.

It was at Execution Dock that the famous pirate Captain Kidd met his end in 1701

The noose below this point reminds us of this gruesome man who later died in The Tower of London

The noticeboard at the Prospect of Whitby proclaiming its most infamous guest. (*Photo: JG Montgomery*)

The gallows on the Thames at the Prospect of Whitby. A gruesome reminder of the many lives sacrificed to the whim of Jeffreys. Hanged men would be left on the gallows until three high tides had washed over them. (*Photo: JG Montgomery*)

Tintern Abbey, Wales. Reputed to be visited on occasion by armour-clad knights and hazy figures of monks and abbots, it is a peaceful and stunning beautiful ruin. (*Photo: JG Montgomery*)

Conwy Castle, Wales. Built between 1283 and 1289 it is the site of many strange occurrences.
(*Photo: JG Montgomery*)

Greyfriars Kirkyard. Pleasant and green during the day, but apparently terrifying after dark. (*Photo: JG Montgomery*)

The author exploring the mausoleum of the seventeenth-century judge and Lord Advocate Sir George MacKenzie in Greyfriars Kirkyard. *(Photo: KW Willcox)*

Kirsten outside the Dragon Inn, Montgomery, Wales. It is believed that the hangman made the inn his regular drinking spot. (*Photo: JG Montgomery*)

Tintagel Castle, Cornwall. A bleak but beautiful place as befits the legendary birth place of King Arthur. What ghosts stalk these lonely ruins?
(*Photo: KW Willcox*)

Hellfire caves. Does the forlorn ghost of Sukie wander the dark passages searching for her long lost love? (*Photo: JG Montgomery*)

The George and Pilgrims Hotel, a fifteenth-century stone building on Glastonbury High Street. Originally constructed to accommodate the many wealthy pilgrims and other visitors to the abbey, it is believed to be haunted by at least two ghosts. (*Photo: JG Montgomery*)

Glastonbury Abbey, a Grade I listed building and a Scheduled Ancient Monument, was founded in the seventh century and is now the site of many unexplained occurrences. (*Photo: JG Montgomery*)

The Ancient Ram Inn. Believed to have been a place of ritual child sacrifice, black magic rituals, suicide, witchcraft, and murder, it is said to be haunted by numerous evil spirits including an incubus or a succubus. (*Photo: JG Montgomery*)

An eerie red glow floods the Priest's Room at the Ancient Ram Inn. (*Photo: JG Montgomery*)

The stairs in the Ancient Ram Inn leading to the first floor. A photograph taken of the stairs in June 1999 appeared to show a white mist, roughly the height of a person ascending the staircase. (*Photo: JG Montgomery*)

Dunster Castle, for many years the site of the ghostly apparitions of a Grey Lady and a phantom soldier and also an oubliette reputedly containing the skeleton of an apparent giant. (*Photo: JG Montgomery*)

The staircase at Dunster Castle where the apparition of a Grey Lady has often been witnessed. (*Photo: JG Montgomery*)

The impressive gatehouse at Dunster Castle. The oubliette is located to the right upon entry through the gates. (*Photo: JG Montgomery*)

Woodchester Mansion. Looming out of the forest like a set from a horror movie, this neo-gothic building is reputedly haunted by a number of supernatural entities, including a small girl, a dwarf, a headless horseman, and a spectral black dog. (*Photo: JG Montgomery*)

The cellar at Woodchester Mansion in Gloucestershire.
A truly eerie place. (*Photo: JG Montgomery*)

Edinburgh Castle. One of the most important strategic strongholds in the entire United Kingdom and haunted by a myriad of ghosts.
(Photo: JG Montgomery)

The George Inn, Alfriston. Surprisingly for such an ancient building it does not appear haunted in any way and yet the town and surrounding district are renowned for ghostly activities. (Photo: JG Montgomery)

CHAPTER 8

†

A Talking Mongoose, a Haunted Rectory, and a House Full of Monks

A house is never still in darkness to those who listen intently; there is a whispering in distant chambers, an unearthly hand presses the snib of the window, the latch rises. Ghosts were created when the first man woke in the night.

—J. M. Barrie

But if poltergeists in quiet London boroughs or ancient Scottish graveyards don't alarm you, or at least pique your interest, then what of the next amazing story that was reported to have happened in a farmhouse known as Cashen's Gap near the hamlet of Dalby on the Isle of Man in the early 1930s?

In September 1931, James Irving, his wife, Margaret, and their daughter, Voirrey, started hearing strange scratching and rustling noises in the attic of their farmhouse. Soon after, these noises seemed to migrate to the farmhouse's wooden panel walls, and the Irvings suspected that they had a rat infestation. However, no rats were ever seen and, more curiously, the unseen creature began making different sounds. At times it growled like a small dog, sounded like a ferret, or gurgled like a baby. And even more remarkably, over time, this gurgling started to turn into words in the way a baby speaks when learning to talk. James Irving was astounded. In a very short time whatever it was behind the walls had effectively learned to speak English.

The hidden entity soon introduced itself as Gef, apparently a mongoose, and claimed to have been born in New Delhi, India, in 1852. According to Voirrey, who claimed to be the only person to see the creature, he was the size of a rat with yellowish fur and a large bushy tail. An Indian mongoose is actually much larger than a rat and does not have a bushy tail.

Whatever the case, Gef often claimed to be clever and suggested that he was an earthbound spirit and a ghost in the form of a weasel. He was reported to have said, "I am a freak. I have hands and I have feet, and if you saw me you'd faint, you'd be petrified, mummified, turned into stone or a pillar of salt."

As well as talking in perfectly acceptable English, Gef also developed a talent for singing. He quickly learned the words to many popular songs and was also a bit of a joker, providing the family with an interesting source of entertainment. However, it has been said that he sometimes took this practical joking too far; one time pretending to have been poisoned, which worried the family immensely.

At one stage Margaret Irving apparently managed to touch Gef through a hole in a wall, and he allowed her to stroke his fur. Unfortunately, she either cut her finger on Gef's teeth or was bitten in the process, but remarkably he seemed to show concern for her well-being and instructed her to put ointment on the wound.

However, even with all this strange phenomena, Gef refused to allow himself to be seen and insisted on remaining hidden, except on occasions when he fleetingly showed himself to Voirrey. Although he lived within the walls of the house, he would often hide in the garden or wander around the island, apparently spying on other people and reporting back to the Irvings with local gossip and happenings. Now and then some of the locals reported hearing odd sounds, which they attributed to Gef.

Overall, it appears that the mysterious mongoose-poltergeist-spirit was friendly, funny, and generally sensitive, although at times could lose his temper. His humour was apparently a little over the top, on occasion so much so that the family once threatened to move out. This greatly upset Gef, who apparently loved their company and was afraid that he would be left on his own. When the family decided to stay, Gef became much more obedient and promised not to be so lively.

Having said that, what can we make of this strange case? In reality, the only real evidence we have as to the existence of the creature was the sound of his voice and a number of other strange phenomenon such as objects being moved and thrown about the house, knocking and rapping, characteristics traditionally ascribed to poltergeists. In 1912, a farmer who owned some mongooses released them hoping that they would reduce the rabbit population on the island as they were becoming a pest. Is it possible that some of these mongooses survived and bred? Could one of these have been the smooth talking Gef?

Whatever the case, the incredible story of Gef the talking mongoose reached the popular press, and numerous journalists made the boat trip to the island to either see or hear the elusive little creature. Of course, with all this publicity it could hardly escape the attention of paranormal investigators, and in July 1935, Richard S. Lambert, editor of *The Listener*, and Harry Price, who we have already met, went to the Isle of Man to investigate.

Price was determined to conduct a proper scientific study of the phenomena and hoped that he would be able to obtain conclusive evidence as to the existence of the mysterious mongoose. The research, however, was inconclusive and, therefore, generally unsuccessful. Price himself never managed to catch a glimpse of the animal, and all the evidence he collected was extremely weak, consisting of a few blurry photographs of something that bore a remarkable resemblance to a cat and some strange hairs, which were remarkably similar to those of the Irving's dog, Mona.

Nevertheless, Price and Lambert later published a book about the case called *The Haunting of Cashen's Gap*. Described as "an essay in the Veracious but Unaccountable," in reality it was little more than a light-hearted story than serious research. In the book the two completely overlooked saying that they believed the story but put forward the premise that it must be viewed with an open mind.

Price did manage to get some paw prints and tooth marks in plasticine, allegedly made by the elusive singing mongoose. These were duly sent to the British Natural History Museum for investigation where oddly enough a curator could not match them to any known animal, although he did note that none of the markings were that of a mongoose and could have conceivably been made by a small dog.

But Harry Price was not the only person interested in this most unusual case as Nandor Fodor, who we have also met previously, also decided to examine the situation. During his investigation Fodor stayed at the Irvings' house for a week but unfortunately neither heard nor saw Gef. However, in interviews with both the family and the locals he became utterly convinced that what he had heard was true. He stated that he found the Irvings "sincere, frank, and simple" and that "deliberate deception on the part of the whole family cannot be entertained as a solution of the mystery."

Fodor, through his research, came to the conclusion that Gef was not a poltergeist as none of the family members appeared to be psychic and that Gef had never showed any real paranormal powers. Apart from that he had been seen, photographed, and touched, something not usually associated with poltergeist behaviour. As well, Gef stated that he was a small furry animal. Price, on the other hand, concluded that Gef was a fantasy, probably like an imaginary friend, who provided entertainment and interest for the Irving family.

Fodor, as we have seen, was influenced by Freudian theory, and later became a psychoanalyst, putting forward the theory that poltergeists were external manifestations of conflicts within the individual subconscious mind rather than autonomous entities existing of their own volition.

In 1937, the Irvings had to sell the farm and move. It was reported at the time that they had to sell for a lower price than the market price as it was reputed to be haunted. What happened to Gef is not known, although many believe he simply followed the family to their new home.

A postscript to the story occurred in 1946 when Leslie Graham, the new owner of the farm, claimed that he had shot and killed Gef. However, when later put on display, the creature was black and white and much larger than the elusive little mongoose. Voirrey Irving was also certain that it was not Gef. In an interview published late in her life, Voirrey maintained that Gef was real and not a creation of her imagination.

Poltergeist or not, Gef the Talking Mongoose certainly stimulated the interest of people, including the celebrated Harry Price who had already built up quite a reputation as a ghost hunter and an expert in the supernatural. But it was not the mongoose case that Price built his reputation around; instead, it was another celebrated case involving a haunted rectory in Essex.

Borley Rectory, like numerous other haunted sites, seemed to suffer not only from various apparitions and spirits, but also from poltergeist-like behaviour. Located in the village of Borley in Essex, it had the reputation of being one of the most haunted places in England, even though the original building was destroyed by fire in 1939. Built in 1863, it still remains an eerie place, and there are still reports of poltergeist and ghostly activity to this day.

A large neo-Gothic brick building, Borley Rectory was built next to Borley Church by the Reverend Henry Dawson Ellis Bull. It was designed by Frederic Chancellor, a pupil of Augustus Pugin, an architect and designer who played a major part in the Gothic Revival style of the early nineteenth century and whose work culminated in the interior design of the Palace of Westminster.

The house was built on the site of an earlier demolished Georgian house that was the home of the previous Rector, a Reverend Herringham, although there appears to be evidence of an even earlier house on the site before the Herringham rectory. The nearby Borley Church, dating from the twelfth century serves the rural community which includes several substantial farmhouses, and the remains of Borley Hall.

There is an old legend about a Benedictine monastery that was supposedly built in the area in about 1360 in which a monk from the monastery had a relationship with a nun from a nearby convent. When their illicit affair was discovered the monk was executed and the nun allegedly bricked up alive in the convent walls.

The very first reports of ghostly activity at the rectory appear to have started around 1863, a year after its construction, when locals began to report hearing strange disembodied footsteps that followed them past the building. A number of poltergeist-like occurrences were also reported.

Over the coming the years, Bull's servants and his daughters were repeatedly frightened by phantom knockings and rappings, unexplained footsteps, and the appearance of various ghosts. In July 1900, four of the Rector's daughters reported seeing the ghost of a woman near the house early one evening. The girls told their father that they had initially tried to talk to the figure, but she disappeared when they moved closer to her. After this, reports of supernatural manifestations became quite regular, including that of a ghostly coach being driven by two headless coachmen.

Oddly, the Reverend Bull regarded these events as grand entertainment, and with his son Harry, constructed a summer house on the property so he and his guests could enjoy after-dinner cigars and wait for the appearance of the phantom nun who walked nearby. Bull, who had inherited the rectory and the job as parson when his father died in 1892, stayed on until his death in 1927.

The Reverend Guy Eric Smith and his wife moved into the rectory in October 1928. Not long after they had moved in, his wife, while cleaning out a cupboard one day, made a rather gruesome discovery when she found the skull of a young woman wrapped in brown paper. Shortly after this, poltergeist activity become a regular event and the family reported the sounds of ringing bells, strange unexplained lights, window glass shattering, footsteps, and their daughter becoming inexplicably locked into a room that had no key. Mrs. Smith also reported seeing a ghostly horse-drawn carriage one night.

The Reverend Smith, quite perturbed at the events, got in touch with *The Daily Mirror* who then contacted the Society for Psychical Research. In June 1929, the newspaper sent a reporter to the rectory and he too witnessed and recorded many strange unexplainable events. Perplexed, the paper contacted Harry Price and asked him to visit the place to see if he could make any sense out of the disturbances.

Price arrived at Borley Rectory in June and, as if finding a new lease of life, the poltergeist activity seemed to increase. Price reported that stones, a vase, and several other objects were hurled around by an unseen hand, and that strange rapping noises were also heard. Price believed these rapping noises to be messages of some sort, and it is abundantly clear that this event firmly established Price's reputation as a paranormal investigator, even though there were some later doubts and criticisms of his methods and integrity.

Understandably, the Smiths found the poltergeist activity too much, and in July 1929, they fled the home, vowing never to come back. In their place, the Reverend Lionel Foyster, his wife, Marianne, and their adopted daughter Adelaide, moved into the rectory in October of 1930. While in residence, Foyster kept a diary of the poltergeist activity that happened, which he later sent to Price.

Price suggested that while he was there over 2,000 strange supernatural-like events had been witnessed at the rectory, including bell ringing, stone and bottle throwing and, most disturbingly and intriguing, strange handwriting that appeared on the walls. Marianne Foyster reported that, apart from witnessing innumerable poltergeist-like phenomena, that she was forcibly thrown from her bed.

It would seem that the worst of the incidents involved Marianne, as she was also slapped by invisible hands, forced to dodge heavy objects, which were apparently thrown at her, and was once almost suffocated with a mattress. Whatever was happening, it was enough to worry the family, especially when the spirit, or whatever it was, attacked Adelaide.

Soon after, a series of scrawled messages started to mysteriously appear on the walls of the house. Written by an unknown, almost childish hand, they appeared to be pleading to Marianne Foyster for help using phrases such as, "Marianne, please help get," "I cannot understand, tell me more," and "Marianne light mass prayers."

Whatever the scrawled writing meant remained a mystery; however, because the majority of poltergeist-like activity occurred when Marianne was present,

Price suspected that she somehow had a hand in the manifestations, very much similar to the Eleonore Zugun case. Having said that, he fully believed in the possibility of the existence of the ghostly nun and other reported supernatural phenomena, even though the rectory did not fit into the preconceived notion of a stereotypical haunted house.

Despite his misgivings regarding the phenomena being centred around Marianne, Price believed that at least one of the spirits in the house had somehow found her sympathetic to its plight, whatever this may have been. As such, he assumed that the scrawled writings were from the ghost of another young woman who seemed to attach itself to the Rector's wife. Price even suggested, from the writings, that she may have been Catholic.

Interestingly, when Price finally published his theory of Borley Rectory, he suggested that the phenomenon was all a result of a tragic tale of murder and betrayal in which the central character was a young nun, although not the one of the Benedictine monastery legend.

Foyster tried twice to conduct an exorcism, hopeful that the ceremony would drive away whatever it was that was haunting the house. However, these were to no avail and the phenomena continued. During the first exorcism Foyster reported that he was hit on the shoulder by a large stone that was seemingly thrown from nowhere. After this episode the Foysters decided they had had enough and, like their predecessors the Smiths, left the house.

After the Foysters' departure in May 1937, the rectory remained vacant for some time until Price took out a year-long rental with the view of investigating the reports of the poltergeist behaviour. He even went to the extent of running an advertisement in *The Times* looking for like-minded people to help record any phenomena that took place. Surprisingly, Price had no shortage of applicants and ended up with a group of forty-eight students to observe and report any unusual phenomenon.

In March 1938, one of these students, Helen Glanville, conducted a séance with a planchette and apparently contacted two spirits, the first being a young nun by the name of Marie Lairre and another by the name of Sunex Amures.

Marie Lairre said she had been murdered on the site of Borley Rectory and her answers were exceptionally consistent with the local legend of a murdered nun. She also indicated that she was originally a French nun who decided to leave the order and marry, and as a result, ended up living in England. The groom, it was suggested, was one Henry Waldengrave, the owner of the original seventeenth-century manor house. Price believed that the ghost of the nun that had been sighted at the house over the years was Marie Lairre and that the cryptic writings on the walls were her cries for help.

However, as much as Marie Lairre was believed to be a benign spirit, the second, called Sunex Amures, seemed to be the one responsible for the poltergeist activity. This spirit suggested during the séance that the rectory would be burned down, and the bones of a murdered person would be found.

Interestingly, the alleged predictions of Sunex Amures came true when, in February 1939, the new owner of the rectory was unpacking boxes when an oil lamp in the hallway was knocked over. The resulting fire spread rapidly and the rectory was seriously damaged. A witness to the fire stated that she plainly saw a figure that looked like a nun in an upstairs window. After the fire Price conducted an investigative dig in the basement cellars of the burnt house and found two bones of a young woman; however, a more thorough excavation of the cellars carried out some time later found nothing of note.

A Christian burial for the bones found in the basement was conducted by the Reverend A. C. Henning and this appeared to deliver the ghost some peace. The building itself was finally demolished in 1944; however, despite this, reports of strange activity still abound, and its legacy as one of the world's most famous houses remains. The nearby Borley Church is also the site of much unexplained paranormal phenomena. Is it possible that the ghosts of Borley simply moved next door?

Remarkably, photos of the rectory that appeared in *LIFE* magazine during the final demolition in 1944 appear to show a floating brick, seemingly suspended in air. However, as compelling as the photo is, sceptics point out that it could simply be a brick thrown by a workman and was accidentally captured by the *LIFE* photographer. Having said that, the photo shows a remarkably clear image with little blurring, suggesting that if it was thrown, then it was moving exceptionally slowly, almost as if it were actually suspended in air.

Price died in 1948, and after his death, three members of the English Society for Psychical Research investigated his claims about Borley Rectory and later published their findings in a book *The Haunting of Borley Rectory* in 1956. The publication sadly concluded that any evidence of a haunting or paranormal activity was hopelessly confused by Price's duplicity. The report suggested that much of the phenomena were either faked or were simply due to natural causes, such as mice and rats and natural noises of an old building.

A book written by Louis Mayerling, who lived at the Rectory, later stated that he faked most of the phenomena and perpetuated the myth of the spectral nun, a family ghost, and paranormal activity in the area. He also suggested that most of the poltergeist activity was perpetrated by various servants and children who were encouraged by the Bulls to exploit the house's many hidden doors and passages. He revealed how a piano that the Bulls claimed was played by spirit hands, was in fact activated by the six-year-old Mayerling plucking the piano strings with a poker while hidden in a nearby gap in the wall.

Mayerling admits though to one incident that he was completely at a loss to explain. At Easter 1935, Mayerling, Marianne Foyster, and a number of others attended a séance at Borley. They held the séance in a badly lit underground cellar at about midnight. As they were sitting in the silence the kitchen bells seemed to clang together in one single clash. Apart from those sitting at the table, the house was empty, and both Foyster and Mayerling knew from experience that it was impossible to make the bells ring at the same time.

One of the group apparently leapt up, and a lightning-like strike of silver-blue light appeared to implode from all walls and the ceiling of the cellar. Following this was silence. Every member of the séance was struck with an instant paralysis that lasted about five seconds, and Mayerling was blinded, although he eventually recovered sight in one eye. Two of the group refused to stay in the house that night. Maybe there was more to Borley Rectory than anyone, including Price, thought possible?

Luminaries, such as George Bernard Shaw, T. E. Lawrence, Sir Montagu Norman, and others were firm believers in the paranormal activities of Borley Rectory and regularly attended séances at the house. Unfortunately, Borley Rectory no longer stands, and, therefore, no one will ever know the complete truth. As such only the legend remains, but this in itself is a powerful thing and perhaps fitting for the title of Britain's most haunted house.

To the present day the Borley Rectory site holds a certain mystique and interest for parapsychologists and ghost hunters alike. Although it is unlikely that all the reported events at Borley were fraudulent, there is enough evidence and testimony to suggest that Price's conclusions were really not that far off the mark.

But if Borley Rectory, legend excluded, appears to have been somewhat debunked, then what of the picturesque Chingle Hall in Lancashire?

Chingle Hall is just north of Preston in the small village of Goosnargh and is a Grade II listed thirteenth-century manor house. The house itself contains a small private chapel, complete with priest holes, and has also been given the title of the most haunted house in Britain due to a number of unexplainable paranormal episodes. It is believed that up to sixteen spirits haunt the rooms and corridors of this ancient building.

Originally, the land around Chingle Hall was owned by Ughtred de Singleton from around the time of the Norman Invasion, and by 1260, Adam de Singleton had constructed a small manor house known as Singleton Hall. The manor was surrounded by a moat and had a studded oak front door, which was accessed via a small wooden drawbridge. This drawbridge was replaced in the sixteenth century by a brick-built bridge, and both the door and bridge survive to the present day, although some of the moat has dried up.

It is reported that the wooden beams used to construct the house were from Viking longboats, something that can possibly be verified in that Goosnargh itself is an old Viking village, though other sources give the derivation of an Old Irish word *Gosan*, or *Gusan*, meaning Gosan's or Gusan's hill pasture. Whatever the case, it is an exceptionally old building, and a lot of its history is now shrouded in the mists of time.

De Singleton was a devout Catholic and as a result built a chapel within the house complete with two priest hiding holes. During the sixteenth century, Catholic masses were illegal and punishable by death, and so any priest performing a mass needed somewhere to hide, if not escape, if authorities happened by the place of worship.

The house, although renamed Chingle Hall, remained in the Singleton family until 1585, when Eleanor Singleton, the last of the line, died. The house was then passed to the Wall family through the marriage of William Wall to Anne Singleton.

Chingle Hall is believed to be the birthplace of John Wall, one of the last English Roman Catholic martyrs and a Franciscan priest. He was believed to very active, conducting secret mass on a regular basis in spite of the Catholic reformation until 1678 when he was apprehended by authorities at Rushock Court near Bromsgrove. From here he was taken to Worcester jail where he was offered his life if he forsook his religion. A man of strong beliefs, he declined, and as a result, he was drawn and quartered at Redhill in August 1679.

Wall's quartered body was then handed over to his friends and was buried in St. Oswald's churchyard. His head, however, was procured by a Mr. Levison, and it was treasured by the friars at Worcester, indeed, so treasured was his head that Catholics took it around the country in a sort of reverential tour of the faithful. It is rumoured that Wall's head is either buried in the grounds or is hidden somewhere in the house. The Franciscan nuns at Taunton also claim to possess relics of the martyr, a tooth and piece of bone. He was canonized by Pope Paul VI in 1970.

With such a history it is, therefore, not surprising that Chingle Hall has a reputation for being haunted. Over the years witnesses have reported seeing the ghost of John Wall himself, who is said to appear as a monk within the walls of the house and in the grounds. Others have reported seeing monks or monk-like figures in the Hall, and one of these ghostly monks is often reported as walking outside the window some twelve feet off the ground. The kitchen is also reputed to be haunted by a reasonably harmless poltergeist-like entity who is said to move pots and pans.

Another room in the house, Eleanor's Room, is also reputed to be haunted. This room is where Eleanor Singleton was held as a prisoner for twelve years, and indeed, she died there at the age of seventeen or eighteen. It has been rumoured that she was murdered in the room. Apart from feelings of overwhelming sadness, people have also reported the strong smell of lavender and sensations of their clothes being tugged or pulled. It is believed that the young Eleanor used to prefer lavender fragrance.

Some visitors have reported seeing orbs in the room, and in 1997, a parapsychologist, while filming a movie outside of the window on the landing just outside of Eleanor's Room, reported being hit in the face so hard by an unseen entity that it knocked him to the ground and caused bruising and swelling around his nose.

Various people have also recorded strange rapping and scratching sounds coming from the priest holes, and when investigated, they have been completely empty but for a shadowy figure and a deathly cold. In 1985, a visitor staying in the Priest's Room reported hearing bricks being moved inside the priest hole.

On inspection the man saw the partial outline of a human hand moving a brick around. The hand then disappeared and the brick stopped moving.

To add to this, a Grey Lady has also been seen in the building, and in one exceptionally strange occurrence, a young couple who had heard of Chingle Hall's reputation, happened to be passing by when they decided to knock on the front door and ask about having a look around. It was late but a little old lady answered the door and introduced herself as Mrs. Howarth. She then happily led the couple around the house telling them all about the ghostly phenomena that had occurred. Later that night when the couple mentioned this to a publican at a local pub, the barman replied that Mrs. Howarth had been dead for a year. As such, it is thought that Mrs. Howarth is the Grey Lady and is a recent haunting in the place, as opposed to the others that seem to be positively medieval.

Ghostly monks appear to be the most widely reported apparitions at Chingle Hall and given its strong religious connections in the past, one can understand why. On one occasion, a number of people attending a nearby dog show asked locals where the local monastery was. Apparently, they had been to Chingle Hall, seen a number of monks wandering around, and assumed that they were from somewhere nearby.

In the early 1980s, Terry Whittaker, an author and radio producer, was recording a series on ghosts at Chingle Hall when, early one morning while he was making some recordings, he heard footsteps outside the room he was in. He and one of his crew went into the corridor but could see no one. The footsteps, however, continued to walk straight past them and they could see the floorboards flex as if someone was walking on them. Then, off in a corner, the ghostly shape of a monk appeared. It remained in full view for about half a minute before drifting off into a nearby priest hole.

Previous to the new owners, who have restricted visitors, Chingle Hall was a popular tourist destination with people arriving for day tours or overnight stays. These visitors reported numerous strange experiences with the most haunted parts appearing to be the Priest's Room, the John Wall Room, and the adjoining corridor between the two, appropriately named the Haunted Corridor.

In the Priest's Room people have reported peculiar apparitions, crashes, bangs, and strange lights. In addition, some reported that the room itself had also appeared to change shape, as if it were from a completely different era. A particular feature of the room is a heavy chandelier that apparently appears and disappears. One tour group, admiring the chandelier in the Priest's Room were completely shocked to discover that it wasn't there when they visited the room a second time. Apparently, a hand rail on the staircase was also known for simply disappearing and then reappearing at a later time, which, like the disappearing chandelier and the changing room, suggests some sort of time-slip, a paranormal phenomenon whereby a person is supposedly transported back to a different age or time, either momentarily or for longer periods of time.

Another incident that reportedly took place in the John Wall Room was when a group of nurses held a charity night at the Hall. They alleged that they were sitting in the room when the figure of a monk appeared over the shoulder of one of them. The nurse that witnessed this was so overcome that she was unable to speak for ninety minutes afterwards. Others that have stayed in the room have reported seeing flashing lights and hearing inexplicable noises.

Despite most poltergeist-like activity being centred on the Priest's Room, the John Wall Room, and the Haunted Corridor, other parts of Chingle Hall can be equally perplexing. Mrs. Howarth, when alive, would regularly smell or see smoke and on occasions called the fire brigade only to be bemused when they couldn't find the source of the smoke. In the Great Hall the ghost of a cat has been seen and heard even though no cat lives in the building. Ghostly monks have also been seen through the window of the entry porch, apparently floating in mid-air from the waist up. It is believed that this is due to the floor level having changed over time. As such, one must wonder if witnesses have ever seen the legs of a monk dangling from a ceiling?

Even when the hall was derelict in the mid-1980s, neighbours would report strange lights in what should have been an empty, unpowered house. Police that attended calls to investigate reported seeing lights as well as hearing talking and music; however, when inspected, they found no evidence of anyone being there at any stage; instead, the house was as it should be: dark, quiet, and abandoned.

In addition, workmen, who later carried out some of the restoration work when it was purchased and restored by Sandra and John Coppleston-Bruce, seemed to be the victims of ghostly pranks. One plumber reported that he had spent a long time installing central heating except when he and his assistant went to inspect newly fitted pipes, they found them gone, as if they had simply vanished. Confounded, the plumber called the owner only to find, literally minutes later, and very reminiscent of the staircase hand rail or the low-slung chandelier in the Priest's Room, that the pipes were back in place.

Sadly, Chingle Hall is currently closed to the public as the new owners simply want the place as a house and a home. Whether the ghosts and spirits are still active is unknown, but whatever the case, there is still a lot that needs to be investigated in this 750-year-old building.

But if Chingle Hall is closed to the public and the ghosts of its past now safe from the prying eyes of investigators and ghost hunters alike, then what of the myriad of popular tourist destinations that dot the landscape? Do visitors to these places experience ghostly phenomena?

CHAPTER 9

†

Haunted Caves, Tunnels, and Ghostly Wales

What terrified me will terrify others; and I need only describe the spectre which had haunted my midnight pillow.

—Mary Shelley

Chislehurst Caves in Kent is a thirty-five kilometre-long warren of secretive and mysterious passages and tunnels in the southeastern suburbs of Greater London. Although they are called caves, they are in fact a vast complex of ancient mines originally carved out by Neolithic man in search for flint and chalk. The caves were last worked in the 1830s, and during the early 1900s they were a popular tourist attraction. In World War I they were used as an ammunition depot, while in the 1930s they were used for mushroom cultivation.

Interestingly, but incorrect, William Nichols, vice president of the British Archaeological Association, suggested in 1903 that the mines were created by the Druids, Romans, and Saxons. This theory was used to give names to the three distinct parts of the caves, and tour guides these days point out supposed Druid altars and Roman features.

During World War II the caves were used as an air raid shelter and soon became an underground city of some 15,000 people with electric lighting, a hospital, and a chapel. In the cramped, dark, and sometimes wet conditions, many of the sick and injured could not be treated and as a result, many died. Although the caves were quickly closed after VE Day, it is believed by many parapsychologists and supernatural enthusiasts that the spirits of these people still haunt the dark and eerie passageways.

In the 1960s, pop luminaries, such as David Bowie, Status Quo, Jimi Hendrix, The Rolling Stones, and Pink Floyd used the caves as a performance venue. In addition, they have also been featured on several television programs, including a *Doctor Who* episode and *Seven Natural Wonders* presented by Bill Oddie.

The caves are immense and frightening. Noises carry for great distances, and the unwary can be tricked into believing something that has been said, or dropped, is happening right behind them. It is an eerie and lonely place and the dark plays tricks on the visitor's mind, so much that one begins to imagine that they can see things in the inky blackness. It is little wonder that people believe this place haunted.

The caves are reputed to be haunted by the ghost of a lady in a white dress who has been seen floating across the dark waters of a pool deep within the bowels of the caves. It is thought that she was murdered by her husband and is now doomed to haunt these waters forever, unaware that she is dead, and unable to be released from her eternal wanderings. People who have witnessed this apparition tell of a beautiful but sad and ultimately lonely figure.

In addition, other visitors to the caves have experienced strange and unexplained noises, such as children laughing, talking, and singing; mournful crying; drilling noises; and, quite bizarrely, a horse whinnying. Others have reported being touched or having the sensation that a child has rushed past them, brushing their legs on their way. People have reported seeing strange mist-like shapes and, quite unnervingly, full apparitions of ghostly children. Whereas the ghostly children appear to mean no harm, the shock of seeing something as such in a place like this is quite confronting and overwhelming.

Much like places like the London Dungeon, mannequins that are part of displays are said to move on their own, and it is not uncommon for staff to find a mannequin has changed its position from a previous tour. Some visitors also report seeing fleeting human-like shapes between the mannequins. The ghost of a Roman centurion who was speared to death nearly 2,000 years ago is also said to appear on occasions.

It is also the place of an infamous supernatural trial called "The Challenge" and, as scary as the previously mentioned ghostly inhabitants may be, this is an even more frightening story.

According to legend, The Challenge originated in the early 1960s as an event whereby anyone who could sleep a night on their own within the caves without running away terrified, would win themselves the princely sum of £5. Given the task and the eerie nature of the caves, it is not surprising that most challengers did not complete the task. Apparently, only one person, a policeman, managed to complete a full night in the dark, claustrophobic depths of the caves, and even then he stated that he felt as if he was being watched the whole time. Not daring to turn around and shine a torch at whatever was in the shadows, he apparently busied himself with carving a horse into the cave walls. At dawn he emerged and said that there was no way that he would ever do it again.

The final Chislehurst Challenge came about in November 1985 when two tour guides decided to experience a night alone in the caves as, at this time, members of the public were no longer allowed to take part. While in the caves one of the guides suffered an unexplained fit, which resulted in the other terrified guide calling for help and being let out.

After the event, the details of what apparently happened in the cave were released. It seems that one of the guides was asleep in his sleeping bag when he heard approaching footsteps. Following the footsteps, a loud scream pierced the darkness. The other guide, not knowing what was happening, ran over to the sleeping man to check his well-being only to find he was having what seemed to be some sort of fit. The guide reported that the man fell silent and opened his eyes and looked straight at him, and that his face had apparently changed shape and now appeared to have skin like an old, ravaged, and emaciated man.

The guide also reported that his colleague's eyes were red and glowing like light bulbs, and that when he got out of the sleeping bag he was frothing at the mouth. He then started getting aggressive and swung a punch at the guide while speaking and growling in a guttural voice, very unlike his normal voice. This was too much for the guide, and he ran to entrance absolutely terrified for his life.

The guide was let out and, with the owner and manager of the caves, decided to go back to help the other man. When they found him he was apparently acting strangely, crawling on all fours like an animal. However, he soon calmed down, yet insisted that he wanted to stay in the caves. The group called an ambulance thinking that he was still having a fit; however, within ten minutes the man began to return to normal.

The events of that night are still shrouded in mystery. Is it possible that the man simply had an epileptic fit and, in a panic, his colleague lost all composure, which led him to believe that the man was somehow supernaturally affected or bewitched? Alternatively, did something evil possess the man rendering him another person for a short moment in time? Interestingly, some people have reported that in some hauntings or séances, people's faces can change form and shape. Is this what happened in the caves?

Whatever the case, The Challenge is now deemed too dangerous, and overnight stays in the cave are prohibited.

After the events of the previous night, the owner reported poltergeist-like activity in the caves, continually finding locks being thrown around, chalk thrown at visitors, cabling torn down, and lamps knocked off pedestals. Indeed, there was so much destructive and annoying behaviour that she had to clean up every morning before the guided tours. In the end, it all became too much, so she enlisted the aid of a priest to perform an exorcism. Whether this exorcism worked or not is unknown, but Chiselhurst Caves remain just as spooky and just as mysterious.

And yet Chiselhurst Caves are not the only haunted caves in England. One of my favourite sites is the Hellfire Caves of West Wycombe in Buckinghamshire, which we looked at in the introduction of this book, "Personal Encounters and Thoughts". Without recounting the complete history of the place and my strange experience while visiting the caves, I can say that it is an eerie place and has a strange sort of atmosphere, one in which you can believe that ghosts exist. Is this because of the dark, the history, and the suggestion that ghosts exist in these depths? Or is it something else? Can the rough-hewn walls and passages of these places somehow record a slice of history and occasionally, under the right conditions replay this slice of history thus creating what we call a ghost?

Whatever the case, my experience in the unnerving underground passages and rooms of the infamous Hellfire Caves left me scratching my head as to what I may, or may not have seen. Did I simply misinterpret a common and normal situation? Or did I actually see a ghost?

But ghost or not, it seems that the Hellfire Caves, along with numerous other underground places across England, are haunted.

Kelvedon Hatch Secret Nuclear Bunker in the Borough of Brentwood in Essex is a large underground bunker, a relic from the cold war that was decommissioned in 1992. It was built in 1952–53 as part of a Royal Air Force air defence project designed to improve Britain's air defence network. During its operational life it provided command and control of the London Sector of Fighter Command, and during the 1960s until the early 1990s, the UK government maintained the bunker as an emergency regional government defence site. As well, it was designed to house up to 600 military and civilian personnel who would organise the survival of the population and continue government operations in the event of a nuclear attack. When the threat of nuclear war eventually subsided in the early 1990s the bunker was sold back to the family who had previously owned the land. Currently it is a Cold War museum.

The bunker is built thirty-eight metres below ground and entered via an ordinary-looking bungalow set amongst the trees. This bungalow leads to a service tunnel measuring ninety-one metres, above which there are two further levels containing generator rooms, command centre posts, dormitories, and a hospital wing.

But why is such a place considered haunted? After all, there was no Cold War nuclear strike and unlike haunted RAF bases around Great Britain, the bunkers never saw wartime service and the death and destruction associated with it. Having said that, ghost hunts at Kelvedon Hatch have been featured on television shows, such as *Most Haunted* and *Great British Ghosts* and, although it never saw operational service, nevertheless has many ghost stories associated with it.

During construction, concrete was poured pretty much non-stop, day and night, for weeks and weeks, and one morning the foreman's hard-hat was found floating on the wet concrete. He was never found and it was assumed that he had somehow tripped and fallen into the wet concrete and was accidentally buried alive. It was rumoured that the excavation uncovered an ancient burial ground, and it is believed that a number of suicides happened within the complex while it was still operational.

Witnesses have reported seeing a number of apparitions roaming the dark interior of the complex, including a grey figure that moves from room to room and takes the form of an unusually tall elderly lady. As well, the ghost of an RAF officer has been spotted on several occasions, and a number of people have had a frightening experience with a woman in uniform who angrily instructs them to leave the building. A similar experience was also reported

by a visitor who was walking through the dormitory when he heard a disembodied voice distinctly tell him to "go back," which he did, quite rapidly.

Apart from this, it seems that the sick bay is a paranormal hotspot with people reporting seeing dark shadowy figures, and mediums reporting the presence of a malevolent figure, which may account for the feelings of dread and despair that visitors often report when entering the room. And, like other poltergeist-like occurrences, stones have been reported to be thrown at people and loud crashing and bangs have been heard from empty rooms. In addition, unexplainable lights and mists have been seen materialising seemingly from thin air and inexplicably strange smells have also been reported.

But if places such as Kelvedon Hatch Secret Nuclear Bunker are haunted, then one must ask why other, much more ancient places are not? Or at least, seem much less so?

And so it is one dreary and overcast morning in early summer that I drive across the mighty Severn River from Somerset and into Wales. Once across this magnificent body of water I swing north towards Chepstow before following the road through delightful green forests until we emerge at Tintern Abbey. Luckily, the sun breaks through, and Kirsten and I spend a few delightful hours exploring the ruins of this once magnificent building.

Tintern Abbey is a truly wondrous sight. Nestled in a small valley and surrounded by glorious oaks and conifers, this once grand Gothic abbey sits serenely beneath blue skies next to the bubbling River Wye. Sadly, little remains of the original Cistercian Abbey, which was founded in 1131, but what remains is breathtaking in its beauty. Indeed, it has been called the finest relic of Britain's monastic period and was the source of inspiration for poems written by both Tennyson and William Wordsworth. Its serene beauty was also the subject for several paintings by the famous artist J. M. W. Turner.

And yet, for all this, it isn't the inspirational qualities of the ruin that I have come to see, as I am more interested in stories of ghostly monks and knights and other supernatural events attached to this most inspiring of places. Tennyson once wrote: "full for me of its bygone memories." Is it possible that Tennyson felt the presence of the spirits of this place? Did he write of those who lived there in long-gone days?

In my book *A Case for Ghosts* I wrote of Tintern Abbey that there are surprisingly few ghostly stories concerning the site. And yet, these few are still interesting all the same. For instance, local folklore says that the devil used to preach from a nearby rocky outcrop, attempting to lure the monks away from the abbey and their faith. Having said this, he was obviously not that successful given reports of a ghostly monk that is often seen praying near one of the arches.

Another piece of local folklore tells of a group of young men who visited the site intent on searching for antiquities. They employed some local men to dig in the nearby grounds but instead of antiquities they turned up two ancient skeletons. Quite unperturbed they stopped within the Abbey ruins to celebrate their discovery. However, within moments, the sky became dark and ominous clouds threatened. Flashes of lightning and huge roaring thunder claps punctuated the previously peaceful day. Then a heavy mist shrouded the ruins and, to the amazement and consternation of the men, an armour-clad knight, with his visor up, rode out of the mist and stared at them. Following this, hazy figures of monks and abbots began to appear and closed in all around them. The men fled in terror and never returned. It appears that the spirits of the abbey had come to life to protect their colleagues.

But apart from these few stories, oddly enough there are few reports of ghostly activity at the site. True, reports of the odd ghostly monk are not unusual, but overall one would suspect such a place to have a rich history of ghosts and hauntings whereas it is not the case.

What then can one make of this lack of ghosts, especially when so many sites all over the British Isles claim to be haunted? Maybe visitors to the site do see ghostly figures but simply assume they are real flesh and blood? Or is it simply that the place is not haunted? Tintern Abbey is quiet and serene, a place where reflection comes naturally, a place where the beauty of the countryside is perfectly blended with the built environment of a bygone age. In fact, it is a romantic place. However, this is not to say that the site would feel so inviting at night when the dark shadows beneath the great Gothic arches hold a more menacing countenance, and the moonlight causes grey shadows to creep across the ruined stones. Whatever the case, the ghosts that haunt this site do not appear to wish anyone malice.

Tintern Abbey lay forgotten and ruined under strands of ivy until the late eighteenth century when rediscovered by romantic artists and poets in search of the sublime. Maybe the ghosts had all decided to move on by this stage?

England and the British Isles are without a doubt some of the most haunted places on earth. The ancient Prehistoric, Neolithic, Medieval, and Industrial ages that have passed have seen many changes, many battles, many wars, and many deaths. It is little wonder that legends and myths have evolved over time in an attempt to explain the unknown during all these periods of time and history.

But can we definitely say that all these places that dot the countryside, towns, villages, and cities are haunted? I would say no; however, the sheer amount of stories suggests that, even if a tiny percentage were true, then ghosts must exist. One simply cannot dismiss such a rich history of supernatural events with complete disdain as to do so would be to simply reject a thousand lifetimes of paranormal and supernatural encounters.

But it is not Tintern that really interests us here as we drive further north into Wales past lush green meadows, forested hills, and rocky outcrops. Soon we drive into Monmouth, situated where the River Monnow meets the River Wye and within two miles of the border with England. Monmouth itself is an old town, going back to at least Roman times when the settlement was the small Roman fort of Blestium, one of a network of military bases established on the frontiers of the Roman occupation.

From Monmouth we continue under rapidly darkening skies, and before long, a torrent of rain impedes our vision. We pull into a small village to stay the night. And while there I manage to get hold of a local publication that lists local folklore, ghosts, paranormal happenings, and other strange stuff.

Wales is an old country. It is a place of mystery where the normal and paranormal blend into one under the mists of time. It is a place of Kings and Queens of antiquity, of dragons and wyverns and elves and other creatures of the night. It is a place where the supernatural is not a flight of fancy but is very real.

Like the Skirrid Inn, which we have previously visited, the Queens Head Hotel in Monmouth is also reputed to be haunted. A sixteenth-century coaching inn, the building is Grade II listed, and the original plaster work ceiling dating from the seventeenth century can still be seen near the bar. Over the years the building has seen many changes with the original stone being plastered over and mock black and white wood framing added to the exterior in 1922.

The pub has a number of secret hiding places, and during the English Civil War, Oliver Cromwell stayed there on a number of occasions. On one of these occasions an attempt was made on his life but the would-be assassin was chased into the bar and shot dead. A plaque on the wall of the pub records that moment:

It is said that when the land was much troubled by civil warr in 1642 secret hiding places be made in the walls of ye Inn—and in ye cellars a passage most secret was dug—hid by a cask half filled a secret door within, on ye 15 May 1648 Oliver Cromwell was harboured at ye Inn— and that on ye 16 May as he slept a Royalist Cavalier did enter ye Inn through ye secret passage in ye cellare, and did go to Cromwell's bedchamber on intent of murder, but was chased downstairs into the parlour by a Roundhead and shot by the fire.

Widely regarded as the third most haunted pub in Wales, the Queens Head boasts sightings of a ghostly male figure sitting by the fireplace in the bar area, the ghost of a small girl wearing a dress and estimated to be roughly four years of age, as well as the ghost of a man who is said to walk about on the landing upstairs.

The current owner, although claiming to be a sceptic, admits that a number of his staff refuse to work alone in the inn after midnight, and also relates tales of staff who claimed to have seen a man in an old-time war uniform sitting by the fireplace. Oddly, they reported that they could only see him from the knees up as the floor has been raised since the English Civil War. Some believe that this man is the ghost of the Royalist Cavalier who died when attempting to assassinate Cromwell.

The owner's daughter also recounts seeing a small girl, probably about four years old, wearing a dress, roaming about the building. She claims to have seen the ghostly child more than once and, on three occasions, also claims to have seen a ghostly old man walking in the halls upstairs. She also had one experience that gave her a bit of a shock when, late one night while getting herself a drink from the bar, she encountered a person sitting beside the fireplace. At first she thought it was someone who had accidentally been locked in after closing time, but when she approached him and spoke he simply vanished.

But the Queens Head Hotel is obviously not the only haunted place in this ancient landscape, and like England and Scotland, it has numerous castles that are reputed to be haunted. And Raglan Castle is one of these.

Raglan Castle is a late medieval castle just north of the village of Raglan in the county of Monmouthshire in south east Wales. A relatively modern castle, it was one of the last castles built in Wales and was constructed between the years 1435 and 1525. In its pomp, it was a luxurious, fortified castle, complete with a large hexagonal keep, known as the Great Tower or the Yellow Tower of Gwent, and was surrounded by superb parklands, water features, and terraces. So great was its grandeur that it was considered to be the equal of any other castle in England or Wales.

During the English Civil War the castle was held on behalf of Charles I, however, like Montgomery Castle in Powys, it was taken by Parliamentary forces and destroyed to ensure that it could no longer be used for military purposes. Sadly, the owners declined to rebuild the castle, and it became a source for local building material. It is now a romantic ruin that attracts numerous visitors to its grounds. A fascinating place to visit, it has its own ghost story as it appears the castle still remains home to a resident from the English Civil War.

The castle once housed a magnificently stocked library and, during the English Civil War, with a siege imminent, the castle librarian reputedly hid books and valuable manuscripts in a secret passageway beneath the castle. However, after the siege the library was destroyed and none of the books or manuscripts were ever seen again. Visitors to Raglan Castle often report seeing a Shakespearian figure who beckons to them from an area above where the library once existed. It is believed that he is attempting to show people where the stash of valuable books now lies or is still attempting to guard his hidden treasure. This figure is believed to be the castle's librarian, and his appearance startles visitors on a regular basis. He was last seen in the summer of 2001 when a girl on a school trip came running from the castle ashen-faced and trembling, insisting that she had seen him gesturing to her from a dimly lit corner.

Whatever the case, Raglan Castle, with its interesting and bloody past, mysterious aura, gloomy passageways, and dark, twisting stairwells provides the perfect setting for such a story. When one stares at its huge, hollow windows and walks the long dark corridors that elicit feelings of dread and a certain spine-tingling menace, one cannot help but believe the place is haunted.

As we travel further across Wales we find ourselves on a narrow, winding country road in the rugged country south of Conwy. We stop at an ancient and brooding gatehouse, made all the more gloomy by a slight drizzle that falls from grey, leaden skies. A heavy, black, solid wooden gate is decorated with medieval iron hardware as well as the date 1555 and the initials and arms of Sir John Wynn, son of the builder of the main house. We have arrived at Gwydir Castle.

Situated in the Conwy Valley roughly a mile to the west of the ancient market town of Llanrwst, Gwydir Castle is an excellent example of a fortified manor house and dates back to circa 1500. Located on the edge of the River Conwy floodplain, it is overlooked from the west by the densely forested slopes of Gwydir Forest and is an area of exceptional natural beauty.

The current site of Gwydir Castle has seen some sort of fortification for the last 1,400 years, and during the Dark Ages the area constantly saw skirmishes between various rival princes. By the fourteenth century, a manor house of sorts existed on the site with the first recorded owner being Howell ap Coetmor, who fought in the Hundred Years War and was a commander under Edward the Black Prince at the Battle of Poitiers in 1356. Gwydir then became the ancestral home of the Wynn family, one of the most powerful and significant families of North Wales during the Tudor and Stuart periods.

At the conclusion of the Wars of the Roses, the castle was rebuilt using recycled material from the dissolved abbey at Maenan. The turret was constructed around 1540. Other buildings in the complex date from 1500, with some alterations around 1540, 1600, and 1828 and, although called a castle, it is in fact a fortified manor or Tudor courtyard house.

Stepping through the small door set within the larger main gate, one gets the sensation that they have somehow traversed time and space itself. In the courtyard peacocks strut and preen much as they have since the early 1800s.

In 1921, the castle was sold by Charles Wynn Carrington, Marquis of Lincolnshire, and the contents auctioned off. In 1922, a fire gutted the Solar Tower. Another fire then burnt the west wing making it too dangerous to live in and it became abandoned until 1944, when new owners moved in and attempted to restore the place. However, after twenty years of effort the new owners ran out of money and abandoned their struggle. The building again became derelict. In 1994, the castle was purchased by Peter Welford and his wife, Judy Corbett, who have continually worked on the restoration and refurbishment of the building to this day.

In 1921, the main dining room, dating from 1640, was totally stripped and the carved and gilded panelling was bought at auction by William Randolph Hearst, the American press baron. On his death, the panels were inherited by the Metropolitan Museum of Art in New York City where they remained in storage. Peter Welford and Judy Corbett managed to track down these long-lost panels and then negotiated their return to Gwydir. The fully-restored dining room was re-opened in 1998 with the Prince of Wales attending the ceremony. The castle is, of course, haunted.

Soon after the new owners moved in, visitors began to make mention of ghostly dogs that kept mysteriously appearing around the place, although they would disappear whenever approached. Later, while excavating the basement, some ancient bones were unearthed, and not knowing if they were human or not, they were sent away for examination. When the results came back, it was found that they were the bones of a dog as in medieval times an animal, usually a cat or a dog, was sometimes buried in the foundations of a building to ward off evil spirits. In this case, the dog bones were reburied, and the ghostly dogs were seen no more.

Apart from ghostly hounds, the castle has the reputation for being one of the most haunted houses in Wales with a number of regular appearances by numerous ghostly figures. Sir John Wynn is believed to haunt the spiral staircase leading from the Solar Hall to the Great Chamber. Eyewitness accounts report him being seen wearing a tall black hat and ruff and walking through walls where a door once existed. In addition, a monk, said to have been trapped in a tunnel from a secret room, is also seen.

On the second floor of the manor are a number of rooms that are said to be haunted by a servant girl who was romantically involved with the son of one of the lords of the manor. The romance soon led to a pregnancy and the girl was murdered, and her body bricked up in a space in the walls beside one of the chimney breasts. It is said that there are times even today when the foul odour can be smelled and the temperature in the area seems to drop notably. In addition she has been known to tap unwary visitors on the shoulder. She is generally known as the "Grey Lady," although some have suggested she is more white than grey. During renovation work a few years ago, a space was found within the chimney breast, and it is believed that it was once used as a priest hole. It is thought that the girl's body was hidden here after her untimely death.

There are many more ghost stories connected to Gwydir Castle; however, one from the present day is somewhat chilling in that it directly affected the family in a physical sense. Before purchasing Gwydir Castle, Judy Corbett was a historic book binder, and to finance the restoration work at the castle, she continued to work in this capacity whenever she had the chance. Being painstaking and detailed work, she chose a secluded room in the castle, known as Sir Richard's Chamber, where she set up her equipment and workplace.

At this time there were a number of inexplicable accidents where Peter Welford felt that he had been pushed or tripped. At the same time Judy started to feel that something was watching her while she was in Sir Richard's Chamber, and gradually, over time she started to think that whatever it was, was trying to make contact with her. However, the more that Judy became familiar with this spirit, the more the accidents kept occurring to Peter, including time spent in hospital after a fall caused a concussion and required stitches.

Some research led the couple to believe that the spirit was that of a lady by the name of Margaret who had married Sir John Wynn in 1606. The marriage was apparently particularly unhappy although short, as Sir John died at the age of thirty-one. It seemed to the couple that the spirit was trying to extract some sort of revenge against males in the household, in this case Peter. Later research also suggested that Sir Richard's Chamber had once been known as the Ghost Room.

Whether or not the ghost continues to harass males is unknown, but Gwydir Castle is undoubtedly a significant place, full of beauty, wonder, intrigue, and just enough tragedy to allow it to be considered haunted.

And another place, similar in beauty and wonder, but on a much grander scale, is Conwy Castle, just a short drive north of Gwydir Castle.

The first view one gets of Conwy Castle is simply awe-inspiring. Driving into the walled market town on the north coast of Wales one is struck by the sheer size of this castle as it sits, grey, bulky, and menacing in the mist that rises lazily off the cold grey waters of the River Conwy. As one gets closer, the Conwy Suspension Bridge, itself a historical wonder and completed in 1826, spans the river next to the castle, its supporting towers designed to match the castles turrets. Next to this is the Conwy Railway Bridge, a wrought iron tubular bridge built by Robert Stephenson and officially opened in 1849.

But it is not the bridges that we have come to see, and as we drive across the bridge that holds traffic on the A55, we are astounded at the sheer size of this place. Conwy Castle and the town walls were built between 1283 and 1289 on the instruction of Edward I as part of his conquest of the principality of Wales. Originally, the site of Aberconwy Abbey, Edward and his troops took over the abbey site and relocated the monks to a new site in the Conwy Valley where they established Maenan Abbey.

Initially constructed as part of a wider plan to create the walled town of Conwy, the combined defences cost an enormous amount for the time, although, over the next few centuries it played an important part in several wars. It survived a siege in 1294–95, acted as a short-term haven for Richard II in 1399, and was even held for a few months by forces loyal to Owain Glyndwr in 1401. Welsh forces led by Glyndwr later attacked the walled town of Montgomery in 1402, and although the castle survived the attack, the town was sacked and burned and remained a ruin for the next 200 years.

After the outbreak of the English Civil War in 1642, the castle was the stronghold of forces loyal to Charles I, and managed to hold out until 1646 when it was surrendered to the Roundheads. As with Montgomery Castle and many others around the country, it was partially slighted to prevent it being used in any further revolt. By 1665, it was a complete ruin when its remaining iron and lead was stripped and sold off.

However, this grand old castle was not to lie down and die and, in the late eighteenth and early nineteenth centuries, it became an attractive destination for painters trying to seek the sublime. Visitor numbers grew and some restoration work was carried out in the second half of the nineteenth century. Today it is a national treasure and has been considered by UNESCO, the United Nations Educational, Scientific and Cultural Organization, as one of "the finest examples of late 13th century and early 14th century military architecture in Europe."

A World Heritage site, the rectangular castle is built from stone and occupies a coastal ridge which originally overlooked a significant crossing point over the River Conwy. It is divided into an inner and an outer ward, and is defended by eight large towers and two barbicans, with a gate and walls leading down to the river, which allowed the castle to be resupplied from the sea. It also retains what has been described as the "best preserved suite of medieval private royal chambers in England and Wales."

A stereotypical medieval castle, almost a fairy tale castle, it stands as a monument to the tenacity of the resistance of the Welsh and is testimony to the immensity of the task of usurping Wales and the Welsh rule. Visitors today can take the opportunity to walk along portions of the castle's walls and even climb the towers from where one is subject to a buffeting wind and breathtakingly spectacular views. From here one can image what it must have been like being a Royalist soldier during the Civil War, cold, wet, hungry, and with the constant threat of violent death. In the dark, dank dungeon located at the base of the Prison Tower one feels a chill run up their spine.

However, history aside, the castle is reputed to be haunted by a number of eerie spectres, including reports of a strong smell of incense on entering the upstairs chapel, and there has been numerous sightings of a black silhouette apparently watching visitors. In addition, people have been overcome with a sense of terror whilst in the towers, which is not surprising given that the apparition of a ghostly monk has been reported, and the silhouette of a large man in armour and wearing a helmet, looking out of a window and lit up as if by candlelight, has also be seen. Tourists have also reported to have seen apparitions in period dress whilst walking past the castle from the street.

While the ghosts of Conwy Castle may not be as prevalent as other reputedly haunted sites, the same cannot be said for Plas Teg Hall, an architectural gem, and possibly one of the finest surviving Jacobean houses to be found anywhere in Britain. Located near the village of Pontblyddyn in Flintshire, it was built by Sir John Trevor I, a Welsh politician, in about 1610. At the time of its construction it was considered the most advanced house in Wales and throughout the early seventeenth century it functioned primarily as a family home. However, after the death of Lady Margaret Trevor and the onset of the Civil War, the house was tenanted out, and the family resided at their other residences.

The estate remained in the hands of the Trevor family until as late as 1930, and later, during the Second World War, the house and outbuildings were used by the war office to house soldiers. Sadly, the grand old house suffered damage and decay during this time and by the mid-1950s it was in a state of advanced decay.

With the house under the threat of demolition there was a public outcry, and as a result, the house was purchased by Patrick Trevor-Roper, a Trevor descendant. Trevor-Roper managed to partially restore the building with funds from the Historic Buildings Council, and he then leased out the house until

1977 when a Mr. and Mrs. William Llewelyn purchased it. Sadly, they only used parts of the ground floor and allowed the rest to slowly fall into a state of disrepair. However, in 1986, Cornelia Bayley, the present owner, acquired the house and poured funds into its restoration. Within ten months of the completion, the house was opened to the public.

Of particular interest is the main staircase, which is believed to be made from original timber from a ship from the Spanish Armada. There is also a sofa in the house, which was a gift from Napoleon, Ruben paintings, imported Italian paintings and a fireplace which is said to have witches markings, designed to stop any evil from entering the house through the chimney.

In addition, the infamous Judge Jeffries, who was born in Wrexham, was also a resident at Plas Teg, when he married into the family. It is believed that he used the house as a personal courtroom in which to sentence criminals. In another story associated with the house, Sir John Trevor V, in 1742, found that his wife was having an affair. Infuriated and distressed, he is rumoured to have rode his horse and trap around the grounds at a great pace until it finally overturned. He was then carried to the Regency Room where he stayed, mortally wounded, until his death a month later.

Not surprisingly, given the age and history of the place, there has been numerous reports of ghostly apparitions within the house, grounds, and outside road, including men, women, and children. Many traffic accidents have occurred on the road leading to Plas Teg, and witnesses have reported seeing *something* on the road. Numerous drivers have also reported having to swerve to miss hitting ghostly figures that appear in the middle of the road.

One of these figures is said to be a "White Lady" who walks up and down the road. In addition, people report seeing a ghostly wolf and the spirit of a witch-like figure. One witness recalled seeing what she thought was a woman dressed in grey holding a child in her arms and walking along the roadside in the dead of night. When she stopped and looked back at the figure, it was gone. Others have reported being prodded in the back, pinched, grabbed, hugged, and had their clothes tugged. Indeed, photos taken on the road, in the grounds of the house and within the house itself have picked up numerous orbs.

The dining room is said to have been used for sentencing criminals before they were sent into the adjoining room to be hanged, and the ghost of Judge Jeffries, who we have already seen seems to haunt a vast number of places, is just one of many who are believed to haunt this room. In the Regency Room there have been reports of drastic temperature drops as well a feeling of despair. It is believed that the ghost of Sir John Trevor the Fifth haunts the room having never recovered from his injuries and broken heart.

As well, dogs tend to whimper and cower and have even fled from the room in terror. Visitors have reported being grabbed, pushed, pinched, and even felt an invisible figure rush by them. A medium who visited the house once reported seeing a lady lying on the bed covered in blood. And to add to that, the bathroom for this room is also said to be haunted with numerous reports of people leaving the room only to hear the mirror repeatedly rattling and banging against the wall.

Equally strange and unnerving things happen in other rooms in the house such as the Twin Poster Bedroom where drops in temperature and heavy, disembodied breathing are a regular occurrence, while in the so-called Parrot Room people report hearing a voice that calls out inaudibly.

On the landing area and stairs a ghostly woman holding a candle has been seen at a window, and there have been reports of two males and one female figure, apparently arguing about something from beyond the grave. In addition, there have been numerous sightings of a spectral lady on the third step of the stairs.

With such a rich tapestry of ghosts and apparitions, it is no wonder that Plas Teg is said to be one of the most haunted houses in Wales. It has been featured on television's *Most Haunted* program on two occasions. Interestingly, the county of Flintshire is said to be a land of spirits and hauntings with one notable case being the ghost of an old lady who is reported to have been seen moving across the A541 road adjacent to Plas Teg and into the path of traffic where she sometimes causes havoc with oncoming vehicles. Plas Teg also appeared on the television program *Country House Rescue* in 2011, although it is unknown whether or not any of the multitudes of ghosts turned up to help.

Whatever the case, Wales, a place deeply enshrined in myth, mystery, folklore and history, is a place where ghosts and ghostly stories abound. And so we must ask, why is it such places have such strong histories of the supernatural? Is it time alone, or the landscape itself that inspires these stories? And if it is the time and landscape that inspires such stories and legends then surely we will find more of the same across the icy grey waters of the Irish Sea?

CHAPTER 10

†

GHOSTLY TALES FROM THE EMERALD ISLES

Now I know what a ghost is.
Unfinished business, that's what.

—SALMAN RUSHDIE

Ireland, like Cornwall and Wales, is a place of mystery and wonder where the mists of time have blurred the edges between the supernatural and the normal between the paranormal and the ordinary. It is a land of fairies and banshees, of ghosts and leprechauns, a place where the mysteries of the past blend seamlessly with the present.

It is a melancholic landscape that has seen war and famine, hardships and good times, and its ghosts seem indicative of this past. It is a land of contradictions, beautiful but bleak, modern yet ancient, rich in places but desperately poor in others. Its ruined castles, crumbling stately homes, and Neolithic stone circles cry out from the wilderness leading the visitor to wonder if he or she has somehow managed to traverse time itself.

As such, there is little wonder that it has a rich history of ghosts and supernatural happenings.

Castle Leslie, apart from being where ex-Beatle Sir Paul McCartney married Heather Mills in 2002, is one of these places. A historic country house built in 1870 for Sir John Leslie, it is located on the site of an earlier castle and is situated some eleven kilometres north-east of Monaghan in County Monaghan.

Although the Leslie family believe that they can trace their ancestry back to Attila the Hun, the first Leslie came from Scotland and was a Hungarian nobleman called Bartholomew. Apparently, he was the chamberlain and protector of Margaret Queen of Scotland. The family motto is "Grip Fast," which is said to have originated when Queen Margaret, while riding pillion on Bartholomew's horse while evading enemies, nearly fell off into a river. As a reward for saving the Queen's life the family was granted the motto.

The Leslies first came to Ireland in the early 1600s and the castle's ownership has since been passed on down through the Leslie family until the present day. Now it is owned by Samantha Leslie, the daughter of Desmond Leslie, a World War II Spitfire pilot.

In the banquet hall the presence of a ghostly monk is often seen and felt. He is said to be very tall and dressed in black. Surprisingly, he is seen more often than not when the castle is hosting some sort of event. Of course, this could simply be because of greater numbers of people at the castle but also raises questions as to why and how ghosts appear given that sometimes they appear to feed on energy from the living. However, if this large ghostly monk seems rather benign then this is not so in the case of the spirit of a child in the Geraldine Bedroom who is, chillingly, often heard whimpering.

The Red Room is reportedly haunted by Norman Leslie who was killed in action in 1914. It is said that his mother, Lady Marjorie, awoke in this room one night to find his ghost standing by the chest of drawers, surrounded by what she described as a "cloud of light." His ghost appeared to be leafing through some letters and seemed to be seeking one in particular. Sitting up, Lady Marjorie asked him what he was doing whereupon he turned to her, smiled, and faded away. Given that Norman was killed in France, it is possible that Lady Marjorie witnessed a "dead" apparition of sorts, as discussed in chapter four of this book.

More recently an employee at the castle reported that she was approached by the ghost of a scary grey man when in the basement, while the spirit of a Lady Constance is supposed to haunt the "Mauve" Bedroom. There is also the story of a woman who lived at the castle called Leonie who, on her death bed, was visited by an elderly woman who spoke to her for a while and then left. A nurse who was caring for the ailing woman quite reasonably assumed that the visitor was one of the family members and thought nothing of it until later; after the funeral, the family and the nurse were sitting in the dining room when the nurse realised that the old lady visitor looked exactly like a portrait on the wall, a portrait of Lady Constance, who had died in 1925.

But Castle Leslie is not the only castle to have a resident ghost. Ardgillan Castle, like Castle Leslie, not a real castle but a country house in Balbriggin, Fingal, is also haunted by various spooks. Featuring castellated embellishments and made of grey stone, the structure sits in an imposing position overlooking Barnageera Beach, the Irish Sea, and Balbriggan.

Built in 1738 by the Reverend Robert Taylor, it remained in the family until 1962, when the estate was sold to Heir Henrich Potts of Westphalia. In 1982, it was again sold, this time to Fingal County Council who renovated the house. It was officially opened to the public in 1992 and is a fine example of early- to mid-eighteenth century finery.

At one end of the property is a bridge, known locally as The Lady's Stairs. This bridge is said to be haunted by the ghost of a woman who waits in vain for her dead husband to return to her. Apparently, the woman's husband was an enthusiastic swimmer and frequently swam in the cold sea waters. One night he did not return from his swim, and the woman went to the bridge to wait for his return. Tragically, however, the man had drowned and it is said that she then waited for his return every day until finally, she died as well. These days her ghost is seen waiting forlornly for her love.

Local legend also claims that if a person is to go to the end of the bridge at midnight on Halloween, the lady's ghost will appear and throw them to their death in the ocean. However, local newspaper reports do not back this theory.

Another theory put forward as to why this bridge is haunted concerns a Lady Langford, who drowned in the sea while swimming in November 1853. Apparently, Lady Langford, real name Louisa Connolly, was very friendly with the Taylor family of Ardgillan and was spending time there while her husband, Lord Langford, was on a shooting excursion in Scotland.

She loved swimming, but on this fateful day the waters were rough, and she was swept out to sea where she drowned, despite the best efforts of her maid to save her. Beaten back by the waves, her maid spotted some men in a nearby field and screamed at them for help. Sadly, none of them could swim.

Fortuitously, a gardener from Ardgillan came upon the scene about an hour after Lady Langford had been swept away. He entered the rough waters and managed to grasp the now lifeless body but was pounded so much by the chilly waters that he had no choice but let go.

Lady Langford's body was later recovered by boat, and a surgeon who examined her body pronounced her dead. Tragically it was believed that Lord Langford had planned to return home that evening, and it is believed that the ghostly woman on the stairs is none other than her tragic figure.

Ghosts, or as they are sometimes called in Irish, *Thevshi* or *Tash,* seem as common in Ireland as they are in the other countries that make up Great Britain. Indeed, in 2007, at the Old Kilbeggan Distillery at Killarney, a number of people reported seeing a dark, robed figure walking around the site leading to speculation that the distillery was haunted by a monk, while at the lighthouse at Skellig Michael a poltergeist-like entity is said to reside. It is rumoured that two lighthouse keepers have been driven away by the eerie and frightening cries, bangs, footsteps, and slamming of doors.

At Wallstown Castle in the River Awbeg Valley in County Cork, the ghost of Henry Bennet, a loyal soldier and defender of the castle who was killed during the siege during the Irish Confederate Wars, is said to wander the lonely ruins. A local man once reported seeing the ghost of Bennet in full cavalier period dress, carrying a pole that he used to stop people from entering the castle. It was said that whenever a person challenged by Bennet asked him to withdraw the pole, he would laugh and let them pass. The man who reported the ghostly cavalier stated that, when he saw his ghost, he asked if he could withdraw the pole, resulting in the ghost laughing loudly and then disappearing.

Built in the late fifteenth century and the ancestral home of the O'Donoghue clan, Ross Castle has a bloody past, including being among the last to surrender to Oliver Cromwell's Roundheads during the Irish Confederate Wars. Now run as a five-star bed-and-breakfast, it is said to be haunted by the ghost of Myles "The Slasher" O'Reilly, the Irish folk hero who was believed to have spent his last night in the castle before dying in battle in 1644. Apart from O'Reilly, it is also believed that the spirit of the daughter of an English lord also haunts the corridors and guests have often complained of hearing disembodied voices, banging doors, and strange unearthly sounds.

Likewise Leap Castle, in County Offaly, about three kilometres north of the town of Roscrea is another to hold a grisly and tragic past. Although no one is exactly sure when the main tower and keep were constructed, it is believed to date from somewhere between the thirteenth and the fifteenth centuries but most likely around 1250. There is evidence to suggest that, like numerous other castles and country houses, it was built on a previous site of importance, perhaps even a Neolithic ceremonial site.

In 1513, the Earl of Kildare tried unsuccessfully to seize the castle, yet three years later he was more successful when he managed to partially destroy it. By the 1530s, a bitter family power struggle occurred when one brother, a priest, was brutally murdered by his brother while holding Mass in the chapel, now known as the Bloody Chapel.

Around the 1900s, workmen who were hired to clean up the castle's oubliette found an incredible amount of human skeletons, the remains of people imprisoned, tortured, and left to die. It was said that it took three cartloads to remove them all. Intriguingly a pocket watch made in 1840 was also found in the bones suggesting that the oubliette could have been used up until quite recently.

Prisoners would have been pushed into this dark cramped room, basically a walled hole in the ground with no doors, where they would have fallen onto steel spikes. Those who didn't die instantly from being impaled would have died a truly horrific death of starvation and infection.

This fortress is considered to be one of Ireland's most haunted castles and is haunted by the type of spirit called an "elemental." This spirit is allegedly a frightening and horrifying apparition that brings an overwhelming sense of dread, hopelessness, and fear. Those who have seen it describe a hideous looking, small grey man-like creature with almost human-looking eyes, a skeletal face, and reeking of death. One would suspect something similar to Golem from Tolkien's *Lord of the Rings*.

In 1659, Leap Castle passed in marriage from the O'Carroll family to the Darbys, an English family who began alterations and renovations to turn it into their family home. In the late nineteenth century their descendants, John and Mildred Darby inherited the ownership and looked forward to raising their family. At this time experimenting with the occult was fashionable, and it is suggested that Mildred Darby, while innocently dabbling, somehow managed to wake the elemental.

In 1909, Mildred Darby wrote a short article for the *Journal Occult Review* in which she described her experience with the malevolent spirit. She stated that: "The thing was about the size of a sheep, thin, gaunt and shadowy in parts. Its face was human, or to be more accurate, inhuman, in its vileness, with large holes of blackness for eyes, loose slobbery lips, and a thick saliva-dripping jaw, sloping back suddenly into its neck! Nose it had none, only spreading, cancerous cavities, the whole face being a uniform tint of grey."

She added, "Its lustreless eyes, which seemed half decomposed, and looked incredibly foul, stared into mine, and the horrible smell, which had before offended my nostrils, only a hundred times intensified, came up to my face, filling me with a deadly nausea. I noticed the lower half of the creature was indefinite and seemed semi-transparent—at least, I could see the framework of the door that led into the gallery through its body."

Reports of this creature have not ceased with time and a filmmaker described how he was attacked by the apparition on 18 June 2002 while making a television documentary. Later, in June 2006, a visitor to the castle reported: "I looked into the darkness of a corridor that exited the spiral stairway. I became aware of the smell of sulphur. It was as if boxes and boxes of matches had suddenly been lit at once. I looked at my friend who had taken me to visit Leap Castle. He could also smell the sulphur. I stared into the darkness of the corridor and had the impression that a beast like a bear or lion was staring back at me."

Local legend suggests that the elemental is the ghost of a former owner of the castle who died of leprosy with the reasoning being that the decaying facial features and the appalling stench of decomposing flesh that accompanies the ghoul's manifestations are entirely consistent with advanced leprosy.

But if reports of a skeletal half-human/half-animal-like ghost with leprosy haunting the dim cold corridors of Leap Castle seem somewhat incredible, than what of Ireland's supposed most haunted place, Wicklow Gaol? Surely such a place, with centuries of pain and suffering must be haunted? Well, yes, if one is to believe numerous eyewitness reports.

Proclaimed as one of the most haunted places in Ireland, Wicklow Gaol has a long history of cruelty, pain, and suffering. Built in 1702 and locally known as "The Gates of Hell," it finally closed in 1924, but not before large numbers of prisoners died inside the gaol due to the harsh and inhospitable conditions and maltreatment, starvation, and disease.

Within the walls of this 300-year-old prison were held murderers, thieves, rapists, and criminals, including women and children. Sadly, it also contained innocent people, victims of the Great Famine who had stolen food to survive. And not only did it hold prisoners from the Great Famine, but also from the 1798 Rebellion and the War of Independence. It was the place where Irish patriots involved in the 1798 rebellion were held prior to transportation to Australia, and included prominent rebels such as Joseph Holt and Michael Dwyer.

One of the ghosts that haunt this silent eerie place is the spirit of a young girl by the name of Grace who died of gangrene after breaking her leg at the tender age of seven. It is believed that she was staying at the gaol with a parent during the famine when she died. People have reported hearing her voice or hearing knocking when they call to her, and on some occasions visitors report feeling an invisible child tugging at their clothing as they walk around the gaol.

The gaol is an eerie place with half-heard whispers seemingly emanating from darkened rooms and half-glimpsed dark shadows slinking in corners. Visitors often report seeing strange mists that appear and then rapidly disappear, as well as odd lights that flash across the now empty cells. In various areas people report strange feelings of being watched and have also reported being tapped on the shoulder or even pushed by an unseen assailant.

In addition, a staff writer from *Irish Central* reported in March 2004 that Dublin-based psychic medium Declan Flynn claimed to have come in contact with the deceased president of Ireland, Erskine Childers, who died in 1974 at age sixty-eight. Childers tragically died just over a year after taking office, and his spirit was apparently anxious that his portrait be restored to its original place of honour in the gaol.

However, even with numerous paranormal enthusiasts visiting the goal on a regular basis, the gaol hardly seems to live up to its reputation of being one of the most haunted buildings in Ireland. As such, where should we go if we are to find something or some place in this mystical place that is apparently more haunted? Perhaps another gaol?

Kilmainham Gaol in Dublin was built in 1796. These days it is a museum, and its disconcerting quiet reminds visitors of an earlier period in history when it was anything but quiet and peaceful. When it was first built, public hangings often took place at the front of the gaol, although from the 1820s these executions ceased.

The gaol was a grim place with no prisoner segregation; men, women, and children were confined up to five in each cell in the cold, damp darkness with only the light of a single candle. Many people died in these conditions, and many were executed for their crimes, so it is little wonder that it is reported that its long, echoing corridors and dank cramped cells are believed to be haunted.

Apart from holding common criminals the gaol was also used in 1916 to hold the leaders of the uprising for independence, and many of them were executed within the gaols walls. And it was here that James Connolly, the Irish republican and socialist leader, was executed by a British firing squad because of his leadership role in the Easter Rising of 1916. As the last of the leaders to be executed, ironically, he had to be carried out to the courtyard for execution as he had been severely wounded in a previous battle and could no longer walk.

With the death and misery that occurred within the walls of the gaol it comes as no surprise that the place is haunted. During its restoration in the 1960s, workmen and tradesmen alike reported strange goings-on, including seeing vague outlines of what appeared to be people. The governor at the time, Daniel McGill, was living in the gaol with his family during the restoration, and his bedroom looked out upon the courtyard where the executions took place. One night just before he retired to bed, he noticed that the chapel on the other side of the courtyard was lit up from the inside. Wondering why this was, he made his way to the chapel, had a look around, and finding nothing there, turned off the lights. Before he could return to his rooms, he glanced back and saw that the lights were on again. Again he returned and looked around, thinking that someone was playing a trick on him, but once again finding nothing, he switched of the lights for a second time. This was to happen a total of three times that night.

Another incident during the restoration of the gaol happened when a painter was working in the dungeon area when he was literally blown off his feet by a powerful gust of wind. The wind then continued to blow, pinning him down for a period of time until he managed to struggle free. From that point on the painter, apparently very religious, refused to enter the dungeon to complete the painting.

In another inexplicable episode a tradesman was working in a corridor inside the gaol when he heard what he thought was the footsteps of a colleague behind him. He turned around to greet the person but was shocked to find no one there. The footsteps, however, continued to walk straight past him and down the corridor.

Others, whether visitors, staff, or workmen alike have reported lights that turn themselves on and off in the prison's chapel, unseen forces that push people over, disembodied phantom footsteps, feelings of being watched, unexplained bangs and tapping noises, plus shadowy figures that are fleetingly seen before they disappear. As well psychics have suggested that an evil presence exists around the chapel balcony area.

But it is not just gaols and stately manor houses that are haunted in this mystical place as, like other theatres around the world, Ireland's Grand Opera House in Belfast is also considered haunted. Designed by Frank Matcham, who also designed the London Palladium and Victoria Palace, it was opened in December 1895 and has been described as "probably the best surviving example in the United Kingdom of the oriental style applied to theatre architecture."

In 1904, it was renamed the Palace of Varieties, although by 1909 it had once again reverted to its original name. The building saw performances by no less than Gracie Fields, and became a repertory theatre during World War II. General Dwight Eisenhower and Field Marshal Bernard Montgomery, 1st Viscount Montgomery of Alamein, commonly known as Monty, attended gala performances at the theatre. Later it was used as a cinema and, although it was almost demolished in the 1970s, it has survived to this day hosting dramas, musicals, plays, pantomimes, and live music concerts. It is also believed to be haunted.

Cast members walking down stairs from the dressing rooms on the top floor of the opera house have often reported seeing an unknown face looking at them as they have passed a round window. Other members of staff have been spooked by the feeling that someone was behind them when no one was there, especially when entering or crossing the stage, and a woman who was working back alone one night reported hearing something behind her and upon turning around was greeted by a figure in a long black robe. It then disappeared leaving her somewhat shaken.

The Northern Ireland Paranormal Research Association recently claimed to have contacted the spirits of Harry and George, who worked there as stage crew in the 1980s, as well as the spirit of a woman who may have been a cleaner during its halcyon days.

And like England and its myriad of haunted pubs, Ireland is no different. At John Kavanagh's in Prospect Square in Dublin the ghost of an elderly man in old-fashioned tweed is said to occasionally appear at the bar sipping on a pint. Interestingly this pub is also known as "The Gravediggers" apparently due to its proximity to Prospect Cemetery and the old custom of throwing a shovel of earth from the cemetery against the pub's wall to order a pint.

At Renvyle House Hotel in Galway witnesses have reported doors opening and closing, groans, bed sheets flying off, people being thrown out of their beds, and other unexplained happenings. WB Yeats, the celebrated Irish poet, even claimed to have witnessed these ghostly incidents himself. Other guests have reported seeing figures in mirrors, but when they turn around the figure has disappeared.

Grace Neill's on High Street in Donaghadee, County Down, is reputed to be the oldest original pub in Ireland. Built in 1611 and originally called the The King's Arms, it is supposedly haunted by Grace Neill who once ran the pub and died in 1916 at the grand old age of ninety-eight. She is said to be seen in the front bar straightening glasses and furniture, and switching lights on and off. In one episode a whisky bottle suddenly split open, dousing the bar in alcohol. When the barman examined the bottle, he could find no reason for its behaviour.

In addition, a customer once saw her glass slide straight across the table. When she told the barman what had happened, they checked the table and found that it was completely level and dry leaving them both completely astounded. Visitors have also reported hearing the shuffling of clothing on the second floor, and glimpsing an old woman wearing Victorian clothing. As well customers and staff have mentioned that they can smell the distinctive aroma of pipe smoke in the bar, even though smoking has long been banned in the establishment. Strangely enough, Grace was known to be very fond of smoking a clay pipe.

The Dobbins Inn Hotel in Carrickfergus, County Antrim, was built in the thirteenth century by Reginald d'Aubin. The family name changed from d'Aubin to Dobyn and finally Dobbins giving this ancient white building its name. The hotel is said to be haunted by Elizabeth Dobbins who lived in the seventeenth century and was commonly known as Maud. Sadly, she became romantically involved with a soldier from the nearby Carrickfergus Castle. At night, it is said she would creep through a tunnel that linked the house to the castle to meet him. Tragically their liaisons were discovered by her husband and she was murdered. The husband then made his way to the castle where he found her lover and beheaded him. The ghost of Elizabeth Dobbin has wandered the building ever since, a sad and mournful figure still searching for her lost love. Staff are now quite accustomed to her presence, although it is said that she sometimes caresses the cheeks of sleeping guests before disappearing into the dark of night.

Likewise, the Kyteler's Inn was established in 1324 and sits proudly on Kieran Street, Kilkenny. The original owner of the inn was Dame Alice le Kyteler who was born in Kilkenny in 1263 and was widely known as the Witch of Kilkenny. Over her lifetime she gained much notoriety mainly due to the fact that she was able to survive four husbands who died untimely and mysterious deaths, and amass a considerable amount of money. Accordingly, accusations of poisoning and witchcraft followed, and she was sentenced to be burned at the stake; however, in 1324, she fled to England, although in doing so her property, including Kyteler's Inn, was confiscated.

The witchcraft trials did, however, take place and a William Outlaw was convicted and ordered by the Bishop to attend three Masses every day and to give alms to the poor. This light sentence was in contrast to the torture dealt out to less wealthy friends of Alice, including her maid Petronella who was tortured, whipped, and then burned at the stake. And it is her ghost that is said to now haunt the pub, although the current owner believes that Alice's spirit also resides within its ancient medieval walls.

Whether Alice le Kyteler was a witch or a murderer is unknown; however, hers is not the only story of witches and witchcraft in Ireland as, about eighty kilometres north-west of Dublin is the Loughcrew Cairns, a set of Neolithic passage tombs built 3,000 years ago and also known as Sliabh na Cailli or "The Hills of the Witch." The tombs are located on three different hills with one of them having a cruciform chamber, a corbelled roof, and some of the most beautiful examples of Neolithic art in Ireland. It is also reputed to be haunted by a witch who, legend has it, once jumped from one hill to the next, dropping stones from her apron to form the cairns.

Of course, stories of witchcraft in Ireland are many but are outside the scope of this book and of course, Neolithic stories of leaping witches, quaint as they may seem, are really the realms of mythology and folklore and not the supernatural. However, as we shall see in the next chapter, some supernatural stories are not quite as quaint.

CHAPTER 11

†

A Ghost in Berkeley Square, the Underground, and Other London Haunts

Some places speak distinctly. Certain dark gardens cry aloud for murder; certain old houses demand to be haunted; certain coasts are set apart for shipwreck.

—Robert Louis Stevenson

Nestled into the quaint, late eighteenth-century streetscape of Berkeley Square in the prestigious London suburb of Mayfair is a fairly nondescript four-story brick townhouse that holds the offices of an antiquarian bookseller. And yet, behind this facade of calm suburban normality is one of the most well-known and interesting ghost stories to ever come out of the United Kingdom.

The house at 50 Berkeley Square was once the home of George Canning, who served briefly as Prime Minister in 1827. He also lends his name to a quaint little pub in Camberwell where I spent quite a deal of time reviewing some of my research or discussing it with others. The house was also the property of Marcus Samuel, 1st Viscount Bearsted, founder of the Shell Transport and Trading Company and at one stage was thought to be the oldest unaltered building in London.

However, this is not what interests us in this case, as this quaint little place was once regarded as being the most haunted house in London. And indeed, it is not so much the ghosts that really interest us, but the number of deaths that have occurred in the house allegedly due to the haunting. Oddly enough, the case also seems to straddle the supernatural/ cryptozoological spheres with some claiming that the ghost is actually some sort of undiscovered semi-aquatic, predatory cryptid.

Some tales suggest that the attic room is haunted by a spirit of a young woman who committed suicide by throwing herself from a top floor window after being abused by her uncle. Her spirit is said to take the form of a brown mist, although sometimes she is reported as being a white figure. She is also said to be capable of frightening people to death. Another legend, however, suggests that the ghost is that of a young man who was locked in the attic room and fed only through a hole in the door until he went mad and died.

Whatever the case, after Canning moved out, the house was bought by a Mr. Myers in 1885. It was said that he had been previously jilted by a lover and would lock himself in the attic room, something that, over time, led to complete madness and eventually his death. During this time the house became somewhat dilapidated and its reputation as being haunted grew.

In 1872, Lord Lyttelton, a British aristocrat and conservative politician, stayed a night in the building's attic for a bet. Knowing the reputation of the place he brought his shotgun with him. Sometime during the night he reported that an apparition appeared, and frightened, he shot at it. In the morning, however, all he could find were the spent shells of his shotgun. Whatever it was that he had shot at was gone. In another version of this story, Lyttelton was said to be armed with two blunderbusses loaded with silver coins. Interestingly, Lyttelton is also said to have had another paranormal experience when he dreamt that a bird and a woman in white told him he would die in three days time. Already in ill health, he travelled to his mansion in Epsom where he promptly died.

In 1879, it was reported in *Mayfair* that a maid who had stayed in the attic room went completely mad and later died in an asylum. However, it was an event, reportedly in 1884, that really cemented the supernatural reputation of the house when Sir Robert Warboys, a nobleman, decided to take up a challenge of staying in the haunted room.

Warboys heard of the haunting while at a tavern in the Holbrook district. Apparently, hot-headed and very single-minded, he dismissed the legend wholeheartedly. Warboys drinking colleagues, Lord Cholmondeley and John Benson, the owner of the house, disagreed with him, and challenged him to spend a night in the haunted room, either on the second floor or the fourth, depending on sources. Warboys, fuelled by alcohol and his overinflated ego, agreed to the challenge and took the bet.

Warboys then proceeded to the allegedly haunted house where he managed to convince the reluctant landlord to allow him to spend a night in the haunted room. However, before the landlord would allow him to do so, he specified that Warboys must be armed with a pistol and that at the first sign of anything strange he would pull a cord that was attached to a bell in the landlord's room below as a warning sign. Warboys ridiculed the notion but agreed to the terms.

According to the landlord, the spectre was a "man-ghost" with a face that was "white and flabby with a huge gaping mouth black as pitch." Others said that it was an animal-like creature with many legs and tentacles, and that it could have crawled out of the London sewers. Whatever the case, it was agreed by all that whatever it was, it was evil.

Warboys then entered the haunted room, closed the door and waited. The room was large and comfortably furnished with a double bed and armchairs. Two big windows overlooked the Square, and a fire was burning in the hearth.

Warboys, not expecting to sleep the night, lay on the bed apparently propped up by pillows.

At his side was a cocked and loaded pistol. The clock chimed midnight, and the landlord assumed that everything was still all right, however, sometime after midnight he was awoken by the urgent clanging of the bell in the haunted room. Leaping out of bed he heard a single gunshot and then silence.

He breathlessly scaled the stairs and opened the door, but it was too late. Warboys, previously sitting at the table when the landlord left him, was now cowered in the corner of the room, the still smoking pistol in his white-knuckles. For all intents and purposes it appeared as if he had died of fright. There were no signs of a struggle.

It was reported that Warboys' lips were peeled back from his clenched teeth in a grimace of horror and his eyes appeared to be literally bulging from his skull. In the wall opposite the body the landlord found a single bullet hole but nothing else. Whatever Warboys had fired at had not only scared him to death, but had also disappeared into thin air. Later, a coroner pronounced that he had in fact died of fright—he was literally scared to death.

Reportedly, only three years after the death of Sir Robert Warboys, the house became the site of another gruesome and unexplainable death. And although the story varies in minor detail, the major premise of the story remains the same.

In 1887, two sailors from the HMS *Penelope*, Robert Martin and Edward Blunden, had wasted their money on a night of drunken celebration at being on shore and, short of funds and a place to stay for the night, noticed a "To Let" sign on the then-abandoned Berkeley Square house. Seeing that no one was around, they broke into a basement window in search of somewhere to sleep for the night. The lower level of the house, however, was unpleasantly damp and rat infested, so they headed upstairs, finally settling down in the haunted room.

Blunden, upon entering the room, expressed some anxiety in that he thought he could feel some sort of presence. These fears were soon dismissed by his shipmate, and as both were drunk, they simply dismissed it as a normal feeling for such an old, dark, and decrepit house. Martin apparently propped open a window with his rifle and then built a small fire with bits of broken furniture and rotting floorboards. The two men then settled down on the floor to sleep.

According to legend, sometime after midnight Blunden awoke when he heard the door to the room creak. Slowly the door opened and a dim sliver of grey light began to creep across the wooden floor. Blunden was frozen in fear but managed to wake his shipmate, and the two men sat on the floor listening as a strange, moist, scraping sound slowly approached them. Martin was later to claim that it sounded as if something was being dragging across the floor, or worse, that something was dragging itself across the floor.

Details are vague, but it appears that the two men managed to snap out of their fear-induced paralysis and came face to face with the creature, whatever it was, which was blocking their only avenue of escape, the door. Blunden reached for his rifle, but the creature lunged at him and wrapped itself around his neck.

Panic stricken, Martin seized the opportunity to escape and ran from the house screaming for help. A passing policeman soon heard his screams and, although sceptical of the tale, decided to follow the agitated sailor back to the house to ascertain what was going on. According to the sketchy accounts, Martin and the officer ran up the stairs but found no sign of Blunden in the room. Martin grabbed the rifle and the two men searched the house for the missing man. However, there was no sign of him until they entered the damp, rat-infested basement where they found the bloodied corpse of the dead sailor. His body reportedly lay in a heap, with his head wrenched violently to the side. The officer reported that Blunden's eyes, similar to those of Warboys' three years previous, were wide open as if they had witnessed some unimaginable horror.

The tale has been recounted in many different guises over the years and indeed, even the dates are now somewhat debatable. It is believed that the most notable variation in the retelling is the description of the creature as a shadowy man-like figure with a deformed face and body that strangled Blunden with cold, misty-looking hands. Another discrepancy in the legend is that Blunden did not perish in the basement, but was impaled on a spike on a wrought iron fence that surrounded the house, suggesting that he had been thrown out of the open window, remembering that it had been propped open by the rifle. Whatever the case, there does seem to be some evidence for something strange happening in the house, however, what this is remains unknown.

Some have described the creature as being an amorphous being, formless and slimy, which makes a gruesome sloppy, sliding noise when it moves. Others have suggested that it is a dark, shapeless, spectral form that attacks its victims with clawed feet and sharp, bird-like talons. Still others have described it as a ghostly mist-like form that moves silently across the room towards its intended victim. Oddly enough, there is a school of thought that it has tentacles and was somewhat similar to an octopus.

Bizarrely, the octopus theory, as unlikely as it is, has led some paranormal and cryptozoological researchers to suggest that the creature may actually be some kind of mutated freshwater octopus, or at least, an unknown, amphibious, marine animal that had somehow managed to migrate from the Thames into London's vast subterranean sewer system, and from there had somehow managed to enter the house at 50 Berkeley Square. Having said that, London sewers at this time were hardly conducive to living beings, apart from rats, although the presence of rats would have provided a ready food source for such a creature.

Personally, I lean towards the supernatural rather than bizarre and speculative stories of mutated freshwater octopi and indeed, in the 1920s, ghost hunter Harry Price revealed that he possessed a great deal of information regarding the house, including an 1840 account of bizarre noises, bells, loud footsteps, and heavy dragging sounds coming from the house. He also came across an 1870 article published in the magazine *Notes and Queries* which stated: "The mystery of Berkeley Square still remains a mystery. The story of the haunted house in Mayfair can be recapitulated in a few words; the house contains at least one room of which the atmosphere is supernaturally fatal to body and mind. A girl saw, heard and felt such horror in it that she went mad, and never recovered sanity enough to tell how or why."

The article continued, "A gentleman, a disbeliever in ghosts, dared to sleep in number 50 and was found a corpse in the middle of the floor after frantically ringing for help in vain. Rumour suggests other cases of the same kind, all ending in death, madness, or both as a result of sleeping, or trying to sleep in that room. The very party walls of the house, when touched, are found saturated with electric horror. It is uninhabited save by an elderly man and his wife who act as caretakers; but even these have no access to the room. This is kept locked, the key being in the hands of a mysterious and seemingly nameless person who comes to the house once every six months, locks up the elderly couple in the basement, and then unlocks the room and occupies himself in it for hours."

Price also noted that, although the house was located on a prime piece of real estate in one of London's most desirable districts, it appeared to remain unoccupied for large periods of time. Price's personal conclusion was that the events and phenomena witnessed in the house were due in the main to, "a particularly nasty poltergeist" that, "had been active at number 50 in the 1840s." He also noted that he doubted that the thing was still at large.

As mentioned, the house is now the premises of an antique book shop, and if one is to believe local reports, nothing supernatural or paranormal has ever happened. But if number 50 is no longer haunted by, well, whatever it was, then it appears that number 53 may have taken up the baton.

During the eighteenth century, it is alleged that a middle-aged man lived at number 53 Berkeley Square with his daughter, apparently an extremely attractive woman. After a few years she eloped, but promised her father that she would return after her wedding. The father waited patiently for her to return, but she was never seen or heard from again, and he eventually died of a broken heart.

Recently, on a moonlit night, the figure of a man, wearing a period-style satin coat and wig with lace ruffles at his neck and wrists, has been seen looking out of the first-floor window of number 53. Witnesses have stated that he appears overwhelmingly sad with a despairing look on his face.

Besides numbers 50 and 53 Berkeley Square, there is another legend of a haunting in Berkeley Square as well. Apparently, a Colonel Kearsey was visiting the unnamed house and on arrival was ushered into a sitting room to await his hostess. In the light of the brightly burning fire he slowly became aware of a woman wearing a long dress and wide-brimmed hat who was sitting in an armchair and apparently crying. Perplexed, as he hadn't noticed her when he walked in, he stood up to lend whatever assistance he could and was astonished when she rose from the chair, walked straight at him, and then vanished.

When he mentioned this alarming incident to his hostess she informed him that the children of the house often heard the sound of a woman crying in that room and that a previous tenant had told her that a woman who had lived an unhappy life had once lived at the house.

But London, for all its brash modern reputation, is an ancient place and stories of the extraordinary and paranormal are commonplace. Steeped in history and legend, the city has the dubious reputation of being the most haunted capital city in the world. Ancient medieval streets wind their way past back alleys and yards and buildings and the River Thames flows on by as it has for countless centuries. At night, when the crowds have receded and a thin mist or fog descends upon the city, it is easy to believe that ghosts and ghouls occupy the narrow streets, alleyways, theatres, churches, and old historic buildings.

From the Underground to the frightening haunts of Jack the Ripper, it would seem that no section of the city is without a grisly secret or a haunting of some type. To some the city is simply an overpopulated conglomerate of humanity's mistakes with a hedonistic weakness for wealth and possessions. However, to others it is a treasure trove of history, culture, myth, and legend, for as much the countryside of England, Scotland, Wales, and Ireland evokes images of imps, fairies, goblins, ghosts, and other creatures of the supernatural, so does this ancient city.

A case in point is the Tower of London, reputedly the most haunted building in England and in fact, so haunted that it would appear that it could contain more ghosts per square metre than anywhere else in the country. Located on the banks of the Thames in the London we have already read of its gory and grisly past and of its amazing array of ghostly historical figures from all ages.

As we have also seen, other ghosts of the Tower include those of Thomas à Becket, Henry VI, the tragic Guy Fawkes, and Sir Walter Raleigh. The ghost of Sir Walter Raleigh is said to wander around the Tower grounds just as he did when he was imprisoned there. In 1983, a Yeoman Guard on duty in the Bloody Tower reported seeing his ghost and a year or so later he was again seen in the same area by a different guard. And like the Hanging Judge, George Jeffreys, Raleigh, who was executed in 1618 at Whitehall, seems to appear in multiple places. Likewise, Thomas à Becket, who was murdered in 1170 at Canterbury Cathedral, also appears at the Tower, as well as at the place of his death.

Sadly, when I visited the Tower I witnessed no ghosts or supernatural phenomena of any kind. However, the wealth of history and culture was quite awe-inspiring and the ancient halls and corridors seemed to reek of history and tragedy in equal measures.

But as we have previously discussed the Tower of London in some depth in a previous chapter we shall move on from the infamous landmark and its great assortment of ghosts to others that appear in all sorts of garbs right across the city. Not surprisingly many of these stories share the same characteristics as each other and the claustrophobic London Underground is no different.

From ghostly figures in the Tower of London to the venerable and loved London Underground with its 140-year history and over 400 kilometres of track, it would appear that ghosts don't seem to care where they appear nor who they appear to. The Tube may seem impersonal, dark, bland, and soulless, but given that its tunnels pass through or under most of London's great historic sites, it would seem no surprise that it too has its share of ghostly inhabitants.

When being built, workmen often came across seventeenth-century plaque pits, a legacy of bubonic plaque outbreaks. Due to the fear of infection, the pits, mass burial sites, were dug deeply into the ground, and over time records of their whereabouts and even existence were lost. In some cases no records were kept, and the souls of those horrifically infected dead remained unknown and unremembered tens of metres below the bustling surface of the modern city. As recently as the late 1960s the Victoria Line ran straight into a forgotten plaque pit at Green Park.

At Farringdon Station the ghost of a murdered thirteen-year-old girl called Annie has been seen, and many people over the years have reported hearing her ear-piercing, horrendous screams. At Hyde Park Station, in 1978, a station supervisor closed the deserted station for the night and shut down the escalators before returning to his office. He also removed electrical breakers so that the escalators were rendered completely inoperable. At about 2:30 a.m., strange noises were heard in the station, and the supervisor and a colleague went to investigate only to find the escalators working. The men quickly shut them down again before going back to the office to ponder what had happened. While in the office one of the men witnessed a disembodied head float through the wall and stare at him. The man reportedly left, never to work on the Underground again.

At the southern end of the London Road Depot on the Bakerloo Line there are two tunnels. One exits onto the line between Lambeth North and Elephant and Castle stations, and the other is a dead-end designed to stop runaway trains. And behind this wall at the end of the dead-end tunnel is a plague pit, so it is not surprising that people have reported strange poltergeist-like phenomena in this region of the tunnels.

But it is not just the plague pits that give the Underground its reputation for ghosts as it has seen its own share of tragedy. Many people have died on the network from natural causes to murders to suicides. Others have died whilst maintaining the lines, while train crashes, derailments, and fires have all claimed lives. Even as recent as July 2007, Islamic extremists cruelly murdered dozens of innocent commuters by detonating bombs to deadly effect.

At Ickenham Station the ghost of a young woman who fell onto the tracks and was electrocuted is often reported. She is said to wear a bright red scarf and waves before vanishing. The Jubilee Line is also said to be haunted by phantom monks, a result of the line being dug through the grounds of several old monasteries, something that led to the re-internment of over 600 graves.

On the Bakerloo Line passengers have reported seeing the reflection in the carriage window of someone sitting next to them but upon turning to see who they are, have found the seat empty. The British Museum Station is bizarrely said to be haunted by the spirit of a long dead Egyptian Princess whose mummified remains are on view in the museum itself, while Covent Garden is haunted by the ghost of a long-dead English actor by the name of William Terriss. Terriss, who was stabbed to death by another actor, said to an actress as he lay dying, that he would return. In 1955, a startled Underground employee who saw his ghost later identified him from a photograph. Covent Garden, in comparison, is relatively quiet, although staff members regularly report strange noises and disembodied footsteps.

At Beacontree Station in 1992 it was reported that a station employee who was working on his own, heard the door to his office rattle several times. Slightly anxious, he began to climb some stairs to find a colleague but felt as if he was being watched. Turning around, he saw a woman with long blond hair standing behind him. However, what really unnerved the man was that she had no face, or at least nothing discernible that could be taken for a face. After talking to other employees he found that he was not the only person to have seen this terrifying apparition.

Interestingly, ghosts and like apparitions are often reported as having no face or facial features. Quite bizarrely the ghost of Anne Boleyn, although often seen without her head, has likewise been reported having a head but lacking facial features. Apparently, in 1882, a Captain of the Guard saw a light burning in the locked Chapel Royal and when he went to investigate witnessed a figure who he thought was Anne leading a slow, stately procession of knights and ladies in old but special clothing. Oddly, although she appeared to have a head in this case, her face was averted. The complete party then disappeared from view, leaving a slightly shaken and puzzled witness.

In this case, Anne's face was said to be averted, or at least unseen, which corresponds with numerous other ghostly reports from all over the world of supernatural figures with no faces. Why so many ghostly figures are reported as having no face or, at least, very blurred features is a complete mystery.

But as we have already explored, the ghost of Anne Boleyn and her many manifestations around the countryside, we shall continue looking at the Underground and its quite amazing number of reported ghostly encounters. In 1981, a station master working alone at Bethnal Green Station late at night heard the soft sounds of children crying. Distressed and thinking that somehow a group of school children had been trapped somehow underground, he went to investigate. As he did the cries grew louder and were soon joined by the screams of women. Perplexed and somewhat frightened, he left the station and reported it to superiors. Later, it was found that 173 died in the station in a single accident during World War II, most being women and children.

Just aside from ghostly apparitions that seem to regularly appear on or in the Underground complex, legend has it that the final resting place of Boadicea, the warrior queen who fought against the Romans, is under Platform 10 at King's Cross Station. Having said that, it is also widely thought that a barrow in Garboldisham Heath, Norfolk could also be her grave. Of course, as we have seen, that her ghost has been reported at King's Cross Station does in no way mean that she died there or that she is buried there.

At Channelsea Depot, in Stratford, it was reported that a former British Rail employee described seeing a tall man wearing a cape and top hat. Apparently, he had a horrific grin and a mouth full of white teeth. Upon being seen he immediately vanished, leaving the witness feeling apprehensive and uneasy. A few months later, in the same area, it was reported that a witness felt a strong tug at her bag as if someone was trying to steal it from her. When she spun around to confront whoever it was there was no one in sight.

A most interesting case involving the Underground is at Bank Station on the Central Line where a female figure has often been seen. Legend states that she had a brother who worked there in an office and who was executed for forgery. After his death she would return each day in hope of meeting him. She is reported as wearing black clothes and is known colloquially as the "Black Nun." In one story a worker at the station mistook her for an intruder and chased her down a corridor in the early hours of one morning; however, she vanished around a corner. In addition, other employees have reported something knocking on the inside of an empty lift door long after closing time and, thinking that someone has accidentally been trapped, have found no one there. There is also a school of thought that this ghost is the same one that haunts, of all places, the Bank of England.

Sadly, in all my time on the Underground I experienced nothing more than any other commuter. And yet, sometimes late at night when I found myself alone at a station waiting for a train to arrive, I would feel as if unseen eyes were watching me from the shadow of the arches and tunnels. There is no doubt that the Underground, when free of the hustle and bustle of commuter crowds, does have an eerie feeling. And when one is sitting alone on a train staring out the black window into the nothingness of the dark depths, one can believe that the place is haunted. Indeed, I don't think that anyone could pay me enough to walk alone down one of the many lonely tunnels that crisscross beneath the ancient London streets.

Aside from the Underground and its ghosts, one of the most delightful aspects of ghost hunting and investigation in a place like London, or anywhere in the British Isles, is the opportunity to enjoy a pint or two in a historic pub. And, as visiting old pubs and drinking pints of beer have always been a favourite pastime of mine, London is definitely the place to be.

The Grenadier is a tiny pub in Belgravia in central London and has long enjoyed a reputation as one of the most haunted pubs in London. Originally built in 1720 as the officers' mess for the 1st Regiment of Foot Guards, it was opened to the public in 1818. On one of its walls newspapers, now yellowed with time, tell of the pubs haunted history. Although once an officers' mess, the basement was used as a drinking and gambling den for enlisted soldiers and it was here that legend suggests that a young soldier, caught cheating at cards, was savagely beaten by his fellow soldiers, so much that he later died of his injuries.

Although the year of his death is unknown, it is believed that he died in the month of September, and it is in this month that the pub seems to experience the majority of its supernatural occurrences. This phenomenon ranges from objects disappearing or mysteriously being moved, various unexplained raps and tapping, footsteps pacing anxiously around empty rooms, inexplicable cold spots that seem to move around various rooms, low moaning sighs from disembodied voices, and even the chilling sight of a solemn, silent spectre that moves slowly across the low ceilinged rooms.

It has been reported that on one occasion a Chief Superintendent from New Scotland Yard was enjoying a drink in the pub when wisps of smoke began to waft around him. Wondering where the smoke had come from he reached out to brush it away only to cry out in pain and pull his hand back rapidly as if burnt.

But it's not just comfortable pubs that help London retain its status as one of the world's most haunted cities. And, as we have seen, there appears to be a ghostly link between the Underground and the Bank of England.

On 2 November 1811, Philip Whitehead, who was described as a man of genteel appearance and who had been employed in the cashiers office at the Bank of England, was found guilty of forgery at the Old Bailey and was sentenced to hang.

News of his crime and execution was, for some reason, kept from his devoted sister, Sarah Whitehead who remained blissfully aware of anything amiss. However, one day Sarah turned up to the Bank of England to ask about her brother when an unthinking clerk told her of his crime and subsequent death. The shock of this was too much for the woman, and she lost her mind. From that day on she would unceasingly turn up at the bank every day to enquire about her brother, unable to fathom that he was dead and no longer worked there. During this time she took to wearing mourning garb, a long black dress with a black veil that obscured her face. As a result onlookers began to refer to her as "The Black Nun," although it is said that the city merchants and traders took pity on her and made sure that she was never short of financial assistance.

Over time her madness increased until she became convinced that the bank was secretly hiding a small fortune of her money. As such she became somewhat exasperating and frequently insulted bankers and merchants alike.

Legend has it that on one occasion Baron Rothschild was emerging from the stock exchange when Sarah accosted him calling him a villain and a robber. To placate the clearly mad woman he gave her some money while telling her to leave, which she did.

By 1818, however, the bank workers, merchants, and customers had grown tired of her daily insults and disturbances, and so gave her a sum of money on condition she agreed never to return again. In a rare flash of clarity and understanding she took the money and never returned. However, that is, not in her earthly life. Since her death her ghostly figure has been seen in the bank on numerous instances and on more than a few occasions her ghostly figure has surprised people on Threadneedle Street by appearing as a forlorn figure in front of them and sadly asking if they know the whereabouts of her brother.

And of course, no account about haunted London would be complete without mention of Jack the Ripper and his victims.

The Jack the Ripper story is one that really needs little introduction except to say that between August and November 1888, the Whitechapel area of London was the scene of five brutal murders with the killer dubbed Jack the Ripper. All the women murdered were prostitutes except for one, Elizabeth Stride, and all were horribly mutilated.

The first murder took place on 31 August when Mary Ann Nicholls was brutally slain. This was soon followed up on 8 September when Annie Chapman was also killed. Elizabeth Stride and Catherine Eddoweson were murdered on 30 September and Mary Jane Kelly on 9 November. These five vicious murders are generally believed to be the only ones committed by the felon, although Martha Tabram, who was stabbed to death on 6 August 1888 is considered by some to be the first victim.

Although there has been much speculation as to the identity of the killer, Jack the Ripper was never caught and he is not thought to have killed again after November 1888. As to who he was is still speculation with various theories suggesting that he may have been a doctor or butcher or even the grandson of Queen Victoria and Prince Albert.

Local tradition suggests that if one stands on Westminster Bridge on 31 December, as the first Chimes of Big Ben usher in the New Year, a shadowy figure will suddenly appear on a parapet before leaping into the cold and murky waters of the Thames. Legend maintains that this is the spot and time when, in 1888, Jack the Ripper killed himself by plunging into the river. Interestingly, at the same spot it is said that, on misty autumn mornings, a ghostly barge drifts towards the bridge and passes beneath it but vanishes before reaching the other side.

Mitre Square is nothing like it was in Victorian days, except maybe for the cobblestones at your feet. It is now surrounded by modern office blocks and bordered on its south side by the Sir John Cass Foundation School. It is also the site, in the south-western corner, of the murder of Catherine Eddowes, the fourth victim of the Ripper. Local legend maintains that her ghost appears on the anniversary of her death, a tragic, mutilated figure lying crumpled and bloody on the ground.

The mutilated body of the Ripper's second victim, Annie Chapman, was found at around 6:00 a.m. on 8 September 1888 at 29 Hanbury Street. But rather than a Victorian era building, the north side of Hanbury Street is now covered by buildings that were formerly the Truman Brewery. It had been suggested by some that in the days of the brewery's operation, a strange chill used to drift through the boardroom on the anniversary of her murder and, occasionally, the ghost of a woman was seen standing by the wall of a storeroom, the exact spot where she was killed.

This area of London is steeped in Jack the Ripper legends, and as I walk through the Old Spitalfields Market, I am reminded that not far from here is another of the Ripper's haunts, the Ten Bells Pub on the corner of Commercial and Fournier Streets in the East End.

The Ten Bells Pub will be forever linked with the legend of Jack the Ripper, and as I cross the street and dodge a bicycle rack I realise that the pub's cream and mocha-coloured exterior and the surrounding buildings have hardly changed since those frightening days of 1888. Once inside I order a pint and sit on a stool at the bar. It is quiet at this time of the day although a lunchtime crowd seems not far away. On the walls are posters and information about the Ripper and worn sofas add to the ambience of the place. It is comfortable and inviting and hardly evokes images of the gruesome Victorian murders, but then again, this is an old pub and as such it could hardly not be haunted.

In the late 1990s, staff that had bedrooms on the upper floors of the building often complained of uneasy encounters with a ghostly old man dressed in Victorian clothing. They reported that they would wake in the night with a feeling of unease and upon turning over would find the ghostly figure of the man lying next them. However, as soon as they cried out, the phantom would disappear. Staff with no prior knowledge of the ghost often reported seeing him and their descriptions were generally the same.

In June 2000, however, a new landlord, while clearing out the cellar, found an old metal box with a number of personal effects in it. These belonged to a man by the name of George Roberts and dated from the early 1900s. Intriguingly, with the items was a brown leather wallet, inside of which was a press clipping which talked of him being murdered with an axe in a Swansea Cinema. Further research soon revealed that a man named George Roberts had been the landlord of the pub in the late nineteenth and early twentieth centuries. It is thought that the ghostly figure that haunts the upstairs rooms is in fact George Roberts.

Other tenants have reported footsteps and faint laughter, even when the pub is empty while others have reported being shoved in the back while walking down the stairs.

A psychic once examined the pub and, coming to the top floor, paused outside one of the rooms and refused to go any further, suggesting that she could sense that something terrible had happened in the room, and that it involved the death of a baby. A few years later a leading researcher and expert on Jack the Ripper was being shown around the pub and managed to get access to the roof space. There she noticed some material embedded in the floor behind a water tank which turned out to be a sack tied at the top. Upon opening it she found it contained a mouldy set of Victorian baby clothes that appeared to have been slashed with a knife. The tank was directly over the room that the psychic had previously refused to enter.

Having said this, the pub is not unknown for having a liking for black humour as, during the 1970s and 1980s, the pub was renamed the Jack the Ripper and sold a dark red ale called "Ripper Tipple." Probably for the best, the brewery decided to return the pub to its original name in 1989.

But if the ghost of Jack the Ripper doesn't actually haunt the Ten Bells then where can we find evidence of his supernatural existence apart from at Westminster Bridge? Interestingly enough, this evidence can be found in a most unlikely place, the London Dungeon, which at time of writing was on Tooley Street near London Bridge Hospital.

The London Dungeon, as we have seen, is essentially a historical-based theme park and was built under some of the existing arches of the London and Greenwich Railway line. And as we have also seen, it appears to be an extremely haunted place for reasons previously explored. It was also where I had a strange encounter of my own, but it is not this encounter that concerns us in this case as in the dark tunnels and corridors a tall male figure dressed completely in black has been witnessed by staff and visitors alike. It has been speculated that this grim, frightening figure is in fact the ghost of Jack the Ripper, something that the television program *Most Haunted* has also speculated.

But not all ghosts in this ancient city are the result of human suffering, misery, and death. Indeed, at Pond Square, Highgate, a ghostly chicken is occasionally said to make itself known to passersby.

Although the water source from which its name derives no longer exists, being filled in, in 1864, Pond Square retains a charming and pleasant atmosphere. Huge, mature plane trees cast long shadows across the gravel walks, and quaint Victorian houses gaze serenely across the small park-like area. Apart from this, it is the place where one may be lucky enough to have an encounter with one of London's most unusual ghosts.

Sir Francis Bacon, politician, statesman, writer, and philosopher was also a highly inquisitive man. He was one of the first people to suggest that refrigeration might be used as a means of preserving meat. Subsequently, one exceptionally cold morning in January 1626, Bacon and a good friend decided to test his theory by purchasing a chicken from a woman on Highgate Hill and, after slaughtering and plucking it, stuffed its carcass with snow.

In an amazingly ironic twist, Bacon suffered from an extreme chill while conducting his experiment and immediately fell ill. As he was too sick to move to his own lodgings, he was taken to nearby Arundel House and placed in a bed where he died a short time afterwards of pneumonia, bringing him the distinction of being a part of a rare historical group of scientists who were killed by their own experiments.

A short poem by Pip Wilson describes the untimely death as well as anyone could:

> *Against cold meats was he insured?*
> *For frozen chickens he procured—*
> *brought on the illness he endured,*
> *and never was this Bacon cured.*

But it is not the ghost of Sir Francis Bacon that interests us in this case, even though his spirit is said to haunt the Gatehouse Pub in Hampstead Lane, as, since his death and the death of the chicken, there have been numerous reports of a ghostly white bird, similar to a plucked chicken, that appears from nowhere to race round the square flapping its wings or to sit ominously perched on the lower branches of nearby trees.

In 1943, a Mr. Terence Long was crossing Pond Square late at night when he suddenly heard the sound of horse hooves and the low rumble of carriage wheels. Perplexed he looked around only to be shocked by the appearance of the ghostly chicken, which shrieked and proceeded to race frantically around before vanishing as quickly as it appeared.

During the Second World War, air raid wardens patrolling the Highgate area often reported seeing the ghostly chicken and one man actually attempted to catch it for dinner. However, the chicken simply disappeared by running into, and *through,* a brick wall.

Then in the 1960s, a motorist was left stranded when his car broke down, only to find that he was subject to the whims of the ghostly chicken who once again ran around hysterically before disappearing. In the 1970s, an amorous couple where enjoying each other's company when it interrupted their embrace by dropping suddenly from above and landing next to them.

In recent years, it must be said that sightings of the ghostly chicken have waned. Is it possible that this foul fowl has finally given up its nocturnal wanderings? And if it has, then what can we make of reports of other, sometimes frightening, ghostly animals?

CHAPTER 12

†

Black Dogs and Other Spectral Animals

Of all ghosts, the ghosts of our old loves are the worst.

—Sir Arthur Conan Doyle

The road that runs between Alfriston in Sussex and Seaford is officially called Alfriston Road, although locals refer to it as The White Way, a legacy of the chalky ground in which the road has been cut. It is associated with legends of fairies but is also reputed to be haunted by the ghost of a white dog belonging to a local lord who was murdered by robbers. The dog is said to appear on Midsummer's Eve every seven years and brings bad luck to those who see it, including accidents and death, and a local song commemorates the event.

> *When evening closes in with shadows grey,*
> *and ghostly vapours overhang White Way,*
> *and the crescent moon hangs gloomy in the west,*
> *'tis then the spirit of young Chowne can't rest,*
> *but walks abroad with melancholy stride,*
> *adown the path that skirts the chalk hill-side.*

There is solid evidence of prehistoric occupation in the area with several Neolithic long barrows discovered on the surrounding downs. One of them, to the west, is the fairly well preserved Long Burgh and is not far away from the quaint medieval town of Alfriston. In Saxon times the village was recorded as *Aelfrictun*, the town of Alfric, and the *Domesday Book* records the town as *Elfricesh-tun*. It is an old village and quite picturesque and welcoming.

Kirsten and I drive into Alfriston after spending the day exploring the magnificent Arundel Castle, itself renowned for numerous ghosts and hauntings. This historically important little town is our chosen place of accommodation for the night and it certainly does not disappoint. We drive past the Star Inn, built in 1345 as a religious hostel and used to accommodate monks and pilgrims en route from Battle Abbey to the shrine of St. Richard at Chichester Cathedral. Later converted to an inn in the sixteenth century, it is intimately connected to smugglers and smuggler gangs, who used it as a base for their nefarious activities. One of the smuggler leaders was caught, convicted, and transported to Australia in 1830. The inn is reputed to be haunted with some servants reportedly refusing to stay after hours and the owner and her daughter having seen a ghostly woman dressed in a modern-looking long gown.

Not far from the Star Inn is the Smugglers Inne. It is an old, Tudor-era building, and a recent archaeological dig in the garden at the rear of the building revealed evidence of long occupation of the site including signs of smuggling, animal butchery, and Neolithic activity. It is also believed to be haunted; however, it is the George Inn where we are staying.

The George Inn, where we are to stay the night, is believed to be over 500 years old, and upon first viewing one can see why. It is a wonderfully charming timber frame building that sits along a thin street in the heart of Alfriston. Surprisingly for such an ancient building it does not appear haunted in any way. However, this is immaterial as one is immediately at ease amongst the exposed wooden beams, comfortable old lounges, and rickety old bar, and more to the point, it is simply a gateway for us to explore Kent and other haunted or unusual sites in the area. And with that in mind I retire to the lounge with a pint of ale and sit in front of a roaring fire whilst examining a book of folklore from the area.

The next morning is crisp and cool and Kirst and I find ourselves standing on the edge of a rough tarred lane some five miles from Alfriston. The sun is still low on the horizon, and a refreshing breeze is blowing in from the south. In front of us, less than 100 metres away, is the truly breathtaking Long Man of Wilmington, a sixty-nine-metre-tall chalk figure cut into the steep grassy slope of Windover Hill.

A scheduled ancient monument, the origins of this wonder are unknown, although archaeological work suggests that it could date from the sixteenth or seventeenth century. However, local legend says differently and suggests that it is the falling place of a giant who was accidentally slain in a battle with another giant.

However, it is not slain giants that we have come to see and we move on through the lush green, rolling countryside. This is a place of legend, myth, and folklore, and it is said that fairies used to live in the area just to the north east of Alfriston at a place called Burlough Castle, a natural feature on the River Cuckmere. Although called a "castle," the top has been ploughed so often that any remnants of a medieval fort have long disappeared.

There is, however, an old-world folklore story about two men who were ploughing the area when they heard a fairy speak to them from under the ground. The fairy explained that he had been baking and had broken his peel, a shovel-like tool used by bakers to slide loaves of bread into and out of an oven. One of the men took pity on the fairy and mended the broken peel and was later rewarded with some fairy beer. The other man, who refused to believe in fairies, died not long after the encounter.

And it is in this area that ghostly dogs have been reported, and if one were to walk these lonely roads late at night, one would not be surprised to find that they were being accompanied by a huge, silent, black devil dog.

Sussex itself has numerous legends involving ghostly Black Dogs with the common name for these paranormal creatures being "Wish Hounds" or "Witch Hounds." One such sighting was of a ghostly black dog in Harewick Bottom, a small valley in the South Downs just south-east of Jevington. In this case the dog appeared to a person, then simply vanished into thin air.

Windover Hill, above the Long Man of Wilmington, is another place that seems to have a glut of Black Dog sightings, and it seems that they often appear near lonely roads or Neolithic barrows. The area of the South Downs is where most of the Black Dog sightings seem to be concentrated.

Alfriston itself has two ghostly dogs, though only one of them black. The ghostly Black Dog in this small town has been seen several times on the full moon running from the Downs through Town Fields where it leaps a flint wall at the side of the road before running away. The second dog, a spectral white dog, is said to be a harbinger of bad luck and doom.

A ghostly Black Dog, somewhat like a Labrador, has been seen walking along the main road that runs in an east-westerly direction to the south of Lewes and Mount Caburn. It also disappears into thin air while in a valley to the east of Philpots Promontory Camp, a ghostly Black Dog is said to wander. Poachers in the area speak in hushed tones about this creature and try not to be out at night in its territory.

Just south-east of Ditchling is Blackdog Hill, which is haunted by the ghost of a headless Black Dog. Interestingly, the path that runs diagonally over the hill points directly towards Westmeston Church and is believed to be remains of an old "Corpse Way" or "Coffin Road," a path along which deceased persons were taken to be buried. This dog has been seen on the road from Ditchling to Westmeston and is believed to be a protector of the souls of the dead.

Not far from Blackdog Hill is Ditchling Beacon Hill Fort where, in 1933, a Wild Hunt was reported to have been heard flying overhead with the sound of horse hooves and yapping dogs. The Wild Hunt, as we have previously seen, is an ancient folk myth prevalent across Europe that tells of a ghostly group of huntsmen madly bounding across the skies in hunt. This same area is said to be periodically visited by a ghostly army, which passes over the area in late May and leaves a memorably pungent smell as it passes.

But the lonely forests and fields of East Sussex and Kent are not the only places where ghost dogs have been reported. All across England these dark, fire-eyed harbingers of doom have been reported, from Cornwall to Scotland, and almost everywhere in between.

Stories of phantom dogs in Britain are common and almost every county has its own variation, from the Yeth Hound of Devon, the Black Shuck of East Anglia, or the Barghest of Yorkshire, which bizarrely is said to also appear on occasions as a ghost or an elf.

Phantom dogs vary in appearance from region to region; however, it is not unusual for them to be described as large to huge, with blazing red eyes and a shaggy coat. Phantom dogs are not always black as we have seen in the case of the dog near Alfriston, and the ghost dog that is supposed to haunt the area around Cawthorpe and Haugham in Lincolnshire is also said to be white. The Cu Sith, the traditional fairy/ghost dog of Scotland, is dark green in colour with a shaggy tail.

Legend has it that Black Dogs are usually associated with specific locations such as old roads, lanes, ancient places, forest tracks, crossroads, old church yards, and prehistoric sites. And this is so in the case of the Black Dog that haunts the rough gravel lane to Woodchester Mansion in Gloucestershire, another place with a serious reputation for being haunted.

In medieval times crossroads were often where gallows were sited, and as such were seen as places of evil where the spirits of the dead wandered aimlessly attempting to find a way back to their previous earthly abode. It is not surprisingly then that crossroads and gallows sites are places where Black Dogs are often sighted.

Tring in Hertfordshire is just one such place as, in 1751, an old woman was unjustly drowned for allegedly practicing witchcraft, and a local chimney sweep was held responsible for the death. Subsequently, he was hanged and gibbeted, and many a sighting of a large shaggy dog with flaming eyes and long teeth has since been attributed to his death.

Many of these places haunted by Black Dogs are associated with local supernatural tales and superstitions and appear to be a point between worlds— that is the real and tangible world in which we live, and the less tangible world of the supernatural or paranormal. Strangely, many Black Dog haunts are said to be on ley lines, which we have seen are alignments of geographical places such as ancient monuments and megaliths, natural features, and waterscapes, which suggests that the apparitions represent, or use some sort of natural earth energy to exist.

If one is to look at various maps, one will find many a lane or road named after a phantom hound, such as Black Dog Walk in Crawley, West Sussex; Black Dog Way in Gloucester; Black Dog Copse near Haslemere, just south of the Surrey border; and a place named as Black Dog near Horsted Keynes.

In most local traditions the sighting of a Black Dog is regarded as an omen of death or doom, and this is especially so when seen in an ancient churchyard. On the morning of Sunday the 4th of August 1577, in Bungay in Suffolk, as the violent storm raged overhead, the parishioners were suddenly confronted with the sight of a Black Dog, which appeared in the church during a service. Two people died instantly when it ran past them, and another was severely burnt. Today, a weather vane in the town depicts a black dog and a flash of lightning.

Meanwhile, in Blythburgh, only ten kilometres away, another Black Dog appeared in the parish church and left odd scorch marks on the front door as well as killing three people, presumably by scaring them to death. Of course, it has been suggested that these tales have been misinterpreted over the years and that the people were simply struck down by lightning, possibly a form of ball lightning, which would explain the scorch marks. Having said that, a large black dog and a glowing ball of light the size of a soccer ball are not really similar in anyway.

In the seventeenth century, Richard Cabell, a local squire at Buckfastleigh, reputedly sold his soul to the devil. Cabell was described as being a cruel man with a passion for hunting and blood sports and was also rumoured to have murdered his wife. When he died in 1677, he was interred, but on the night of his interment a phantom pack of hounds came loping across the moor to howl at his tomb. From that night on it is said that on the anniversary of his death he can be seen leading the phantom pack across the moor.

Local legend also tells of how the ghostly hounds could be found around his grave howling and yelping, and the villagers, quite rightly concerned about these devilish entities, constructed a building around the tomb, hopefully to allow Cabell's soul to rest in peace. Then, just to be sure, they placed a huge slab of rock on top of the grave. With this the sightings of the ghostly Cabell and his hellish pack of hounds apparently ceased.

However, it would be incorrect to say that all ghost dogs are part of the devil's minions as Augustus Hare, who once wrote an article in relation to a vampire at Croglin Grove in Cumbria, recalls a tale in his book *In My Solitary Life* about a man called Greenwood from Swancliffe who had to ride through a wood in darkness for a mile to reach his destination. Upon entering the woods he became aware of a huge black dog that pattered alongside him until he emerged from the trees, where it promptly and mysteriously disappeared.

On the return journey he was again surprised when the dog reappeared and walked alongside him until he had reached the safety of the road. Again the mysterious ghostly dog disappeared. It emerged some years later that two prisoners who, about to be hanged, confessed that they were going to rob and murder Greenwood that night in the wood but that the presence of a large black dog had stopped them.

In summary, it appears that the phenomena of phantom and black dogs is a multifaceted blend of folklore, alleged sightings, and local superstition, which has its roots in the distant past, so distant that it is now impossible to really make any judgement upon the veracity of sightings. As such, there are probably innumerable different explanations for modern-day sightings, and the phantom Black Dog has become a powerful standard, now well ensconced into modern stories such as the *Hound of the Baskervilles* by Arthur Conan Doyle.

But Black Devil Dogs are not the only ghostly creatures that haunt these isles as is evident from a strange story that originates from the Mendips Hills, a range of limestone hills to the south of Bristol and Bath in Somerset that run east to west between Weston-Super-Mare and Frome overlooking the Somerset Levels to the south and the Avon Valley to the north.

Whether or not this story qualifies as a ghost tale or a haunting is questionable; however, there is no doubt that it is exceptionally strange and has a particular paranormal angle. The story is based in the Mendips Hills at a place called Charterhouse, once a small mining community, including fifty or so houses, a pub, a church, and a school, which is now owned by the Somerset County Council as an educational establishment for outdoor pursuits. It has been renovated to include conference rooms and accommodation with the headmistress' former premises now offices and the upstairs turned into two bedrooms, one a sick bay for students and the other a staff bedroom.

The lead and silver mines at Charterhouse were first operated by the Romans although human habitation in the area goes back as far as the Bronze Age and evidence of this can be seen in a number of Neolithic cave burials in the area. By the start of the nineteenth century, the silver was long gone and only lead was mined in the area. However, in the smelting process it was noticed that much of the lead was actually lost, carried away in the fumes and smoke. To ensure that lead was not lost in this process, a system of horizontal chimneys were constructed so that, as the smoke passed through, the lead would be deposited in the ash. Young orphan boys would then climb into the chimneys and scrape out the lead, and in time, this contributed to their early deaths from lung disease and neurological complaints.

Some believe the ghosts of these children still haunt the old lead mining areas, and in 1982, Richard Gardner, a teacher at Haygrove School in Bridgewater, experienced a ghostly encounter in an isolated area some five miles from a village when he and some of his students distinctly heard children laughing and singing. No explanation for the voices has ever been found, except that maybe these were the voices of those tragically poisoned children who once worked the mines.

But it is not this that interests us as the warden of the Charterhouse Centre, an ex-Royal Marine called Terry, had an even more perplexing and terrifying encounter while staying at the centre. Terry was described as being a man not prone to fantasy or hyperbole and having excellent leadership qualities as well as being tough and well disciplined—exactly what one would expect of a Royal Marine. It has also been suggested that he was very reluctant to tell his tale, given the odd circumstances.

The Charterhouse Centre, as well as being an educational institute, is also used by the Mendips Cave Rescue Team as a store for their equipment. Terry was alone at the centre one night cleaning and checking cave rescue gear, and knowing he had a lot of work to do, he phoned his wife to tell her that he would stay overnight in the centre.

At about 10:00 p.m., he decided to finish his work. He recalled that he made a bowl of soup and watched television for a while before deciding to go to bed. He grabbed a sleeping bag and headed off to the sick bay where he fell asleep on the bunk with his back to the door and facing the outside wall.

Sometime around 1:00 a.m., he reported that he was woken by an odd snuffling noise from outside, something that reminded him of an animal, possibly a badger rustling around in the leaves and grass. He dropped off to sleep again but was surprised when he was woken again by the noise, except it was no longer coming from outside the building but downstairs within the hall.

Terry thought about this and was convinced that he had closed and locked the doors. Still, he couldn't really be bothered getting up and checking, so he decided to not worry about it and go back to sleep. Besides, if an animal had found its way in, then surely it could find its way out again.

However, as he lay there he could hear the animal getting closer, in fact, slowly climbing the stairs and snuffling and scratching around on the landing outside the closed door of the sick bay. This time Terry was somewhat alarmed as it is rare for an animal to explore so deep into the building. And for some reason, he felt threatened by the sound.

The snuffling continued and Terry lay there wondering what it could be. Then to his horror, the sound changed from the scratching and snuffling, and it sounded to Terry as if it were trying to squeeze under the door of the room, something that was impossible as the gap between the door and floor was only half an inch.

And yet it continued. The sound was something like a stiff brush being pushed under the door and Terry froze. Whatever the creature was, it was somehow managing to enter the room under the door. Then it stopped, and he realised that it had finally managed to do the impossible and was now in the pitch black room with him.

Then the sound of the snuffling and scratching started up again, this time immediately behind him, in fact, only inches away from his back. His body was frozen in terror as the noise terrifyingly continued. The bed then started violently rocking, so much so that the ex-Royal Marine had to hold on tightly so as not to be thrown off.

And then, after thirty seconds, the jerking and thrusting of the bed stopped, and he lay there exhausted as he heard the snuffling and scratching noise make its way from the bedside back towards the door. Again the unknown creature seemed to drag itself under the door and descended the stairs before returning outside.

Terry lay there in complete silence but managed to look at his watch, which showed 2:00 a.m. The creature had apparently been there for a complete hour, and although intrigued by what it was, he was simply too scared to open the door and go down the stairs to find out. Instead, he slept fitfully until daylight when he woke, tired and sore. Looking around he was horrified to see that the bed and room were covered in plaster from the walls, seemingly torn off by the claws of the creature. As well, all the electrical cabling had been pulled from the walls.

This incredible encounter has a postscript. A year after, Terry once again encountered the same unknown creature, and once again was simply too frightened to do anything. Whatever the Mendips Beast is remains a complete mystery, and students boarding at the little building have been known to wedge chairs against the doors at night just in case the bristly creature decides to return.

The Mendips have been the locale of several reported big cat sightings in recent years and savaged carcasses of sheep have been discovered adding weight to claims that a giant alien big cat may be living in the area. Having said that, the ex-Royal marine is adamant that what he encountered was no cat, and indeed, was no animal he could even imagine.

209

But was this creature a ghost? Who knows? As we have mentioned, most people believe that ghosts are the spirits of deceased persons and that it is the soul of the person that continues after physical death. However, this is probably not the case as we will see in the next chapter, and yet, what then are we to make of the reports of ghostly pets and other animals? Is it possible that these animals somehow acquired some of the soul of their owner due to a lifelong close association with humans? Is it possible that animals have spirits of their own, remembering that Native American legends often speak of ghostly spirit animals. Or maybe some humans later appear as ghostly animals? Of course, others believe that animal spirits could be non-human or even demonic apparitions as is the case for Black Dogs.

Although modern accounts of Black Dogs and hellhounds are few, contemporary reports of other ghostly animals, mainly pets, are fairly common. Pet owners often report the sounds of claws on the floor or the jingle of a familiar set of dog tags or a collar. Intriguingly, cats seem to return more frequently than dogs and often as a physical presence with owners either seeing the animal or feeling it lying next to them in bed at night.

My partner Kirsten, who remains open-minded but generally sceptical about ghosts, claims to quite often see her long-dead cat around our house, and I believe that I may have seen him now and then as well. I also had a similar experience many years ago in another house when I saw a large, white, and slightly fuzzy-looking cat walk past my lounge room and then turn off into a hall. As I did not own a cat at the time and all the doors were shut, I was at a loss to explain what I had seen. I'd leapt up from my seat and looked down the corridor, which had a closed door at the end. Inexplicably, there was no fluffy white cat.

But it's not just the ghosts of dogs and cats that people report. In Melsonby in Yorkshire a farmer was reportedly driving along a lane leading to the village one night when his horse suddenly shied, bucked, and then bolted as if it had been terrified by something. The farmer held on for dear life but managed to gain some control over the animal. As he did he looked around to see if he could find the source of terror for the horse, but all he could see was a big white goose waddling along by the side of the trap.

The horse and trap, however, were moving at a rapid rate, and yet the waddling goose appeared to keep up. At first the farmer was quite astonished but then recalled stories of the village being haunted, and the more he looked at the goose, the more he became convinced that the bird was not of this world. The goose continued to keep pace with the horse and trap but, upon passing the village churchyard, entered it through a closed gate and disappeared, much to the relief of the farmer.

On another occasion, it was said that two poachers were returning home one night when they saw the ghostly goose waddling along the road ahead of them. Being poachers, they couldn't believe their luck and so snuck up behind the bird and tried to grab it. However, it simply vanished, leaving the poachers bewildered and somewhat apprehensive.

Interestingly, in St. George's Church in York, it is said that a phantom rabbit scurries up and down the aisles, and all attempts to catch it have failed. Locals believe that it is the ghost of Dick Turpin, who we have already seen seems to spread himself widely across the country. In this case, it is believed that Turpin was buried in the churchyard, so maybe there is a grain of truth in the whole thing.

Athelhampton Hall in Dorset is another wonderful old building that typifies upper-class living of the period and is now open to public visits. Built in the fifteenth century, it is Grade I listed and is considered one of the most haunted places in the county holding a host of ghostly happenings. These include a pair of duellists dating back from the Civil War who are said to haunt the Great Chamber and once interrupted a woman who was reading in the room. Not realising that she was seeing a ghostly duel, she admonished the two and asked them to stop. However, they ignored her and continued fighting. Annoyed at being disturbed by such an outburst, she again asked the two young men to stop, but they both ignored her and fought on. The woman pulled continuously at a bell rope to summon a servant, but no one arrived. Still annoyed, she sat back down and was surprised to see the two exit the room. When she later asked the owner about these duellists, the owner replied that there was no one dressed like that and that he had no idea what she was talking about.

The Grey Lady of Athelhampton has also been seen on many occasions, and on one occasion, Mr. Robert Cooke, the owner of Athelhampton, saw her ghostly figure one morning as she passed through the walls of the East Wing from the landing to a bedroom. She has also been witnessed by a housemaid who noticed her sitting in a chair of one of the rooms. Thinking she was a visitor, she politely suggested that she should leave soon as the house was being closed for the night. The grey figure then rose and disappeared through a wooden panelled wall. The housekeeper also witnessed the same apparition sitting in the same room and described her as wearing, "a rather full, plain dress and a gauzy sort of head-dress." The ghostly woman then gradually faded away.

One of the housemaids has also reported the sighting of a ghostly black priest while she was doing her chores. Apparently, she heard footsteps behind her and on turning was confronted by a "hooded monk, dressed in black, standing outside the bathroom door." It is believed that this ghost may have been that of a Catholic priest. As well, next to the Great Hall is a wine cellar where a tapping sound is said to be made by the ghost of a cooper who once worked in the house.

However, in this chapter we have been looking at ghostly animals and Athelhampton does not disappoint in this regard. On the Great Stairway the sound of cat paws padding across the wooden floor is often reported. Apparently, the cat was once owned by a gardener and had been run over and killed while crossing the main road outside the house.

And yet, perhaps the famous of all the ghosts in Athelhampton is that of a pet ape, which was accidentally imprisoned in the secret passage leading from the Great Chamber. Though it has never been seen, it is thought that the ghostly sound of scratching can be heard from the panels as the ape tries to escape. In another version of the story, a teenage girl who lived in the home became depressed and locked herself into a secret room in the house. Although she thought she was alone, she soon realized that a pet monkey, or ape, had also entered the room. The girl wasn't found for months, but when she was, the monkey was still at her side, having starved to death. And it is the desperate scratching of the ape that can be heard.

Ghost horses are also reported from all over the country with headless horsemen being the most well-known example. Phantom horses are also seen with ghostly carriages and coaches, as well as with soldiers, and make up a great deal of the folklore of the British Isles. For instance, at Crichton Castle in Midlothian, Scotland, witnesses not only report seeing the ghost of William Crichton, one time Lord Chancellor of Scotland, but his horse as well, as the two canter through the broken and ruined gates of the castle.

A ghostly white horse is also said to haunt Clumly Farm in Orkney. Legend suggests that a beautiful young woman came to work on the farm in the late nineteenth century, and the farmer's two sons both fell in love with her. In the end, the sons came to hate each other as they played for the woman's affection. Tragically, this rivalry turned lethal and one son struck the other with a flail, cracking his skull open and killing him. Fearing he may be caught and tried for murder, he disposed of his brother's body at the cliffs at Yesnaby.

As he left he felt as if the ghost of the dead man was pursuing him so he rode as fast as he could. The horse's hooves struck a stone dyke causing many stones to fall over, and it is now said that nobody has since been able to repair that part of the dyke. The phantom horse and rider are also said to be seen on stormy nights, galloping wildly along the road.

And so, are ghostly animals similar to ghostly people? Do they operate in similar ways? Of course, when speaking of ghostly animals we must also recall the phantom bear of the Tower of London which, in 1815, emerged from a doorway where a terrified sentry lunged at it with a bayonet, finding to his dismay that it simply met with thin air. This encounter, and others, suggests that ghostly animals are no different than those of people.

But if spectral animals appear to be no different than spirits of people, then what are we to make of other, quite bizarre supernatural encounters that have been regularly reported from all over Britain? Stories like the Tall Man of Brook and time-slips?

CHAPTER 13

†

The Tall Man of Brook, Time-slips, and Other Anomalies

Science fiction is no more written for scientists than ghost stories are written for ghosts.

—Brian Aldiss

It was a fine, clear Sunday in May 1924 when Betty Bone, her brother, and a friend, Ewart Pope, set off from Southampton on their bicycles. Betty, who was in her late teens, often cycled to Southampton to visit her family. However, lately there had been a number of upsetting incidents whereby gypsies had been threatening violence and demanding money from passersby, so for this trip her father arranged for her to be escorted back to Breamore, a village where she was staying.

Twilight was still an hour or so away as the trio cycled past Cadnam and onto the road that connects New Forest and Fordingbridge, now the B3078. The road was understandably empty as cars were rare in those days, especially on minor rural roads, and although late in the day, visibility was good, even in the forested areas.

Coming up to an avenue of trees, the trio were surprised to find themselves about to pass a tall man who was walking the same direction. Strangely, although they were riding on a straight section of road, no one had noticed the man until they were almost upon him, some twenty yards or so, as if he had simply appeared out of thin air. And secondly, he was exceptionally tall, at least seven feet in height if not more. One of the trio commented that he was so tall he thought at first that he must have been on stilts like a circus performer. And not only this, he was also wearing odd clothing, a long coat and a tall top hat. Still, as strange as this man seemed, the trio took little notice and cycled past on their way to Southampton.

This should be where the story ends; however, it just gets stranger and stranger as roughly a quarter of a mile further down the road, they again ran into the strange tall man who, once again appeared from nowhere just ahead of them, steadily and purposefully striding along the road. From his height and clothing the trio had absolutely no doubt that this was the very same person they had just passed minutes ago, which of course, was impossible as the road was dead straight so there was no way known that he could have overtaken them.

The trio felt somewhat apprehensive and anxious about this second sighting, and pedalled past the strange figure once again. However, if they thought that was it, then they were in for an even greater surprise as, after another quarter of a mile they were approaching a crossroads when to their complete amazement they came upon the same man, again, purposefully striding along the road. However, this time it was not in forested land but now in completely open country where visibility was exceptionally good.

Again, he seemed to appear from nowhere as the road ahead was empty as far as the eye could see. This time the trio was alarmed and pedalled furiously past the strange man, determined to get away from whatever it was. So alarmed were they that no one even turned back to have a look at whether he was still behind them.

Safely back at Breamore, the two young men saw Betty safely home before starting out on the return trip through the now rapidly darkening forest. Although they saw no sign of the tall man, they were apprehensive even to the point that, when a lamp fell off one of the bikes, they didn't stop to pick it up. Whoever or whatever they had seen before was now gone and has never again been seen.

Whatever the three young people had seen is unknown, but all were adamant as to what they had experienced. Whether this figure was a ghost is unknown as it doesn't appear to follow the normal characteristics of ghostly appearances. However, having said that, what is a *normal* ghostly occurrence? Who is to say that this peculiar encounter was not that of a ghost? And this can also be applied to our next set of case studies, the little understood but seemingly very real time-slip phenomena.

Imagine walking into a completely familiar place, say a shop that you know quite well, and finding that the complete interior has changed, and that the people behind the counter and the actual products themselves seem to be from a different era, indeed, from an era well before your lifetime? Imagine also that you are walking along the street when you pass a friend or an acquaintance who is going the opposite way. You acknowledge each other and continue on your separate ways only to turn a corner and come face to face with that person once again, even though you know it is completely impossible for that person to be where they are. Perhaps, you think, he has an identical twin or this person is just very similar in appearance, right down to the exact same clothes and shoes. But no, you acknowledge him again and have no doubts. This is the same person and you have seen him twice in completely unexplainable circumstances.

Even though these situations seem completely and utterly implausible, there have been many occasions when perfectly rational and sane people have reported instances as such. And such instances are what are commonly referred to as a time-slip.

Imagine time being a piece of string stretched out tightly and tautly in a perfectly straight line. Then imagine people moving along this piece of string as time passes. All are going the same direction at the same pace and will apparently, never meet. However, what if this piece of string suddenly develops a loop of some

kind? If this were to happen then the occurrences previously described could actually happen. Either you or your friend has somehow managed to step off the straight and narrow part of time and found yourself on the loop.

On the morning of 18 June 1968 in Tunbridge Wells, Charlotte Warburton was shopping with her husband when they decided to separate for a while with the view of meeting later. Unable to find a particular brand of coffee that she usually enjoyed, Mrs. Warburton went into a supermarket on Calverley Road. Once in the shop she noticed a small old-fashioned café that for some reason she had never seen before. The place had wood panelling on the walls and no windows but was lit by electric lighting. Two women in long dresses were sitting at one table and a number of men in dark suits were milling around chatting and drinking coffee.

Mrs. Warburton did not stay and indeed didn't really think about it much at all until the following day while passing the supermarket with her husband when she decided to call in to the little café. When she entered the supermarket there was no sign of the place and although the two searched up and down the street they could find no evidence that the place had ever existed. They later learned that the Kosmos Kinema used to stand on the site of the supermarket and that the cinema apparently had an assembly room and to the rear a small bar with tables for refreshments, exactly as Mrs. Warburton had described.

The cinema, bar, and assembly room had all disappeared many years previous and yet, it appears that on that day in June 1968, Mrs. Warburton had somehow stepped into the past.

But Charlotte Warburton's strange tale is not really that unique as we shall see in 1935 Wing Commander Victor Goddard had an equally perplexing experience while flying from Andover to Edinburgh in a Royal Air Force Hawker Hart biplane.

About forty kilometres out from Edinburgh, Goddard flew over an abandoned World War I airfield by the name of Drem. After landing in Edinburgh he drove out to Drem and had a look around at the dilapidated and ruined base which had been mothballed for years and now was in a state of disrepair with the hangars now being used as hay sheds and the runways fenced off from grazing cattle. He then returned to Edinburgh.

Taking off the next day to return to Andover, Goddard found himself in a violent storm that pummelled his little biplane so much that it plummeted thousands of feet towards the ground as Goddard fought for control. Levelling out and flying only feet above a stony beach with fog and rain obscuring all distant visibility, he managed to locate his position, which was the road to Edinburgh. He followed this for a while until he could make out the dark silhouettes of the hangars at Drem Airfield, the same airfield he had visited the day before. Fearing that the storm may force him down he headed towards Drem. What he saw was something that he would never adequately be able to explain.

Suddenly, the rain stopped and the sky turned to brilliant sunlight. Drem airfield appeared under his aircraft. However, it no longer appeared abandoned, in fact, to Goddard's eye it had been refurbished and was currently in use, something that was obviously impossible. On the tarmac were four bright yellow painted aircraft, three being standard Avro trainers that Goddard was familiar with, and one that Goddard had never seen in his life, in fact, no one had, as it was a monoplane, and in 1935, the RAF had no monoplanes. In addition, all the ground staff were wearing blue overalls, not the standard brown that was worn by ground staff in 1935.

Goddard was only over the airfield for a moment, but no one appeared to notice him, even at the low level he was flying at. As he passed the airfield he was once again engulfed by the storm and climbing hard was able to escape it and return home safely. After landing he told a fellow officer about his experience and was treated as if he were drunk, or crazy. Fearing discharge from the RAF, he decided to keep quiet about the experience.

By 1939, as war clouds gathered over Europe, Goddard watched as the RAF began to paint its trainers yellow and its ground staff move to blue overalls. And they introduced a new aircraft called the Miles Magister, a trainer monoplane. Drem was also refurbished and became a vital training base.

Goddard remained silent about this strange event for many years but finally concluded that he must have glimpsed the future, or even travelled into it for a brief moment, something he recalled in his book *From Flight to Reality* in 1975. "It took me by surprise and shook me more alarmingly than had that vision shaken me when I experienced it in 1935." He concluded. "For I had then to rationalise the fact that time and happenings are not as I supposed."

And so we must ask, is this conclusion so unreasonable? Our senses determine our reality and Goddard was under extreme stress at the time. Is it possible that in that instant when his life was threatened, his sense of reality changed, allowing him to see another, very different, but no less tangible reality? Or had he simply slipped forward in time, much like in our earlier explanation concerning a piece of tight string?

And if so, what of the people on the ground at Drem? What would they have seen from their ground vantage points? Would they have seen a ghostly aeroplane from the past? How would they explain what they had seen? Was Goddard in fact a ghost without knowing it? Are the ghosts we see today real people from the past, just in a different reality, a sort of time-slip? Not surprisingly we find that this sort of experience is not that uncommon. And yet we must ask, is it connected to ghosts and hauntings in any way, or is it just another strange phenomenon that we cannot explain?

In another strange occurrence, this time in 1935, a Dr. E. G. Moon, apparently a down-to-earth Scots physician, was visiting a patient, Lord Carson, who lived at Cleve Court near Minster-in-Thanet. After spending a short time speaking with Carson, Moon left his patient and proceeded downstairs into a hallway. He had left instructions with a nurse regarding Carson's prescription, but at the front door he paused and wondered if he should go back and ensure the nurse had fully understood.

Looking out Moon noticed that his car seemed to be missing. He had parked it alongside a thick yew hedge but, oddly enough, that too was missing. Even the drive that he had driven down to get to the house was gone, now just a muddy track. Even more astonishing was a man who was walking towards him dressed, as far as the doctor could tell, in old-fashioned wear with several capes around his shoulders, a top hat, riding boots, and a long-barrelled rifle over his shoulder. As he walked he smacked a riding crop or a cane against his riding boots. The man looked at Moon and stared at him.

Moon, remarkably, did not seem alarmed at this bizarre change in scenery, quite possibly because what he was seeing hadn't really registered in his brain. Preoccupied as he was with the script, he turned back to the house, and then, as if checking to confirm what he had seen, he turned back to have another look. Remarkably the car was back, parked where it should have been next to the hedge, and the drive was no longer a muddy track. The man in period costume had also disappeared and it was at this stage that the doctor realised that something strange had just occurred.

As it all took only a matter of seconds, it is easy to see why Moon at first didn't think anything of it. And for the same reason it is understandable why he didn't say anything to the man in period dress. After thinking about it for a while and running over the events in his head Moon came to the conclusion, as unlikely as it seemed, that he was either in a hallucinatory state for whatever reason, or he had somehow been projected into the past for a fleeting moment. Later, he described to Lady Carson what had happened but was adamant that no one should know what happened lest it proved non-beneficial to his career in that patients may have questioned his judgement and sanity. The story was only released after his death.

And so, as with the case of Goddard and the ghostly Drem airfield, is it possible that Moon, when he fleetingly viewed the past, was seen by the man in period dress as a ghost? That is, Moon materialised in front of his eyes and then completely vanished when he approached, exactly like many ghost reports and experiences.

Interestingly, Cleve Court, which spans Tudor, Elizabethan, and Georgian times near Minster-in-Thanet, was purchased by Lord Sir Edward Carson in 1920 and has a reputation for being haunted. Soon after the Carsons moved in, a neighbour mentioned to Lady Carson that there had been some alarming and inexplicable incidents in the house that were due, it was believed, to the ghost of a woman who once lived in the house in the late 1760s.

Apparently, a man had inherited the house along with a large fortune and, so he could enjoy the inheritance, locked his wife up while he drank and entertained many other women, including prostitutes. Over time the wife grew frail and depressed and died, and her ghost is now believed to walk the lonely corridors at night, her high heels tapping along the corridors. In addition, drawers are said to open and shut of their own accord.

In another supernatural happening, the Carson's five-year-old son, Edward, told his mother that he didn't like the grey lady that walked past his room at night. When she quizzed him about her appearance he said that he didn't know what she looked like as she always walked away from him. Edward's bedroom was in the Elizabethan part of the building.

Later, Edward's cousin, Patricia, was sleeping in one of the Elizabethan bedrooms when she too saw the lady, quite alarmingly, leaning over her bed one night. Another time Patricia pointed the lady out to Lady Carson, but she could see nothing. Another member of the family also reported seeing the ghost of a lady walking the corridors.

This grey lady is believed to be the ghost of a Mrs. Fuller Farrer, who died at a young age and, although she had a son she adored, longed to have a larger family. As such, it is said that she appears whenever children are in the house, although offers no threat to anyone.

The ghost was again heard in 1949 by the wife of the now-grown Edward who reported hearing her footsteps late one night. However, it wasn't until late 1949 that Lady Carson witnessed her when she appeared on the staircase wearing a long, old-fashioned dress, a grey cape with a white ribbon in her hair. Apparently, descending the staircase towards her, the ghostly woman turned sideways into another part of the house and disappeared as if into thin air leaving an icy chill that made Lady Carson shiver.

This event alarmed Lady Carson and she told her story to a local newspaper, which not long after published a letter from a woman who had been a maid at the house and also claimed to have seen the ghostly apparition. Whatever the case, the ghost of the grey lady of Cleve Court has never done anyone any harm and has always seemed benevolent in its nature.

But ghostly grey woman aside, this chapter is more about strange, supernatural anomalies that may be in some way related to ghosts. Having said that, time itself is not something that we will attempt to cover in this book, suffice to say that although there exists an infinite amount of time, there never seems to be enough of it. Time itself seems to be an unstoppable force that continually pushes towards an uncertain future with humans bound up in the present and unable to break its boundaries. As such, the past, once it is gone, can never again be. The present is fleeting, in fact, so fleeting that it possibly doesn't exist, and the future unknown.

And, yet, for all this, there exists many extraordinary reports of people from all over the world experiencing time-slips. Generally these occurrences appear to be where a previous era has somehow briefly intruded upon the present in a spontaneous and local nature.

Of course, it is debatable whether figures, such as the Tall Man are ghosts as we understand them and the same is true for time-slips. True, there is no doubt that they come under the umbrella of the supernatural or paranormal, but whether or not they are of the same nature of classic hauntings such as is seen in places like the Tower of London or numerous pubs across the land is debatable.

And as such we shall have a look at ghosts and ghost theories, that is, what are ghosts and how and why do they exist?

CHAPTER 14

†

A Final Word on Ghosts

Indians scattered on dawn's highway bleeding
Ghosts crowd the young child's fragile eggshell mind.

—Jim Morrison

As we have previously seen in chapter four, *Glastonbury, the Bloody Assizes, and a Hanging Judge,* Thomas Lethbridge put forward stone tape theory, which hypothesizes that ghosts may be recordings of a past event that have somehow become visible in the physical environment in which the apparition appears.

The theory suggests that, just like a magnetic recording tape, stones can somehow store information and replay it similarly to music or video tape. The theory also applies to buildings, fields, and other sites and objects.

The theory also notes that ghosts often behave like recordings in that they repeat their actions time and time again over a long period of time while never deviating from the original sighting. It also notes that in a lot of ghost sightings, the ghost in question exhibits no acknowledgement of its surroundings, environment, or even people around it, and in some cases it appears as if the ghost is in a completely different building to the one that now exists. An example being when ghosts have been reported walking through walls where a door used to exist, or being seen only from the waist up suggesting that the floor was once lower in the past.

However, having suggested that a place can somehow reproduce a moment in history does throw up a lot of questions. For one, we have no idea how to turn this ghostly recording on or off suggesting that it is atmospheric conditions that cause apparitions to appear. Secondly, not all ghosts or hauntings happen in this way as we have seen that ghosts can be somewhat intelligent, which would suggest that they can interact with their present environment and, therefore, are not a simple recording of the past. Thirdly, we really have no idea if a stone can record events that have happened while it has been in existence, and lastly, why would a stone or a building or place simply record one tiny slither of history and not everything it has witnessed?

As we can see, the stone tape theory, although quite reasonable and something I tend to agree with, is fraught with problems.

Of course what we haven't addressed here is that there appears to be more than one sort of ghost. From the innumerable accounts of ghosts and hauntings we see that they have widely differing characteristics, and so it is reasonable to suppose that they all have different reasons and explanations for being. The idea that there is simply one sort of ghost just doesn't seem logical. Therefore, if we accept that there are different types of ghosts with different reasons for existing, then we can attempt to come to some conclusions about what they actually are and the reason for their being.

And so let us look solely at the stone tape theory ghost. This recording-style ghost is a phenomenon whereby the entity or apparition acts out the same actions in the same place, time and time again, exactly like a recording. In fact, it is so clockwork that it is quite possible that the event witnessed is actually a real recording of a past event somehow imprinted into the very fabric of a building or site, that is, the local surroundings in which the phenomena is occurring. And if this is the case we must be open to the suggestion that what people are witnessing is actually history replaying itself.

Of course, we know of no technology that can record history in the way that a video camera can as stones and rocks simply don't record. And yet, some stones do have strong magnetic properties as does the earth in general, and we do know that magnetic tapes can record sound, vision, and all sorts of information. However, this still doesn't explain how something from the past can be so imprinted on the present as to manifest itself at certain times.

Let us have a look at a classic-style haunting or ghostly apparition. For instance, many people in the British Isles have reported seeing Roman soldiers marching by, although only from the waist up, which suggests that these ghosts are marching along, not an existing path, but one that existed many years in the past. This makes perfect sense, and a great example of this sort of ghost is seen in the celebrated tale of Harry Martindale, an apprentice plumber who, in 1953, was installing a heating system in the cellars of the Treasurer's House in York when he witnessed the ghosts of Roman centurions. He heard a horn in the distance, and then a dishevelled Roman soldier on a horse emerged from the brick wall. This soldier was followed by others, all looking dejected and tired, carrying swords and spears. They appeared from the knees up which suggests that they were walking on a road that was buried below them. It was later confirmed that an old Roman road was located fifteen inches below the cellar.

After this bizarre procession had passed, Martindale made a hastily escape from the cellar and sat at the top of the stairs quite bewildered when an old curator saw him and asked if he'd seen the Roman soldiers.

However, even this brings up questions. For instance, if we are to believe in the stone tape theory, then what of the environment that the apparition once lived in? Why is it we cannot see this as well? And if we can't, then what are we then to think of the world as we know it? What would be real and what would imagined?

There have been numerous reports of ghostly encounters where the witness has reported seeing whole environments being recreated, but this raises another question in that, is this a ghostly encounter, or is the witness actually seeing a real event and environment somehow transported through time? It would appear that the stone tape theory, or residual theory, for all its shortfalls, is reasonable and appears to explain the vast majority of ghostly encounters. But for all this, it can't explain all ghostly encounters, as we have seen in poltergeist activity.

And so where does this leave places such as the Red Lion in Avebury? The ghosts that haunt this quaint old pub seem to act in a stone tape theory way but also at times appear intelligent, so it is reasonable to assume that they are in fact different types. As an example, we have the ghost of Florie who, apart from throwing things around rooms and making a chandelier spin, seems to be able to wander around and interact with people. Secondly, we have the ghosts of the cowering children who, apart from scaring visitors half to death, don't seem to do anything more than just appear. Thirdly, we have the lady in the same room as the ghostly children and who doesn't even acknowledge their presence.

Of all the ghosts at the Red Lion one could suggest that the stone tape theory could apply to the last two, the lady and the children. But then what of Florie? Obviously she cannot be acting out a recorded event as she appears to be able to move independently around the pub rather than follow a predetermined course. And yet, although displaying some poltergeist-like tendencies, she appears to be much more a classic of traditional-style haunting.

As such we need to look at ghosts in a different light and not simply in a contemporary way where ghosts are returned spirits of the dead. As we have seen, ghosts and hauntings appear to exist in many and varied forms, some intelligent, some semi-intelligent, and others completely oblivious to anything. There are odd noises, tappings, voices, whispers, unexplained lights, cold spots, draughts, object movements, smells, feelings, shadows, misty shapes, and occasionally human figures.

How is it possible that all of these are the same phenomenon? Could it be that some spirits are much stronger than others and are able to appear in a fully-formed human figure while others can do no more than make a light dim or move a glass on a shelf? And what of poltergeists? Are they really ghosts at all? For sure they are from the realms of the paranormal and it would appear that they are delicately intertwined with ghostly behaviour, but as we have seen, they seem to be a source or form of energy that manifests itself generally in the presence of a young girl.

And surely, if a poltergeist can lift beds, throw objects, and move furniture, then one would think that they could manifest in a visible form? Surely something as powerful as a poltergeist would be able to do so especially when you think of other benign hauntings where people claim to see full human figures.

As such we must ask if the entire phenomenon for ghosts and hauntings is so different and varied then how did we arrive with the idea that all ghosts are the same and that all ghosts are returned or returning spirits of the dead? It would seem that the answer to this lies in popular and contemporary culture.

Throughout history people have recorded stories of ghosts and ghostly happenings, and in almost every case what they speak of is the returned spirit of a dead person. These ghosts are generally described as an apparition that often takes the form of a person, but also can be seen as mist, a black shape, a flash of light, a cold spot in a room, unseen footsteps, voices, smells, or a fleeting glimpse of something. Ghosts are also generally supposed to haunt places of previous significance in their once-living lives.

This belief, that ghosts are somehow lost souls, is an ancient concept closely related to animism. In the past the soul was not only the living essence of a person but was also believed to be an exact reproduction of the person as they once were in life.

Ghosts are also regularly described as comprising a misty cloud-like sort of substance, and as such, one could suggest that the soul is in fact what people see when they say that they have seen a ghost. This can also be demonstrated by the fact that anthropologists have shown that, in some cultures, there exists a belief that a ghost is the person within a person and that, mainly in cold temperatures, the exhaling of breath, which appears as a visible mist, is part of a person's soul. Indeed, in some languages the words breathe or breath pertains to soul, such as *spiritus* in Latin and *pneuma* in Greek. In addition, the Bible states that Adam was brought to life by God's breath.

Even without any strong evidence for the existence of ghosts, the belief in them is persistent and extensive throughout all cultures and times. Historically and contemporarily, ghosts are seen as an intangible part of a dead person stuck in some sort of limbo between life and death. Generally, it is thought that these ghosts, while living, have suffered an awful or traumatic death and have not realised that they are dead, as such they are imprisoned on earth but in an ethereal existence.

Pliny the Younger described in a letter how a philosopher named Athenodoros had rented a haunted house in Athens in roughly 100 AD. In the letter he described a ghost that was a dishevelled, aged spectre, bound at feet and hands complete with rattling chains. Apparently, after digging up the bones and giving them a proper burial, the haunting ceased and normality returned.

In the current day almost every ghost movie we see on film or television is based upon the tragic or untimely death of an individual who then comes back to haunt the living, sometimes to extract a grisly revenge, or to raise awareness of their plight, such as the circumstances of their death. Programs such as *Supernatural* and *Ghost Whisperer* follow the same script as did Shakespeare in a great deal of his writing. After all, it was Banquo's ghost who visited Macbeth in the great halls of Dunsinane Castle, while Hamlet also received a visit from his ghostly father on the ramparts of his castle.

And so it would seem, we have popular culture to blame for the stereotypical view of a ghost and, as we have seen, this view appears to be incorrect.

In popular ghost lore we are mainly exposed to classic or historical hauntings. That is, old or traditional reports that are continually retold over the years, in many cases, hundreds or even centuries of years, such as those from the Tower of London. These are the ghosts of guidebooks, history books, tradition, and legend. However, although they may be classed as traditional or legendary, it does not mean that they are any less valid than modern reports as many of them have been investigated and reported numerous times over many years.

However, in this case it must be remembered that the original witnesses are usually long dead and the investigator is reliant upon secondhand knowledge, hearsay, rumour, and history books. This is not to say the ghostly phenomenon is not witnessed again, but more to suggest that facts can often become confused and misreported. This can lead to a doubt as to the legitimacy of the case in question especially in comparison to modern cases which have witnesses that are alive and still able to recount the stories. However, to think this would be wrong as historical traditional cases do have one very solid piece of evidence going for them, and that is the fact that the ghost or haunting will have been seen or experienced by numerous people with no apparent connections over a long period of time thus validating that experience.

A perfect example of this would be the ghost of Florie in the Red Lion who has allegedly haunted the same place for hundreds of years doing pretty much the same thing and being witnessed by numerous people on numerous occasions. However, old and traditional as this story is, the Florie case can also be lumped into another category, that being modern hauntings.

Modern hauntings can simply be described as those that have been carefully investigated by serious paranormal research groups and have occurred in recent times. Generally, these will be new hauntings that have come to light, such as the 2013 Manning Coventry poltergeist tale we previously examined in chapter seven. In incidents like this investigators will have access to witnesses and will have been able to examine the actual site in detail at much the same time, indeed, sometimes during, the supernatural event. The same could be said for the classic Enfield poltergeist although the main investigator Maurice Grosse died in 2006.

And why should this distinction between historical and modern hauntings have so much bearing on ghost reports from all over the world? Simply put, it is easier to validate a modern haunting as the information is more likely to be up-to-date and accurate, thus not prone to the exaggeration of the years as well as the hearsay of traditional cases. And importantly, most modern reports tend towards strange phenomena such as lights, noises, moving objects, and cold spots, rather than full-scale ghostly apparitions by human-like forms.

Of course, we cannot discount the idea that ghosts come in many different guises. Having said this, only a very small percentage of ghosts are readily identifiable as a distinct person or individual. However, positive identification is often based upon hearsay or insubstantial evidence. For example, a place may be reputedly haunted by the ghost of a Victorian gentleman by the name of George. Therefore, the witness, upon seeing something unexplained, will identify George as the ghost they saw, rather than using paintings or photographs or some more reliable evidence.

Most people will spend their lives never seeing a ghost or experiencing anything that they could suggest is of a supernatural origin, and given that a large portion of the population does not believe in ghosts, this make sense. However, even in people who believe that ghosts exist, there is still only a small percentage who report seeing a ghost. Of course, there appears to be others who seem to see ghosts quite often, but generally it has been found that a person will only see one ghost in his or her lifetime.

Interestingly, in a group, there may only be one person who witnesses any visual phenomena. And even if all in a group witness the event, they are unlikely to report the same thing. This may suggest that ghosts are simply figments of imagination brought on by suggestion or sensory hyper-arousal. However, as I mentioned previously, many people may not at first realise they are witnessing a ghost due to the ghost looking like a real, living human. For example, if a person is alone in a building at a certain time, and they see someone else they may think nothing of it until later when they realise that there was no way that anyone else could have been in the building at that time. And the more they think about this the more they may come to believe they have seen a ghost.

But what of multiple witnesses to an event? And what of multiple witnesses to separate but similar events over a long period of time? Is it possible for a group of people to see something unexplainable and then, maybe years later, another group to see exactly the same thing?

When an individual experiences a ghost sighting it could be put down to a number of things including hallucinations, remembering that hallucinations are not simply restricted to people with mental disorders or suffering from the effects of drugs or alcohol. But even if we discount drugs, alcohol, and major mental disorders, there are still a number of perfectly normal reasons as to why a person can suffer from hallucinations, ranging from minor but undiagnosed epilepsy, sleep paralysis, hypnologic hallucinations, sensory deprivation, repressed memory, paranoia, or fantasy proneness.

Of course, this is not to suggest that everyone who experiences a supernatural event or witnesses a ghost is suffering from any of the above. What it does show, however, is that common psychological and psychiatric disorders may contribute to a witness experiencing a paranormal episode.

In cases where multiple witnesses report a ghost sighting or shared paranormal experience, explanations can vary from suggestion to induced hallucinations. For instance, we already know that if a place is reputed to be haunted then a witness is more likely to misinterpret regular noises, sights, and movement as unexplainable and, therefore, supernatural. Indeed, if the place happens to be cold, dark, damp, old, uninhabited, or ruined then there is an even more likelihood of paranormal events happening and being witnessed. As such it is not impossible for a group to witness something and misinterpret what they have seen or heard. If one person in a group hears something and tells others that he or she is unsure about what it is then another in the group who has heard the same thing will doubt what they previously thought, thus leading to confusion as to what actually was experienced, and as such, a supernatural explanation.

In addition to this are low-frequency magnetic fields which, laboratory experiments have confirmed, can cause certain people to suffer ghostly visions and feelings of dread. These fields can be created by commonplace objects, such as household electrical goods, street lights, and other electrical appliances. Strangely, these magnetic fields appear to affect people in different ways in that some report visual hallucinations while others report seeing or hearing nothing.

Interestingly, EMF meters have become extremely popular in modern-day ghost hunting, and in some cases are seen to be actual ghost detectors of sorts. This is because it has been claimed by many ghost hunters that ghosts are associated with, or maybe create, electromagnetic fields. As such, an elevated reading on an EMF should indicate the presence of a ghost. Of course, a problem exists with this theory in that there is absolutely no way of proving whether or not this is true. In addition, EMF meters have a tendency to pick up all sorts of electrical fields from a number of sources.

Having said that, is it possible that EMF meters are picking up electromagnetic fields which, while not being ghosts, actually affect the brain in a way that makes a person believe they have seen a ghost? Put simply, is the magnetic field responsible for small physiological changes in the brain that produce hallucinations? If so, then the ghost myth is dead, and yet, ghosts have existed long before electricity.

These low frequency magnetic fields may explain a number of individual or even group sightings of ghosts or ghostly phenomena yet how does it explain people reporting seeing items apparently moving by themselves, or sightings of ghosts where there is no electrical power whatsoever? Again, could this be a simple misinterpretation of events or another case of hallucination? Perhaps gases such as carbon monoxide?

Whatever the case, one can fairly confidently say that ghost sightings and paranormal events are usually the result of misperceptions due to a number of different reasons. However, this does not account for all cases.

Most hauntings and ghost sightings take place in buildings. These are usually homes, offices, workplaces, or places of great historical or social value, such as prisons and castles. Some hauntings occur outdoors but this is generally only a small percentage, and usually in the vicinity of an old or important landmark or ruin. Older buildings are much more likely to be reputed to be haunted than newer buildings, but this may simply be a reflection of the expectations of the visitor. Activity can occur at any time, night or day.

Strangely, paranormal phenomenon does not appear to randomly and evenly distribute itself around a building or site. Generally, activity will be confined to an area such as a room, a battlement, a hall or stairs. These rooms more often than not are said to be colder and to have a certain feeling about them. Indeed, some places are so specific that haunting or supernatural occurrences happen regularly and repeatedly in that place and nowhere else. For instance, in certain rooms footsteps may be heard, whilst not being heard anywhere else. Knockings or scratching may also be heard, and even physical phenomena, such as being pushed, scratched, or even sat upon will occur only in specific rooms.

Cold spots are another phenomena that is generally confined to a specific area, although they may come and go. As such it seems unlikely that a ghost would haunt an entire building, rather, just a small section of it. Therefore, the idea of a haunted house seems a little farfetched, yet the idea of a haunted room is quite plausible.

This, however, leads to some inevitable conclusions about hauntings. As the phenomenon is restricted to a certain area then surely a certain explanation can be found? For instance, maybe a room that has a history of moaning and knocking may have old plumbing behind its walls? Or another room may have a window that creates shadows that appear to be in a human form? Cold spots and unexplained drafts could come from unseen fissures in walls or under windows and objects moving could be the result of drafts.

Central heating, creaking floorboards, cracked masonry, rattling pipes, and wind that noisily swirls around in a place can all add to misperceptions encountered by people when they say they have witnessed a ghost or experienced something unexplained and, therefore, by association, paranormal. And once a place has a reputation for being haunted it is hard to dispel as people will experience the same events and phenomena and, therefore, come to the conclusion that they too have seen, or experienced, something supernatural. As well, once a ghost or haunting has been reported, it is not hard to see how others come to that conclusion, given what we have discussed previously.

But one must ask, if hauntings are not simply the result of misperceptions then what is their purpose? As opposed to poltergeist activity, hauntings appear to have no real intelligence behind them. There have been cases where people have reported that objects have fallen from the atmosphere and hit them and in other cases they have reported objects being thrown at them, yet this still does not show intelligence in any meaningful way. As such we can confidently say that some hauntings generally show no real purpose or logic.

And yet, as predictable as hauntings can be, they are just as unpredictable in their reliability. For instance, a room that is reputed to be haunted may see as many as a dozen witnesses to the haunting in as many days, and then may not show any phenomena for months afterwards. The phenomena may also fade with time for no obvious reason although this may simply be a result of witness reactions and reporting of the event.

Perhaps fittingly, hauntings seem to decrease when being intensively studied or examined. Sceptics will point out that this proves the non-existence of ghosts and the paranormal, but it can also be argued that not everyone appears to experience supernatural phenomena even when they are in a building or site where regular activity happens. Maybe there is intelligence in hauntings after all?

All through this book we have accepted that normal people like you and I genuinely see things that we believe are of a supernatural origin. However, as we have also seen, these ghostly occurrences do not always follow the same pattern, in fact, so different are these patterns that it is logical to assume that there are one or more types of ghosts, or one or more types of hauntings. For instance, most would assume that a ghost and an apparition are the same thing; however, whereas ghosts may be seen, heard, felt, or even smelt, apparitions are generally just seen.

Sight is undoubtedly the most powerful of our senses and, therefore, any ghost sighting is going to be of far more interest than a simple noise or feeling. And as we have previously covered, most ghost sightings are not of anaemic wispy bits of ectoplasmic mist nor are they dark shadows lurking in doorways, halls, and basements. On the contrary, they are much more likely to look like solid flesh and blood people, almost indistinguishable from you or me.

Having said that, in these types of sightings it is often reported that the ghost bizarrely has very little facial features. In fact, sometimes it is reported that the ghost actually has no face whatsoever. Why this is so I have no idea and I cannot even begin to put forward any explanation except to suggest that there exists many different types of ghosts and that faceless ghosts could possibly be completely different from those with visible facial features. Maybe such a ghost is unsure of its own existence and therefore of its own identity?

Of course, they could just as easily be the same thing yet be viewed in a different way by different people, remembering that we have already seen that different people have different experiences when subjected to low frequency magnetic fields. Is it possible that ghosts have the same effect? Or is it that one is a ghost, and another is an apparition? And if so, then what is the difference between a ghost and an apparition? Is a ghost an apparition, or is an apparition a ghost? Are they one and the same?

The word "ghost" is the most common, most popular collective term for paranormal phenomena. As such, pretty much everything can be attributed to ghosts and ghostly behaviour. However, we have seen that poltergeists act very differently, using psychokinesis in their hauntings while our common, run of the mill, garden variety ghosts generally use simple phenomena such as noises and flickering lights as evidence of their existence. Of course, the spectrum is so wide that it is difficult to generalise; suffice to say the two are very different. Of course, it goes without saying that poltergeist activity can be malevolent and apparently intelligence driven.

Hauntings such as ghosts, however, tend to be more sedate. They are heard, smelt, seen, felt, and sensed but generally do not appear to be able to, or want to, cause harm. If anything they are, as we have discovered, like a tape recording of a historical event, and as such, adhering to the stone tape theory of hauntings, one could logically assume then that there is no intelligence in these hauntings.

And then we have apparitions which we also examined in chapter four, *Glastonbury, the Bloody Assizes, and a Hanging Judge,* another form of supernatural occurrence but one that may not actually be a ghost and has been suggested by some to be where a part of the brain can be artificially activated in sleep or in periods of great stress such as near death experiences and out-of-body experiences.

Obviously ghosts can and do fill a wide spectrum of human senses. We have seen that there apparently exists stone tape theory ghosts, intelligent ghosts of the dead, apparitions, and poltergeists. And yet not all people report ghostly experiences at the same time even when in a group. Often people will report a feeling, a sighting, or smell whilst in a group where no one else has witnessed anything. Are these people simply more sensitive to supernatural energies or powers or are they just in the right place at the right time, or wrong place, depending upon your point of view?

There is one ghost, however, that we have only briefly touched upon and this is a ghost that people suggest has never actually existed as a life form. It is a ghost that logically cannot exist if we are to believe that ghosts are simply the spirits of dead people. It is a ghost formed by, or comprising residual or collective built-up energy.

If we are to follow this, then logically it cannot exist as a ghost and yet they appear to do so. As such, if we adhere to the seemingly valid argument that ghosts are a form of energy, then we can surmise that sites such as buildings, rooms, caves, or even trees can somehow store this energy, which at a later date manifests itself as a ghost. With this in mind, what if a particular place had a particularly evil history? For instance, a dungeon in a medieval castle where people were tortured day in and day out over many, many years? The energy of such a place would be negative, dark, and malevolent. Therefore, if a stone tape haunting can record a historical event from the energy absorbed into the fabric of the building, why cannot a place absorb negative energy in the same way? This does not necessarily mean that you will find an evil ghost, but more so will find an evil presence made up of all the negative energy that has been present in that area over time. Put simply, a conglomeration of evil thoughts and deeds forming as a singular energy or entity capable of intelligence.

Of course, we have already seen something similar to this in poltergeist experiences, which by and large appear as malevolent spirits. However, whereas poltergeists attach themselves predominantly to prepubescent girls and sometimes boys, a malevolent spirit is always attached to a place. And if this were so, surely one could experience this just as one experiences a "normal" ghost, which would mean that ghosts can not only be spirits of the dead, but collective memories or emotions of people. Indeed one could even go as far as suggesting that a person may haunt two places at once given that it is likely that a ghost is a sort of energy source attached to a place.

But where does this leave us? Are we any closer to understanding the phenomena that is a ghost? We have studied numerous ghostly visitations and hauntings, including a number of my own, from all over the British Isles. Does this apparent abundance of ghosts occur due to the rich and ancient history of the place? Why is it that some places that have suffered war, death, disease, and suffering are haunted whereas other places that have equally seen the same are not haunted? Why do some people see ghosts whereas others do not?

I am a sceptical believer in that, although I believe in ghosts, I believe that there is more often than not, a rational explanation for ghostly happenings.

There are many factors that determine what a person believes they have seen or heard. And even if they have seen something genuinely supernatural, then what is it they have actually experienced? In addition, if ghost sightings are so prevalent then why can't science explain these occurrences? How is it that so many people with no connection to each other and over such a length of time report similar ghostly happenings as seen in cases such as the Tower of London, the Spaniard's Inn, Leeds Castle, Avebury, or a vast number of pubs? Surely all these witnesses cannot be lying and have simply invented their stories, even though these stories are almost exactly the same and occur over a period of years, if not decades, thus legitimising the experiences and proving that ghosts do exist?

Or is it a case of us looking in the wrong direction? Is it possible that some people are predisposed to believe in ghosts, or even hardwired to see them? Are the imaginary friends of our childhood really imaginary, or are they in facts ghosts, entities that we as adults have somehow lost the ability to see?

And what of places that seem to convey a certain feeling, a certain depressing or ominous feeling? Without doubt everyone reading this book would have visited such a place whether it be a morgue, a cemetery, an ancient battlefield or a dark, ruined castle. Who among us cannot say that they have walked into a room, or have wandered along a lonely road at night and felt the hairs on the back of their necks rise and their heart beat faster? Is this "fight or flight," an evolutionary response to a once real threat but now lost in the mists of time, a lost human sense, one that seems to have been abandoned in this new and maddeningly fast modern world?

Ghosts and the supernatural seem to have become more and more important in this modern world where spirituality appears to have been traded for technology. From new-agers to reborn neo-pagan beliefs, people appear to be embracing a new interest in their quest for the truth about the unknown, much like the Victorian age of spiritualism. Witness popular television and one will be bombarded with programs based on the supernatural and ghosts. And yet, one must ask, why this is so? Do we yearn for something more in our lives, something to suggest that maybe there is life after death? And is it possible that ghosts provide this link, a link to our past?

Whatever the case, does it really matter? After all, no less an author than H. P. Lovecraft once wrote that, "the oldest and strongest emotion of mankind is fear and the oldest and strongest kind of fear is fear of the unknown."

A Final Word
from the Author

Although this book has attempted to cover ghosts and other supernatural activities across the entire United Kingdom, I will admit that there are hundreds, if not thousands, of other ghostly reports that I could have used. For instance, there is the now famous Hampton Court ghost CCTV footage that apparently shows a skeletal-like figure in a cloak or long coat closing a set of double doors, and whereas sceptics write the sighting off as simply a real-life person, others have suggested that this footage could be the best proof yet found that ghosts really exist.

But Hampton Court is not the only unmentioned place that can claim ghostly visitations as Britain is an old country, one founded on violence and cruelty, one that has seen innumerable wars, battles, death, and brutality. It is the place where the Picts battled the Romans, and the Royalists battled the Parliamentarians. It is a place that saw kings and other royalty murdered and hanged for the most trivial of reasons. It is a place where Vikings pillaged and raped and, in living memory, it is a place that was bombed remorselessly during the Second World War. Whichever way you chose to look at it, underneath the green and pleasant fields and majestic castles and country manors is a place of bloodshed and suffering.

From Chatham Dockyards to Highgate Cemetery to ghostly miners in Cornwall and eerie phantoms in cold stone castles in Ireland, forgotten brochs in Scotland, and damp timber framed houses in Wales, stories of ghosts abound. And although sceptics may sneer, in these places they are very, very real. They haunt the ivy clad ruins of the monasteries and overgrown graveyards of medieval churches. They are the creaks and groans and half-heard whispers in the night, and footsteps that scrape upon old wooden staircases. They are the eerie spine-tingling tapping of fingers on glass, and the clanking of chains in neglected gaols. They are the mysterious hooded figures that haunt our dreams, the headless horsemen who appear out of the cold swirling mist of the moors. They are, it would seem, the souls of corpses now long gone.

At this point, I believe it prudent that I add that, although I do believe in ghosts and paranormal activity in general, I am generally sceptical about many reports and truly feel that most supernatural or paranormal experiences can be logically explained. Having said that, in this book I have simply presented the stories as I have heard or read them, and so one needs to take it with a grain of salt, even though it has been written in good faith. Of course, one must also ask, how is it that so many people with no connection to each other can report the same events over and over again?

One must also remember that, when in pursuit of ghosts and so called denizens of the night, that many of the places described are in fact private property and to intrude upon this is trespassing. True, there are many public buildings mentioned as well as hotels, museums, and pubs and these can be easily visited. Having said this, just because a place is mentioned in this book does not necessarily mean that the people mentioned believe in ghosts or even want to discuss the subject. As such, one needs to be sensitive in these matters.

And, as anything to do with ghosts is fraught, especially when trying to describe exactly what they are and why they exist, I shall leave you instead with this thought by Richard Matheson:

Yet, despite all, it is a difficult thing to admit the existence of ghosts in a coldly factual world. One's very instincts rebel at the admission of such maddening possibility. For, once the initial step is made into the supernatural, there is no turning back, no knowing where the strange road leads except that it is quite unknown and quite terrible.

JG Montgomery
2016

Bibliography and Further Reading

Ackroyd, P. *The English Ghost. Spectres Through Time.* London: Random House, 2010.

Baring-Gould, S. *Myths of the Middle Ages.* London: Cassell, 1996.

Boar, R & N Blundell. *The World's Greatest Ghosts.* Hamlyn: Berkley, 1994.

Brennan, Z. "What IS the truth about the Enfield Poltergeist? Amazing story of 11-year-old London girl who 'levitated' above her bed." *Daily Mail,* 5 May 2015.

Brooks, JA. *Ghosts and Witches of the Cotswolds.* Peterborough, Jarrold Publishing, 1986.

Cohen, D. *The Encyclopedia of Ghosts.* New York: Dorset Press, 1984.

Danelek, JA. *The Case for Ghosts.* Minnesota: Llewellyn Publications, 2006.

Daniel, G. *A Short History of Archeaology.* London: Thames and Hudson, 1981.

Enoch, N. "Don't let the bed bugs and randy sex demon bite: Britain's most haunted B&B where terrified guests have jumped out of windows." *Daily Mai,* 28 October 2013.

Evans, S. *Ghosts. Mysterious Tales from the National Trust.* London: National Trust Books, 2006.

Evans, SJ. "Is this proof of a ghost in 750-year-old pub?" *Daily Mail,* 18 February 2014.

Fairley, J & Welfare, S. *Arthur C .Clarke's Mysterious World.* New York: HarperCollins, 1982.

Felix, R. *What is a Ghost?* Derbyshire: Felix Films Ltd, 2009.

Felix, R & W Anthony. *Ghosts of Derby.* Derby: Breedon Books, 1995.

Fodor, N. *Between Two Worlds.* Paperback Library Inc., 1967.

Fodor, N. *On the Trail of the Poltergeist.* New York: The Citadel Press, 1958.

Goddard, V. *From Flight to Reality.* Winnipeg Manitoba: Turnstone Books, 1975.

Goldman, J. *The X-Files Book of the Unexplained.* Simon & Schuster: London, 1995.

Green, A. *Ghosts of Today.* London: Kaye & Ward, 1980.

Guiley, RE. *Harper's Encyclopedia of Mystical & Paranormal Experience.* San Francisco: Harper, 1991.

Gye, H. "Is this the ghost of a pub landlord who hanged himself? Spooky figure of a man is pictured in supposedly haunted bar." *Daily Mail,* 26 October 2015.

Johnson, WH. *Kent Stories of the Supernatural.* Newbury Berkshire: Countryside Books, 2000.

Kidd-Hewitt, D. *Buckinghamshire Stories of the Supernatural*. Newbury Berkshire: Countryside Books, 2008.

Lilley, S. (with Richard Felix). *The Ghost Tour of Great Britain. Derbyshire.* Derby: DB Publishing, 2005.

Lockley, M & G Roberts. "Gotcha! 'Ghost' caught on camera after years of spooky goings on at England's most haunted castle." *Mirror*, 7 October 2014.

Macrae, F. "Is this another ghostly image caught on camera at Britain's most haunted castle?" *Daily Mail*, 2 April 2009.

Matthews, R. *The Ghosthunters Guide to England. On the Trail of the Supernatural.* Berkshire: Countryside Books, 2006.

McCulloch, J & A Simmons. *Ghosts of Port Arthur* (Revised Edition). Tasmania: AD Simmons, 1995.

Michell, J & B Rickard. *Unexplained Phenomena*. London: Rough Guides Ltd., 2000.

Middleton, J. *Ghosts of Sussex*. Newbury Berkshire: Countryside Books, 1988.

Montgomery, JG. *A Case for Ghosts*. Adelaide: Ginninderra Press, 2012.

Myall, S. "Story behind The Enfield Haunting: Mirror reporter recalls flying Lego in Britain's best-known poltergeist incident." *Mirror,* 30 April 2015.

Naylor, R. "Ghostly 'black-robed monk' spotted lurking in window of medieval castle in tourist's snap." *Mirror,* 21 October 2014.

O'Neill, K & R. Stubbs R. "Ghost of 'guilt-ridden nanny' spotted staring from the window of haunted B&B." *Mirror,* 7 November 2014.

O'Neill, S. "Haunt is on for Pub Ghost." *The Sun,* 13 Aug 2004.

Puttick, B (Ed). *Supernatural England*. Berkshire: Countryside Books Newbery, 2002.

Puttick, B. *Ghosts of Essex*. Berkshire: Countryside Books, 1997.

Rial, B. "Haunted Hull and East Riding: 25 ghost stories for Halloween." *Hull Daily Mail*, 31 October 2014.

Righi, B. Ghosts, *Apparitions and Poltergeists. An Exploration of the Supernatural through History*. Woodbury: Llewellyn Publications, 2008.

Schama, S. *A History of Britain*. New York: Hyperion, 2000.

Simpson, J. *The Folklore of Sussex*. B. T. London: Batsford Ltd, 1973.

Smith, S. *Wiltshire Stories of the Supernatural*. Berkshire: Countryside Books, 2007.

Spence, J & A. *The Ghost Handbook*. London: Macmillan, 1998.

Stevens, RA. *Local Ghosts*. CLX Publishing, 1996.

Tabori, P. *Harry Price—Ghost Hunter*. London: Sphere Books, 1974.

Thurston, H. *Ghosts and Poltergeists*. London: Burns Oates, 1953.

Tim the Yowie Man. *Haunted and Mysterious Australia*. Sydney: New Holland, 2006.

Tongue, RL. *Somerset Folklore*. Folklore Society. October 1965.

Underwood, P. *This Haunted Isle*. Poole: Javelin Books, 1986.

Underwood, P. *Nights in Haunted Houses*. London: Headline, 1994.

Warnes, S. "GHOSTS: Where is England's most haunted place and what should you look out for this Halloween?" *Mirror,* 24 October 2014.

Wilson, I. *In Search of Ghosts.* London: Headline Book Publishing, 1995.

"Don't turn out the light! Terrifying photos of ghosts that will keep you up at night." Author unknown. *Daily Mail,* 15 August 2012.

Weblinks

darkdorset.co.uk
http://hauntedwiltshire.blogspot.com.au
http://paranormal.about.com
news.bbc.co.uk
www.avebury-web.co.uk
www.bbc.co.uk
www.castleofspirits.com
www.dailymail.co.uk
www.dailymercury.com.au
www.fatemag.com
www.ghostsofgettysburg.com
www.ghost-story.co.uk
www.graceneills.com
www.guardian.co.uk
www.haunted-britain.com
www.hauntedhappenings.co.uk
www.hauntedrooms.co.uk
www.hauntedwales.co.uk
www.hevercastle.co.uk
www.irishcentral.com
www.jorvik.co.uk
www.kytelersinn.com
www.mysteriousbritain.co.uk
www.scotsman.com
www.spookyisles.com
www.strangedayz.co.uk
www.thegoldenfleeceyork.co.uk
www.thesun.co.uk
www.thisissomerset.co.uk
www.wales.com

Every effort has been made to ensure all source material is listed. However, it is possible that I have missed some references and if this is so, then I apologise to the original author or publication.

İПDEX

About the Author

JG Montgomery is a forty-something-year-old public servant, born in Cornwall in the United Kingdom and son of an Australian Air Force officer. *Haunted Britain* is his seventh book. He is also the author of *A Case for Ghosts* (2012), the illustrated children's book *The Oomee Mau Ma* (2012), *WYRD—A Journey into the Beliefs and Philosophies of the Known and Unknown* (2014), *Meditations in Orange* (2014), *Summer to Summer* (2016), *Haunted Australia* (2017) and contributed and edited poetry in *Capital Reflections* (2014). Mr. Montgomery is a bass player, guitarist, vocalist, and songwriter in a mod-pop band and has served in both the Australian Army Reserve and Australian Air Force. He has university degrees in cultural heritage and teaching and was once a cricket coach. He is also a decorated state emergency service volunteer and lives in Canberra, Australia, with his partner Kirsten, three cats, a short black dog, six ducks, and a lot of goldfish.